The Freudian Metaphor

• ─────────────────────────────

TOWARD PARADIGM CHANGE
IN PSYCHOANALYSIS

Donald P. Spence

W. W. NORTON & COMPANY • NEW YORK • LONDON

Published simultaneously in Canada by Penguin Books Canada Ltd., 2801 John Street, Markham, Ontario L3R 1B4.

Printed in the United States of America.

First Edition

Library of Congress Cataloging-in-Publication Data

Spence, Donald P.
  The Freudian metaphor.

  "A Norton professional book."
  Bibliography: p.
  Includes index.
  1. Psychoanalysis — Philosophy. I. Title.
RC506.S65   1987   616.89'17'01   87-7720
ISBN 0-393-70042-9

ISBN   0-393-70042-9

W. W. Norton & Company, Inc., 500 Fifth Avenue, New York, N. Y. 10110
W. W. Norton & Company Ltd., 37 Great Russell Street, London WC1B 3NU

1 2 3 4 5 6 7 8 9 0

To my parents,
Rita and Ralph

Contents

Foreword by Jerome Bruner   ix
Acknowledgments   xvii

I · The Metaphorical Nature of Psychoanalytic Theory   1
    Freud's Use of Metaphor   8
    Breadth vs. Depth   11

II · The Metaphorical Unconscious   17
    A Defense Against Skepticism   27
    Features of the System Ucs.   31
    The Seething Cauldron   38

III · The Myth of the Innocent Analyst   43
    The Role of Projection   53
    Empathy or Pathetic Fallacy?   62
    Uncoupled Metaphor   69

IV · The Metaphor of Psychoanalysis as Science   71
    The Search for Historical Truth   77

Explication de Texte   91
Why History Cannot Be Science   109

V · The Sherlock Holmes Tradition: The Narrative
Metaphor   113
Narrative Appeal of the Dora Case   122
Narrative Smoothing   133
Paradigmatic and Narrative Modes   142
Alternatives to the Sherlock Holmes Tradition   154

VI · Rule-Governed But Not Rule-Bound: The Legal
Metaphor   161
Narrative as Resistance   169
Parallels Between Psychoanalysis and Law   179
Three Specimens and Their Commentaries   188
Psychoanalysis and Literature   198

VII · The Post-Freudian Metaphor   203

References   217

Index   225

Foreword

Intellectual historians of the future, looking back on our time, will surely be tempted to call it "the epistemological awakening," or know it by some such emblem. For ours is the generation, perhaps more than any other since Descartes', that has been preoccupied not simply with *nature* or with *mind* but with how we know about them, in what sense we can ever have access to their "reality," and what the limits of our knowledge are. Our skepticism, moreover, is deeper than that expressed in Descartes' Principle of Doubt, for he, after all, had no doubt about the aboriginal realities to which he had a more or less direct access, though his knowledge might be subject to error and to the dislocations of passion. In our times — after Einstein's relativity, Bohr's complementarity, and the riddles of discontinuity in quantum theory — even physics has acceded to the uncertainty that is inherent in the concept of nature. It is not at all clear how one should characterize what is "real" in nature and what is a construct in the mind of the physicist. Nature itself has become a construct, its "facts" subject to the perspective of the theory that drives the search for them. Indeed, as the philosopher, Nelson Goodman, once put it, we know now that facts are not found, but made. Or, as W. V. Quine states it, physics turns out to be ninety-five percent speculation and five percent observation. And it is sometimes puzzling what status to give the latter.

But it is not only the sciences of nature that have been forced to re-examine their epistemological foundations. The awakening, indeed, has spread to the human sciences, to literary theory and linguistics, to legal philosophy and jurisprudence, and to history. All have been forced to shed their nineteenth-century positivism; all have been faced with such questions as how we can know the past "objectively," or how in fact we go about interpreting the law under changed circumstances, or in what sense art imitates life rather than vice versa, or how in any non-ambiguous way a word or expression refers to anything extra-linguistic. Perfect objectivity in any guise is a claim that is viewed with austere suspicion in today's intellectual world.

It is not surprising, then, that philosophy itself is gripped by an epistemological revolution, one centering not only upon the nature of knowledge, but upon the knowledge-acquiring processes. And it is the latter — revisions in philosophical views about how knowledge is acquired and how verified — that has challenged our way of life as psychologists. For if it is a matter of radical doubt how we know nature, it is the more so when it comes to such questions as how we know others' minds or, to take the furthest extension of that question, how we know the unconscious. What is this "knowing" process, how interpretive, how indirect, how uncertain is it?

It is with questions of this order that Donald Spence concerns himself in these pages, with their expression in psychoanalytic theory and practice. To our benefit, Spence is mindful of the broader setting in which these issues have arisen in philosophy and the human sciences generally. Until recently, psycho-analysis has been a most reluctant recipient of the new inherit-ance. For most of its century-long life it has clung to the positivist epistemology of Freud, its founding genius, belying his hope that his followers would be as skeptical about received wisdom in their time as he was in his.

Psychoanalysis has protected itself from change by preserv-ing its store of founding metaphors in their original form. These were metaphors of mind that had had their origins in a dramatism that looked to myth and literature for its inspira-tion. Psychoanalysis invoked positivism to legitimize its claim to being a deterministic science that dealt in causality, while at the same time robing its concepts in the metaphoric language of drama that effectively kept them from being testable, for metaphors have virtually no limit on their extension.

This Janus-like stance has characterized psychoanalysis as a theory of mind and of therapy, and even dominated the manner in which it presented its data in case histories. It is not surpris-ing, then, that psychoanalysis is being subjected to a new scru-tiny both from within and without its ranks. This can only add strength to the enterprise. And I believe that this will be the effect of this book. For what is striking in Spence's account of past and present troubles is that, far from rejecting psychoanal-ysis either as theory or as mode of treatment, he proposes ways in which it can be made to grow again, ways in which it can be protected against being frozen by its entrenched metaphors and can be brought abreast of modern developments in philosophy and in the sciences of mind.

Let me comment briefly on some of the critical issues he raises, some of which will be familiar from his earlier *Narrative Truth and Historical Truth*, though they are much more fully devel-òped in the present volume. The first is the key concept of the unconscious. Spence rightly refers to it as a "free floating meta-phor," and it is to the clarification of such metaphors that his book is addressed. Initially proposed in the metaphoric imagery of "seething cauldrons," secretiveness, depth, and the rest, the concept has over the years been hardly at all converted into hypotheses that could be corrected or modified by confrontation with the rich materials of complete case records. Moreover, psychoanalytic case histories present not the gritty material on which difficult interpretations are based, but vivid selections from that material that support the causal "story" of the interpreter. The story tradition of case interpretation too often overlooks what is involved when one makes *any* interpretation of any text — a patient's case record being, after all, only a text, however special it may be. The patient's story is itself "smoothed" by an interaction with the analyst that is, as it were, tinged with psychoanalytic theory. And the analyst's interpretation of the patient's story is smoothed further by the requirements, so to speak, of the standard psychoanalytic narrative, the kind of narrative that would be acceptable in a standard psychoanalytic journal. And in the process, the very data on which alternative interpretations might be based are omitted in the interest of making the account seem causal rather than interpretive. Not even an historian would be permitted such interpretive licence, even if he were working on a rare and privileged archive! As a result, the psychoanalyst has had to wrap himself in a mantle of authoritative omniscience based on his presumed complete knowledge of the case and on the claim that his training and his own analysis assure him direct and objective access to his patient's unconscious.

Closely linked to the notion of the unconscious are two central tenets of psychoanalytic procedure — ideas, again, that have been allowed too long to live uninspected lives. One is the idea of "free association" in the patient; the other is "freely hovering attention" in the listening analyst. A half-century of experimental psychological research on thought, memory, and attention — work that has discovered a rich world of psychological processes — brings deeply into question the claim that association (or any mental processes, for that matter) can in any sense be "free" or that attention can "hover" in an uncommitted manner. Rather, they are both driven by an "effort after meaning," to use Sir Frederic Bartlett's happy term. Effort after meaning in the realm of human affairs almost inevitably takes the form of narrative, of story. Stories are ways of constructing an account of what happened. As such, they are interpretations, and as interpretations they are themselves amenable to interpretation. The stories one tells—either as a patient on the couch or as an analyst trying to make sense of what the patient is saying—do not and cannot reveal causes or "explain" events in the manner of a series of controlled experiments that can properly make such a claim. For narrative is built out of context, expectancies, conventions, the nature of the interaction in which it is told. Narratives are not "true" or "false." To make sense of stories requires interpretation, and a theory and procedure for interpretation is precisely what is at issue.

The "interpretation of interpretations"—hermeneutics—for all its recent *réclame*, is a subject that is as old as the hills. Born as a branch of speculative theology, it has had rebirths in virtually every domain where men have had to make sense of utterances and texts. Today, for example, the theory of interpretation and its alternate formulations is at the center of legal debate. How shall a judge interpret the Constitution in its application to such modern phenomena as television, or how shall a statute be applied to a specific instance of dispute? When a judge "decides" a dispute in the light of the language of a statute that must be extended to include new events, he or she is (often more than he or she would wish it) *making* law, doing so by an act of interpretation—whether he claims to be bound by the text (the so-called letter of the law) or bound as well by the context of the specific case in the contemporary setting. The psychoanalyst, Spence argues, has as close a kinship to the judge interpreting case law as he does to a scientist in search of "causes." Yet, while the discipline of jurisprudence has developed a rich and complex intellectual apparatus for exploring the bases and rationale of legal interpretation, psychoanalysis has until recently taken interpretation for granted as a given of the psychoanalytic procedure, has indeed even taken the *rightness* of interpretation for granted, as a matter settled by Freud's brilliant original insights.

Interpretation *never* achieves univocal understanding, and certainly it does not discover "causes." Whether it is interpretation in psychoanalysis, in the law, in literature, in history, what it requires for its success is multiple perspective, including the perspective of the patient, if it is psychoanalysis that is at issue. The "hermeneutic" approach, an approach that asks only that we be aware of and explicit about the principles of interpretation that we apply to an utterance or story or account, cannot be dismissed on the ground that it is "soft" science or that it cannot produce an account of cause. One of the psychoanalytic critics of the hermeneutic approach cited by Spence dismisses it as akin to the "soft" psychology of the South Germans, referring (I suspect) to E. G. Boring's distinction, in his *History of Experimental Psychology*, between "northern" *content* psychology (as represented by Wilhelm Wundt) and "southern" *act* psychology, more concerned with process. Content psychology is concerned with how physical stimuli make their impress on consciousness as sensations, act psychology with the processes of ordering experience. I found this criticism particularly amusing, since psychology in the half century since Boring first made that distinction has moved steadily and increasingly toward interpretivism. We have discovered in this past half century that even an allegedly simple "sensation" is an interpretation on the part of a "subject." It can be shown to be dependent not only upon physical input, but also upon context and the immediate history of the perceiver. And in the end, Wilhelm Wundt himself, writing about perception, ended up as an interpretivist. I mention this example, for after all, it was the prevailing positivism of the latter nineteenth century that influenced both the young Freud and the young Wundt, as well as E. G. Boring.

History has gone that way because we have come to appreciate the degree to which psychological processes are bound by the contexts in which they occur. The meaning of any utterance, for example, cannot be understood without knowing its context, including its dialogic context. Psychological processes are inevitably located in time, space, and circumstances and the interpretation of the output of those processes is impossible without the rich detail of their situatedness. As Mies van der Rohe once commented, "God is in the details." To deny the difficulties of interpretation by making claims to a scientific status is to weaken the central claim of psychoanalysis as a human science. In a deep sense, the difficulties of contemporary psychoanalysis inhere precisely in its claim to being a "science" in the positivistic sense of the term and by avoiding the thorny issues of interpretation and hermeneutics. By trying to live up to such a claim, it achieves the ironic outcome of being not only questionable science, but an incorrigible form of interpretation as well. It is bad science because, given the textual nature of its data and the metaphoric concepts used in their interpretation, it can never establish the conditions for the establishment of causal connections. And it is bad interpretation because, in trying to be a science, it throws away the record and the possibility of open debate that would be needed for rich and corrigible interpretation. It substitutes for rigorous interpretation a Sherlock Holmes story in which the analyst as detective-archeologist comes up with the "right answer," as if there were ever a single right answer to be found in a complex case record.

In the end, Spence urges us to take more seriously the "open texture" of psychological (and social) processes, the extent to which they are rule-governed rather than rule-bound. He urges that we free ourselves from the temptation of the good Sherlock Holmes story when we do our case reporting. Its narrative smoothings, cogwheel causalities, and deft deductions only serve to distort the difficulties. We should adopt instead rich and debate-susceptible documentation and procedures that are akin to the lawyer's or the judge's ways with a case, a more honest, open, and modest ideal of interpretation whose uncertainties are more than counterbalanced by its riches. That way psychoanalysis would produce an understanding of the many alternative ways in which life can make sense — for the analyst, for the patient, and for the scientific community.

Jerome Bruner

Acknowledgments

Many people have helped to make this book possible. Richard and Carol Bernstein, Anton Kris, and Philip Rubovits-Seitz all read the next-to-final draft and responded promptly and thoughtfully. I owe a special debt to Philip for his sense of what the whole was trying to become and for showing me how to bring this about. David Richards read the chapter on the legal metaphor and offered valuable advice.

Two seminars and two conferences on interpretation helped me to enlarge the range of issues being discussed and place the main thesis within a much broader framework. I am grateful to Jerome Bruner for the chance to participate in his seminar on interpretation at the New York Institute for the Humanities; to Shlomith Rimon-Kenan for inviting me to a conference on discourse in literature and psychoanalysis at the Hebrew University of Jerusalem; to Pauline Young-Eisendrath for the chance to attend an interdisciplinary seminar on interpretation at Bryn Mawr College; and to Stanley Messer who enabled me to take part in a hermeneutics symposium at Rutgers University. Preparation for this last event helped to create the final chapter.

My thanks go also to the following journals for permission to reprint portions of published articles: *Contemporary Psychoanalysis, Journal of the American Psychoanalytic Association*, and *Psychoanalytic Inquiry*. I am also grateful to Praeger for permission to reprint portions of a chapter from *Narrative Psychology* (T. Sarbin, ed.).

I owe a special debt to Mrs. Charlotte Hardy who typed the final manuscript (and all earlier drafts). Her unfailing good humor was always welcome; her careful eye for detail a continuing source of reassurance.

Perhaps every science must start with metaphor and end with algebra; and perhaps without the metaphor, there would never have been any algebra.

— Max Black
Models and Metaphors

CHAPTER I

The Metaphorical Nature of Psychoanalytic Theory

To mention both metaphor and Freud in the same breath may seem somewhat unusual — but certainly not unappreciative. I use the word metaphor in the spirit of Max Black and believe that it is a necessary first step along the way to a rigorous theory. At the same time, however, we must recognize that much of psychoanalytic theory is still hypothetical and therefore a piece of undeveloped metaphor.* Many of Freud's conventions were intentional uses of figurative language, which allow us to see clinical happenings in a new and different manner, but have no necessary connection with reality. Much of this figurative usage has been lost in the Strachey translation (the so-called Standard Edition of Freud), as recent writers have pointed out (see Bettelheim, 1983, and Ornston, 1985), and as we are more and more distanced from the poetry of the original German, we are in increasing danger of losing sight of

---

*For a somewhat different discussion of the role of metaphor in Freud's writings, see J. Edelson, 1983.

the metaphor as well. The pseudo-scientific language invented by Strachey contributes to this danger.

Not only is metaphorical language becoming more respectable, but it is also increasingly clear that it represents a critical means of representing the world. "Metaphor," we are told, "is one of our most important tools for trying to comprehend partially what cannot be comprehended totally. . . . These endeavors of the imagination are not devoid of rationality; since they use metaphor, they employ an imaginative rationality" (Lakoff and Johnson, 1980, p. 193).

Building on a line of thought first expressed by Vico in the eighteenth century, metaphor has come to be seen (in the words of Isaiah Berlin) as a

> fundamental category through which at a given stage of development men cannot help viewing reality—which is for them reality itself, neither mere embellishment, nor a repository of secret wisdom, nor the creation of a world parallel to the real world, nor an addition to, or distortion of, reality, harmless or dangerous, deliberate or involuntary: but is the natural, inevitably transient, but, at the time of its birth or growth, the only possible way of perceiving, interpreting, explaining, that is open to men of that particular time and place, at that particular stage of their culture. (1976, p. 104)

Only a century before Vico, the use of metaphor was generally frowned upon in educated circles; it carried connotations of a pre- or anti-scientific state of mind.

> Thomas Sprat, one of the founders of the Royal Society, declared that "specious tropes and figures" should be banished "out of all Civill societies as a thing fatal to peace and good manners"; the Royal Society should avoid "myths and uncertainties," and return to "a close, naked, natural way of speaking . . . as near the Mathematical plainness as they can." So, too, Hobbes banished metaphor from all writings aimed at "the rigorous search for truth." Locke, Hume, and Adam Smith say much the same, although Hume allows that rigid adherence to "geometri-

cal truth . . . might have a disagreeable effect upon the reader. (Berlin, 1976, p. 104)

We can see now that the widespread fear of metaphor reflected by such philosophers as Locke, Hobbes, and Hume contained its own metaphor — an underlying belief in "geometrical truth" or in what Lakoff and Johnson call the myth of objectivity. The attacks on metaphorical thinking contained their own metaphorical pitfalls: all the time the critical philosophers were attacking this or that figure of speech, they were applying an objective metaphor to the world and thus committing the very crime they were attacking.

What does it mean to speak of the Freudian metaphor? In the first place, such usage highlights the poetic nature of Freud's language and underscores his revolutionary campaign to put the unspeakable and the unthinkable into words. These attempts, as he has made clear in many passages, were often groping, tentative, and exploratory: first approximations to phenomena and experience which, even now, have a way of slipping between our fingers. It is partly because it remains hard to capture that the experience tends to be replaced by the metaphor. But the experience may disappear in the process. The word — no matter how experimental or tentative or metaphoric — tends to replace the thing being described and we lose sight of the fact that the word is often more poetic than otherwise. A return to the original German (see Bettelheim, 1983) might repair some of the damage, but it would not solve the problem. To the extent that the language becomes more fanciful and romantic, it may only make it worse.

More specifically, the Freudian metaphor tempts us to believe in the idea of a dynamic unconscious which is actively and continuously influencing the contents of consciousness. It tells us that the contents of this unconscious "proliferate in the dark" where they develop "with less interference and more profusely" than in the light of conscious thought. It strongly suggests that

evenly suspended attention, in conjunction with free association, provides the analyst with the opportunity to uncover the
contents of the dynamic unconscious and the contents of key
happenings in the patient's past — the historical truth of his
early life. And finally, the Freudian metaphor trains us to see
the transference as a faithful replication of critical past experiences.

Each of these assumptions can be seen as a critical part of
Freudian theory, and for some, they have the status of established axioms. But they are also metaphors, as will be made
clear throughout this book. Once we lose sight of their metaphoric nature, we are in danger of turning psychoanalytic theory into a blueprint of the mind — or rather, into what we think is
a blueprint. In actual fact, however, the reified metaphor is
probably closer to a kind of mythology which acquires its own
reality and which deludes us into believing that now, at last, we
understand. This is the worst kind of metaphor; because of its
figurative, poetic nature, it resists falsification and turns into
what Black has called a "self-certifying myth." Metaphor of this
kind quickly turns into stereotype. If we are indeed living with
a Freudian mythology, we have lost touch with science.

The central issue facing us at the present time is not one of
confirmation or disconfirmation — a metaphor, after all, can
never be validated — but rather, which metaphors to choose and
whether they facilitate or interfere with the discovery of clinical
wisdom. Whatever metaphors we finally adopt, it is important
to realize that they are functioning primarily as models, as a
kind of extended sensory apparatus (see Lakoff and Johnson,
1980) which allows us to see certain sorts of phenomena and
certain kinds of causal relationships that would otherwise go
unnoticed. But the paradox is this: Their power as an aid to
comprehension is directly proportional to our awareness of
their metaphoric nature.

To keep alive the Freudian metaphor — that is the challenge
of the moment. To keep it uppermost in our awareness and

prevent it from becoming transparent allows us to keep its metaphorical nature clearly in mind, to avoid the trap of projecting its terms onto the clinical domain and finding things that are not really there. But to take the Freudian approach for granted, to deaden the metaphor and rule out other approaches, is to reduce our options to only one and mistakenly transform the theory into pseudo-science and the practice into a certain kind of religion.

Metaphor works, it would appear, by

> transferring the associated ideas and implications of the secondary [figurative] system to the primary system [domain of observation]. These select, emphasize, or suppress features of the primary; new slants on the primary are illuminated; the primary is seen through the frame of the secondary. In accordance with the doctrine that even literal expressions are understood partly in terms of the set of associated ideas carried by the system they describe, it follows that the associated ideas of the primary are changed to some extent by the use of the metaphor, and that therefore even its original literal description is shifted in meaning. The same applies to the secondary system, for its associations come to be affected by assimilations to the primary. Men are seen to be more like wolves after the wolf-metaphor is used ["man is a wolf"] and wolves seem to be more human. (Hesse, 1980, p. 114)

So it comes about that for the committed Freudian, a certain kind of unexpected outburst by the patient is literally *seen* as a piece of the unconscious which has remained too long in the dark and acquired an unexpected and frightening face. What is metaphoric in the original Freud becomes transformed into a literal description in the case report. When the Freudian metaphor is operating insistently (and invisibly), almost any piece of the clinical material can be seen in the literal language of the initial formulation. Under these conditions, however, the metaphor is no longer being used metaphorically; distorted perceptions of the analyst are projected onto the clinical material and there is no sense in which a particular model has been chosen or—what is just as distorting—that a set of alternatives has been excluded. As Hesse and other writers make clear, metaphors both emphasize and suppress: To see man as a wolf is to not see him as a grown child; to see all events as determined by an actual unconscious is to exclude the view that some events are random happenings.

When the Freudian metaphor operates in completely transparent fashion, it has shifted its status from alive to dead.

> Once such literalization has occurred and a "live" metaphor has been regressively transformed into a "dead" one, one no longer compares the "leg" of a table, let us say, to the leg of a person . . . but *literally* thinks of the supports of a table as its legs. (Carveth, 1984, p. 496)

On the other hand, to step outside the reigning metaphor and see it as one possibility among many is to carry out what Carveth calls a process of "deliteralization." By this means

> We are capable of achieving . . . the cognitive flexibility to intentionally diversify and alternate our conceptual frameworks and languages such that reality may be approached first from one angle and then from another. (Carveth, 1984, p. 509)

To carry out this goal and step outside the reigning metaphor is part of a central theme in modern philosophy.

> It would seem that we must abandon our quixotic attempts to discover *the* meaning (as opposed to a range of *complementary* meanings) of anything, not least ourselves. A great deal of the very best thinking in various fields of modern thought suggests that our grandiose positivist aspirations to godlike omniscience must be relinquished and replaced by a principle of uncertainty—a sacrifice through which, from conceit of knowledge, we might possibly advance toward a rudimentary knowledge of our conceit. (Carveth, 1984, p. 512)

To see the Freudian metaphor more clearly does not make it disappear and need not reduce it to triviality (as in saying, "Well, it's only a metaphor"). Because metaphors are central aspects of our understanding, we will always continue to use them; by the same token, we should not be used *by* them. But we will never step out from under the reigning metaphor unless we have a metaphor to take its place. In the last chapter we explore a possible alternative.

Once we see more clearly into the metaphorical nature of psychoanalytic theory, we begin to see the possible limits of validation and verification. Both metaphor and empirical laws carry explanatory force, but the kind of explanation provided by the first is significantly different from that provided by the second. The explanatory force of the Freudian metaphor of the unconscious is not diminished by the fact that it is seen as a manner of speaking; indeed, its credibility may even be strengthened. To become aware of its metaphoric foundation does, however, sensitize us to the fact that the Freudian system is not a lawful set of axioms which calls for explicit testing — either inside or outside the clinical arena. Its overthrow (or confirmation) will not come from experimental evidence precisely because of its heavy reliance on metaphorical explanation; for this reason, calls by Grünbaum (1984), Edelson (1983), and Holzman (1985) for systematic testing of psychoanalytic concepts seem more than a little misplaced. It might even be argued that calls for such testing represent a serious literalization of the Freudian metaphor and a mistaken belief that the critical psychoanalytic concepts possess a testable reality. To test the Freudian system as if it contained a set of falsifiable propositions is to overlook its essential metaphorical nature and to seriously concretize its most important concepts.

To keep alive the Freudian metaphor would seem to go beyond the argument of hermeneutics vs. science or truth vs. illusion; instead, it looks for different kinds of truth depending on what questions are being asked and what metaphors are being assumed. To make the fullest use of the Freudian metaphor requires a flexibility in approach which raises questions as to the conditions in which it seems relevant and a guide to understanding — and the conditions which call out for some other approach. To identify the Freudian metaphor as a description for a certain approach and a certain set of assumptions opens the way to specifying other metaphors which would illuminate other parts of the clinical picture and thus enlarge and further our understanding.

To keep the Freudian approach alive as metaphor is to extract its fullest potential and to make the greatest use of other options when the need requires. To speak metaphorically in full awareness of this fact is to be reminded that we are using language figuratively and tentatively — but at the same time, extending its use in significant ways. But to take the Freudian system for granted — to deaden the metaphor and rule out other approaches — is to reduce our options to only one and mistakenly transform metaphor into pseudo-science. To use it in this way is to diminish the poetry of Freud's original inspiration and, in the long run, to miss the spirit of the whole adventure.

Freud's Use of Metaphor

Freud was well acquainted with the explanatory power of metaphor. At the start of his paper on instincts, he had this to say about the language of science:

> We have often heard it maintained that sciences should be built up on clear and sharply defined basic concepts. In actual fact, no science, not even the most exact, begins with such definitions. The true beginning of scientific activity consists rather in describing phenomena and then in proceeding to group, classify, and correlate them. Even at the stage of description it is not possible to avoid applying certain abstract ideas to the material in hand, ideas derived from somewhere or other but certainly not from the new observations alone. Such ideas — which will

later become the basic concepts of the science — are still more indispensable as the material is further worked over. They must at first necessarily possess some degree of indefiniteness; there can be no question of any clear delimitation of their content. So long as they remain in this condition, we come to an understanding about their meaning by making repeated references to the material of observation from which they appear to have been derived, but upon which, in fact, they have been imposed. Thus, strictly speaking, they are in the nature of conventions — although everything depends on their not being arbitrarily chosen but determined by their having significant relations to the empirical material, relations that we seem to sense before we can clearly recognize and demonstrate them. It is only after more thorough investigation of the field of observation that we are able to formulate its basic scientific concepts with increased precision, and progressively so to modify them that they become serviceable and consistent over a wide area. (Freud, 1915a, p. 117)

It can be seen that Freud was well aware of the distinction between explanatory concepts which opened up a field of investigation and provided the initial (although possibly erroneous) glimpses into an unexplored domain, and later models which are more closely fitted to emerging observations and which may differ in both form and content from the earlier concepts. He was perhaps less sensitive to the underside of metaphorical usage — less concerned about the fact that the concept which sensitizes us to one part of the domain will blind us to another, and that if the wrong metaphor is chosen in the first place, it may never be possible to refine the "basic scientific concepts with increased precision, and . . . modify them that they become serviceable and consistent over a wide area."
It should not be assumed that the idea of replacement was unfamiliar; only the year before, he had discussed the way in which science begins its work with "nebulous, scarcely imaginable basic concepts, which it hopes to apprehend more clearly in

the course of its development, or which it is even prepared to replace by others" (1914, p. 77). But then he goes on: "For these ideas are not the foundation of science, upon which everything rests; that foundation is observation alone. They are not the bottom but the top of the whole structure, and they can be replaced and discarded without damaging it" (p. 77).

We can see two problems. Observation, first of all, is not the foundation of science; observation is always mediated by metaphor. And the metaphor is never innocent, never peripheral to the elaboration of theory, never flexible enough to accommodate *all* observations. If the wrong metaphor is chosen, some of the "observations" will not be seen in the first place because we will be looking in the wrong part of the clinical arena; others may be noticed but set aside because they make no "sense" against the background of the prevailing model.

As Freud developed and extended his theory, his metaphors tended to become more reified and less tentative, and this tendency made it all the more unlikely that they would either be influenced by new findings or replaced by more fitting models. In the next chapter, we look in some detail at the unconscious; it will appear that Freud's 1915 model was extraordinarily specific on a variety of levels. With the advent of the structural theory, however, the topographic unconscious was turned into the id; many of the original details specified in the original (1915c) paper were never referred to again; and they were replaced by such figures as "a chaos, a cauldron full of seething excitations" (1932a, p. 73). A seething cauldron can hardly be falsifed by the data, no matter how careful the observations; as a result, it tends to become uncoupled from the clinical observations and exist in a protected domain where it is free of influence and yet always available for rhetorical mischief. Not only is the use of these "free-floating" metaphors epistemologically empty, but so long as they remain in circulation, they interfere with the formation of other kinds of models and may actually reduce or totally eliminate our awareness of certain clinical happenings. Protected by its vagueness, the free-floating metaphor can never be falsified and therefore always exists as a kind of presumptive explanation, a working hypothesis which invites us to believe that validation is just around the corner. Here is Freud's extended description of the id:

> It is filled with energy reaching it from the instincts, but it has no organization, produces no collective will, but only a striving to bring about the satisfaction of the instinctual needs. . . . Wishful impulses which have never passed beyond the id . . . are virtually immortal; after the passage of decades they behave as though they had just occurred. (1932a, pp. 73–74)

Breadth vs. Depth

We have seen how Freud was in the habit of using figures of speech to capture the phenomena which he wanted to study, and we have seen how he was quite deliberate in this attempt and well aware that the metaphor was being brought in from the outside. To the extent that it represents a convention, a certain way of thinking about the phenomenon under investigation, the metaphor has no necessary connection to the observations. In this regard, metaphor in psychoanalysis operates no differently from metaphor in physics. The early theory of the atom, for example, represented the atom as a miniature "solar system" in which electrons were represented as revolving around the nucleus. Since it could never be visualized concretely, it could never be tested directly.

But the Bohr model was not *merely* a metaphor — and that fact makes all the difference. The "solar system" metaphor led to a number of testable hypotheses; it could predict, for example, the spectrum of light emitted by a specific element. Results of these tests could be used to further refine the metaphor, elaborate the underlying model, and arrive at a clarified conception of the "solar system" which would be even more relevant to the nature of the atom.

Psychoanalytic metaphors, by contrast, have not generated testable predictions in ways that lead to specific alterations of the model. As we will see in the next chapter, we know very little more at the present time about the form and content of the unconscious than was proposed by Freud (1915b) in his original paper (some might say a good deal less). As is the case with any number of Freud's innovative figures of speech, the metaphor of an unknowable, timeless, and content-rich unconscious which "proliferates in the dark" has neither given rise to new observation nor led to a better understanding of earlier findings. The same criticism could be leveled against the metaphor of psychic structure or psychic energy. We have no precise way of visualizing either the structure or its energy; we cannot even propose a plan of study which could make this possible.

Cut off from systematic elaboration, unrelated to the clinical findings, the central (free-floating) metaphors of psychoanalysis have tended, as we have seen, to take on a life of their own; they have become reified prematurely and treated as something more than figures of speech. The desire to make psychoanalysis into a science may accelerate this process. It seems closer to science to speak of psychic structure in place of pieces of the mind, or of diminished libido in place of reduced interest in sex. To speak of a specific unconscious fantasy with knowable content and predictable derivatives takes on its own kind of reality. The models then become doubly misleading; they support Freud's original aim to capture phenomena in concrete images while also enhancing the metaphor of psychoanalysis as a science.

Something else happens as well. The more sanctified its use and the more established it becomes in the literature, the more we are tempted to assume that the free-floating metaphor is literally true. Given that assumption, the more likely we are to see the world through its eyes, and the more we are cut off from other models and other ways of seeing. Consider Freud's philosophical heritage from Descartes and Brentano, the foundation for many of his favorite models. As part of this tradition, he carried forward the idea that the mind is a set of mental states, with each of these states presumed to have a content, to be *about* something: This is Brentano's intentional conception of the mind. By this metaphor, elaborated by Freud's concept of the unconscious, the mind can be represented as a set of mental states, some in awareness and some not. (I am indebted to Dreyfus and Wakefield, 1987, for this way of representing Freud's epistemology.)

The view of the mind as a layered collection of representations leads directly to Freud's well-known archeological metaphor, to the model of *depth* psychology, and to the family of tropes representing the mind as a storehouse of memories and conflicts. It leads to the model of neurotic distress as somehow situated *in* the mind. By contrast, as Dreyfus and Wakefield (1987) have recently made clear, the problems of the patient and his difficulties with the world could just as well be represented by a *breadth* psychology in which the mind is not mentioned at all. In this view (inspired in particular by Heidegger and Merleau-Ponty), there is no need to believe that the objects in the world have a fixed representation in the mind, taking a library or an archive as the model. In their theory,

> the pure representational [Freudian] view leaves out a crucial part of the story. . . . The shared practices into which we are socialized provide a background understanding of what counts as objects, what counts as human beings, and ultimately what counts as real, on the basis of which we can direct our mind toward particular things and people. (Dreyfus and Wakefield, 1987, p. 00)

This background understanding or clearing (*Lichtung*) can be compared to the illumination in a room.

> The illumination allows us to perceive objects, but is not itself an object towards which the eye can be directed. [Merleau-Ponty] argues that this clearing can be correlated with our bodily skills and thus with the bodily stance we take towards people and things. It is our preparedness for a particular kind of bodily interaction, with a thing, such as using a hammer, or sitting in a chair, or exploring the other side of a wall, which gives us our sense of the reality of such things. It is only on the background of our bodily sense of our potential interactions with a thing that a representation of it can form and make any sense. (p. 00)

The metaphor of the clearing (breadth) may not necessarily be superior to the metaphor of archeology (depth), but that is not the point. What seems clear is how difficult it is to believe in both at the same time. If we think of the mind as a collection of representations of the world, each idea having a fixed meaning, then it is tempting to see therapy as an attempt to rearrange this collection and change their relation to awareness (the metaphor of therapy as "shrinking" tries to capture this attempt). It is also tempting to see the world as a fixed reality through which we move and in which we live. The view of the world as a given set of objects, each having a fixed meaning, leads naturally to Freud's metaphor of free association in which the patient is represented as a passenger on a train, reporting the changing scene (the contents of his mind) to his seatmate, the analyst.

If, on the other hand, the world is not a collection of fixed objects but a shifting set of meanings, the names of which depend on who is looking, then the patient's view through the train window is not so easy to either capture or understand. If the world depends for its description on who is looking, then the representations in your head may be significantly different from the representations in mine. The meaning and usefulness of empathy are immediately brought into question. And if problems in living are a function of problems in categorization, then attention should be focused on how the world is seen rather than how it is stored. If the meaning of an object depends on who is looking and his sense of what it is used for, then it follows that experiences will always be colored by issues of time and place. The absence of early memories, for example, could be seen, using this metaphor, as the problem of having access to specific codes — not as the outcome of repression.

The well-known theory of Ernst Schachtel (1947) makes use of this alternative model. According to this formulation, infantile experiences are registered in a language which is more responsive to the emotional, nonverbal, sensual, and positional correlates of experience. Many of these experiences impinge on the child before his language is well developed. As he moves into an adult world, he acquires new categories of meaning and classification, categories which "are not suitable vehicles to receive and reproduce experience of the quality and intensity typical of early childhood" (1947, p. 4).

We begin to see in more detail how metaphor can contract as well as enlarge our view of the world. Steeped in the archeological metaphor and trained to believe in a real unconscious which has both depth and content, we may be somewhat shocked to be told that these are only figures of speech and that alternative metaphors are also available which might make even better sense of the clinical findings. The die is cast when we lose sight of the metaphoric nature of the theory. A dead metaphor, as noted, comes close to being confused with what we are trying to describe. Despite Freud's sensitivity to this issue, he frequently overlooked the distinction between model and observation and tended to treat his metaphor as if it were a confirmed piece of reality. Many of his followers have made the same mistake.

The danger of reification becomes all the greater when we are working with free-floating metaphors — the kind that psychoanalysis contains in abundance. Uncoupled from the clinical observation, unresponsive (because of their global nature) to subtle changes in observation, the central Freudian images threaten to completely dominate our view of the discipline and fool us into thinking that precise explanation is just over the horizon, that our main task is one of validation, not discovery, and that the main outlines of the theory have long since been settled. In his 1979 Presidential address, Kaplan stated that "it is becoming much more evident that any progress in psychoanalysis must include our evaluation of the psychoanalytic process . . . with the hope of verifying the data of observation" (1981, p. 19). Kaplan's address emphasizes confirmation over disconfirmation and carries the implicit message that Freud's guiding metaphors are largely correct. Psychoanalysis is represented as a science which has now entered its final phase.

From a more skeptical point of view, prospects are not quite so bright. We still seem to be in the early stages of choosing the right metaphor; many of our favorite models have not developed much beyond their early formulations; and most sobering of all, we have no metaphor which has been turned into algebra. When the metaphor becomes free-floating and uncoupled from the clinical observation, the danger becomes all the greater. Shielded from elaboration or emendation, the chosen metaphor becomes all that more easily reified, and instead of a provisional model, we are left with a fully-formed structure which masquerades as science.

In the next chapters we look at two of the central metaphors in psychoanalytic theory.

CHAPTER II

. ———————————

The Metaphorical Unconscious

Conceived as the ultimate cause of any complex behavior, a kind of distant field of force whose effects can be sensed but whose shape is never seen, the dynamic unconscious continues to play a central role in psychoanalytic theory and to be routinely invoked in the course of clinical discussion. Its form and function are, by definition, never directly observed; therefore, they must be reconstructed from conscious behavior. Indeed, it was partly because of gaps in the conscious record that Freud (1915c) was impelled to postulate the existence of the unconscious. But there is a significant difference between the initial drawing up of such a hypothesis — a perfectly legitimate undertaking — and its subsequent validation and verification, and I will argue that there is as yet little hard evidence for its support. In this chapter, I will draw heavily on the distinction between the unconscious as a system with clearly defined rules of operation (the substantive unconscious) and unconscious as an adjective, used in the popular way to mean not available to awareness or referring to processes operating outside of awareness (the descriptive unconscious). We will continue to use the second in any number of contexts (see Shevrin and Dickman, 1980, and Bowers, 1984, for recent reviews); it is less certain whether we should continue to use the first.

Faced by gaps or perturbations in the conscious record — a slip of the tongue, for example, an unexplained piece of forgetting, or the emergence of an out-of-context tic or other symptom — Freud found it convenient to suggest that these symptoms could be defined as manifestations of the substantive unconscious. Just as he constructed infantile events on the basis of the patient's dreams and associations which could be used to account for his present behavior, moving the construction backward in time so that it became a cause of the present (Jacobsen and Steele, 1979), so he constructed a structure from the patient's conscious responses which was moved outside of awareness to become the cause of these responses (the unconscious, usually conceptualized in the form of an unconscious fantasy). Both infantile constructions and unconscious fantasies are screened off from direct observation; both are useful postulates to account for what can be observed; and both play an important role in psychoanalytic explanation. But if they are no more than hypothetical constructs, shielded from verification, then the explanation based on these concepts may be empirically empty.

We are first confronted by the problem of circularity. Jacobsen and Steele (1979) show in great detail how the constructions which Freud produced to explain the Wolf Man are useful in adding plausibility to the final account but have next to no status as confirmable facts. Given the evidence produced by the patient, Freud's constructions go a long way toward adding coherence and narrative polish to what was originally a rather bizarre story; given their seemingly good fit with the facts of the case, these constructions take on a certain narrative truth and may even be thought of as semi-factual in status. But their essential truth value does not go beyond the surrounding narrative; what is more important, they do not even validate Freud's theory of infantile fantasies. And why not? Because it can be seen that we have no independent verification of the role of these constructions in the patient's development. Given the same set of facts, other sets of infantile events could be hypothesized, and even though all attempts might be convincing, the *theory* — that early infantile experience is significant in accounting for later behavior — could still be wrong because each set of explanations might be nothing more than ad hoc.

Similar problems appear when we examine unconscious motivation. For each instance of unexplained behavior, one or more "unconscious" propositions or fantasies could be supplied which would explain the occurrence. But this kind of account is much the same as attributing the failure of an airplane engine to gremlins. Used in this manner, the structure unconscious is little more than sophisticated demonology. So long as fresh pieces of the unconscious are invoked to explain each new occurrence, we will simply be restating Freud's original hypothesis of unconscious motivation. And countless applications of a wrong-headed theory — in the absence of accumulated evidence — add nothing to its validity.

What is missing, of course, is any evidence of convergent effect or cross-validation. What is deduced about a patient's unconscious fantasy life from symptoms A, B, and C must be validated by its use in explaining symptoms D and E. A, B, and C must be independent of D and E; therefore, D and E cannot be known at the time that A, B, and C are used to formulate an unconscious proposition. (If they were known, there would be the suspicion that they somehow biased this proposition and that it accounted for D and E partly because it was designed with them in mind.)

Given two or more independent sets of events, we next need to reach an understanding of confirmation or pattern match. The theory of unconscious motivation makes this a difficult decision to reach because of the critical roles of transformation and displacement. Psychoanalytic theory tells us that although a certain unconscious idea, A, may be prevented from becoming conscious, it may sometimes emerge in disguised form as A'. But Freud (1900) gave us only a rudimentary grammar of transformations (the seventh chapter in *The Interpretation of Dreams*). There is the further problem that what appears to be a transformation from A to A' (which I have labeled a soft pattern match) may often be a pair of unconnected events. This error comes about because of the richness of the real world; as a direct consequence of this richness, most of us find it incredibly easy to establish links between any two of its pieces, whether or not they are meaningfully related. Because soft pattern matches can happen by accident and because we have only an incomplete transformational grammar, the loose fit between unconscious proposition and clinical event cannot be taken as evidence. Before the unconscious hypothesis can be meaningfully applied, some way must be found to separate true transformations from their bogus counterparts because of the fact that the concept of transformation is a central part of Freud's theory of the unconcious.

Thus, a conviction that unconscious motivation is at work can be faulted on at least two grounds. First, if the form of the unconscious fantasy cannot be established independently of its presumptive effect, we may have a piece of circular reasoning. Second, if we claim that a previously established unconscious fantasy can be used to account for a new clinical event, we may have demonstrated no more than the chance overlap between two unrelated happenings. We must show that the pattern match (between presumptive idea and new event) conforms to certain transformation rules (by means of a presently non-existing grammar) and that these rules allow us to define the pattern match as hard rather than soft.

For an example of how an unconscious fantasy is typically inferred from manifest content, consider Langs' (1981) recent re-analysis of an anecdote originally reported by Greenson (1967). In the original hour, the patient felt tired, irritable, and recalled a weekend which left him bored and depressed. After further associations, Greenson pointed out to the patient that he seemed depressed and angry but was also holding back his feelings. The patient then responded that he "felt disgusted and enraged at Greenson's saccharine tone, and that he had been furious with him before his last hour on Friday because he had been kept waiting while Greenson gave a pretty woman patient some of his time" (Langs, p. 207). Langs labels the feelings of irritation and tiredness as Type Two derivatives of being re-jected on Friday in favor of the woman patient — another way of saying that the unconscious meaning of these feelings must have been the response to being rejected by the analyst. This conjecture constitutes a plausible hypothesis and, in keeping with similar conjectures along the same lines, tries to build two seemingly disparate events into some kind of continuous pat-tern.

What is at issue is the question of validation. After criticizing Greenson for keeping him waiting, the patient goes on to de-scribe how he had made a wrong turn while driving home from the session and had almost hit another car. Langs chooses to see this association as a validation of the unconscious interpreta-tion. "The mismanagement of the patient's time was experi-enced quite validly as an assault, and generated an image of a hypocritical analyst who professes to be helpful while uncon-sciously behaving in a destructive way" (p. 208). Greenson's decision to see the woman patient was seen as a "wrong turn" which produced a "near collision."

Langs' analysis of the account can be represented as a partic-ular "reading" of the Greenson "text," and as such, it has added to the plausibility and coherence of the patient's associations. But Langs intends much more by claiming that he has uncover-ed the unconscious meaning of the original feelings of tiredness and irritability. He is making a claim about the cause of these feelings and, in the process, a claim to understanding the con-tent of the patient's unconscious at the time these feelings were expressed. And this claim is presumably validated by the subsequent association about making a wrong turn. Possibility turns into certainty; thus "the mismanagement of the patient's time *was experienced quite validly* as an assault" (p. 208, my italics). We no longer have one of many possible readings of the event; we have arrived at its only meaning.

With such a strong claim at stake, we need to be more than usually cautious about interpretations of pattern match, and here the formulation is vulnerable to the second type of error described above. The correspondence between taking a wrong turn and the analyst making a technical mistake is based more on analogical reasoning than a clear similarity of events. We can, if we choose, look at the mistake as a kind of "wrong turn" which may have come close to a "near collision," but in reasoning this way, we are drawing on the metaphorical looseness of language to find similarity between two separate events. And such a metaphor simply allows us to generate a possible similarity; it says nothing about the first being the necessary cause of the second. It seems clear that a causal attribution requires a pattern match that is beyond reproach and from a clearly different domain than the word play we use in literary analysis.

A second cause for concern lies in the lack of cross-validation (the first error listed above). Langs makes no attempt to show that his representation of the patient's unconscious can be used to account for subsequent derivatives. If we have, as claimed, identified a portion of the patient's unconscious, then these ideas are presumably active over a finite period of time and should affect other pieces of behavior and emerge in related derivatives. In fact, it could be argued that *only* when we can achieve cross-validation can we make a meaningful statement about the substantive unconscious.

Now one might ask, can a hard pattern match and independent verification ever be established? Can we ever make a verified claim that such-and-such was—beyond doubt—the contents of the patient's unconscious? Can we ever say that this interpretation is not just another reading of the hour but represents the true cause of a particular piece of behavior? If we can, then we obviously have need for the substantive unconscious; if we cannot, we may be appealing to an empty construct. There may still remain a metaphorical use for this construct, but we should be clear that there may be no referent (for a similar view, see Bernstein, 1987).

For another example of how the unconscious functions primarily as a metaphor, we turn again to Greenson, this time looking at his discussion of technique. In a section entitled "Understanding the Unconscious," he lists the following skills required of the psychoanalyst:

> The most important skill which the psychoanalyst must possess is his ability to translate the patient's conscious thoughts, feelings, fantasies, impulses, and behavior into their unconscious antecedents. He must be able to sense what lies behind the various subjects his patient is talking about in the analytic session. He must listen to the obvious melody but also hear the hidden (unconscious) themes in the "left hand," the counterpoint. He must look at the fragmented pictures the patient paints and be able to translate them back into their original and unconscious form. (Greenson, 1967, p. 365)

This description captures very well the assumption we have been discussing, the assumption that there is a concrete *something* which "lies behind" the manifest content of the patient's associations, a hidden something which can be uncovered and brought to light. We are reminded of Freud's archeological metaphor and his fascination with antiquity; psychoanalysis, by this model, can be described as an excavation of the mind. The nature of Greenson's description is worth particular attention because it suggests that there is only one answer and that it is discoverable. The specificity of the unconscious fantasy stands in significant contrast to the ambiguity of the manifest content; the clear-cut, hoped-for answer is almost the direct opposite of the confusion and chaos of the problem.

Now consider one of Greenson's examples of unconscious deduction:

> A young man talks in his hour of his anger and disgust at his older sister's toilet habits. She leaves the door slightly ajar so he can accidentally see her ugly naked breasts. He can even hear the different toilet noises and they are disgusting. When he goes into the bathroom afterwards he tries not to breathe, but he can still smell her body odors and her powder. The sight of some of her hair in the tub makes him feel like vomiting. Despite the loud conscious anger and disgust it is quite easy to hear in the background the young man's sexual interest in his sister's bodily activities. His unconscious fantasies of taking the different parts of her in his mouth make him feel disgust and nausea. He is not angry at her for being ugly; quite the contrary, he is angry at her for being exciting. (Greenson, 1967, pp. 365–366)

The explanation is not only concrete; it is unambiguous. The patient's sexual fantasies about his sister are the clear and certain cause of his reaction; there seems no possibility for error or for the contribution of other factors. There is no discussion of the possibility that what Greenson "hears in the background" may not be "heard" by other readers, or—much more damning—that what Greenson thinks he "hears" is really being projected onto the material.

It can be argued that much of the absolute certainty of this form of explanation derives from the assumption that the dynamic unconscious exists as a real entity and is being continually transformed into the manifest content of everyday behavior. This assumption is a central part of the Freudian metaphor. Belief in a dynamic unconscious—what might be called the "unconscious postulate"—would seem to contribute directly to the inflexible nature of the usual psychoanalytic explanation, and thus to close off a more thoughtful, problematic, and probabilistic form of reasoning. Now we have still another reason why the hypothesis has remained alive for so long: It leads directly to simplified argument and to an authoritarian approach to the evidence, which greatly facilitates the job of explanation. When Greenson writes, "It is quite easy to hear in the background . . . ," he is mainly making an appeal to his authority and using that to settle the issue.

But something is missing—namely, conviction. The skeptical reader is not convinced by this form of reasoning because what is being asserted as a conclusion is really no more than a possible hypothesis. *If* the patient has an unconscious fantasy of oral sex with his sister, and *if* this fantasy leads to disgust and nausea, *then* we have a possible explanation for his behavior. The argument falters because we have no independent evidence for such a fantasy or evidence that disgust would be the result. (He might, for example, be sexually aroused or disappointed.) Most damning of all, we have no independent evidence that the dynamic unconscious has an independent existence, and therefore that it is anything more than a metaphor.

It is important to appreciate how forcefully the strength of Greenson's argument depends on what might be called the unconscious postulate. Its axiomatic status is implied in the discussion of psychoanalytic skills, in the description of how the analyst listens, and in the rather summary explanation for the patient's behavior; its abbreviated form implies that because of the unconscious postulate, no more evidence is necessary. But if this postulate is found wanting or if its hypothetical standing is better appreciated, then Greenson's explanation changes from a final account to a tentative formulation. The paragraph quoted above would then become only the initial statement of the argument; it would have to be followed by confirming and disconfirming evidence and end in some kind of decision as to whether the hypothesis should be accepted, modified, or simply scrapped.

To reason in this more tentative fashion not only leads to

greater conviction, but may also provide evidence bearing on the unconscious postulate. Such evidence is significantly lacking in the Greenson explanation, largely because it is taken as a given — its status is beyond argument. Because we have been claiming for many years that the unconscious exists, we have tended to treat as irrelevant the evidence pro and con; now when its status is called into question, such evidence is in short supply.

For a third example of how the unconscious can be taken for granted and treated as a concrete field of force instead of an explanatory concept, consider the following claim by Brenner: "If the unconscious cause or causes can be discovered, then *all* apparent discontinuities disappear and the causal chain or sequence becomes clear" (1955, p. 14; my italics). To speak in this manner seems to suggest that the unconscious has a fixed content; that a finite cause or causes can be discovered; that we will know when we have discovered them correctly; that there is no room for multiple interpretation or other kinds of ambiguity; and that when the unconscious becomes clear, *all* problems of understanding and *all* uncertainties will dissolve. A literal reading of this quotation turns psychoanalysis into a wonderfully exact science; to speak in this manner holds out the hope that the day will come when we will discover that psychic functioning is every bit as lawful as any other part of the physical universe. The unconscious is no longer a metaphor; it is a discoverable entity with a knowable content and a clear connection to manifest behavior.

It would appear that a troubling change has occurred in the status of our theory. What was originally intended as a working hypothesis which could be used to further our understanding of the clinical material and whose nature could be clarified by a careful reading of this material has been transformed into a piece of knowledge whose standing is beyond question and whose significance has increased in direct proportion to its inaccessibility to study. As its significance has increased, direct knowledge has diminished. Legitimatized as an axiom, it has been largely screened off from study, and a careful review of current conceptions would probably show little advance over Freud's model of 1915. We have little more precise knowledge, at the present time, of the workings of the primary process, of the rules and conditions of transformation, or of what might be called the half-life of the typical unconscious fantasy than we did in 1915. Nor do we have even approximate answers to any of the questions raised by Freud in his original monograph.

It could be argued that the unconscious postulate has become our collective fantasy, a ghost in the machine which can explain almost anything and which only we can identify. William James called it "the sovereign means for believing what one likes in psychology" and the "tumbling ground for whimsies" (quoted in Shevrin and Dickman, 1980, p. 432); even though written almost one hundred years ago, his description is still largely true. As with other fantasies, its life is not touched by fact; as with other fantasies, it is kept alive by wish; as with other fantasies, its existence depends purely on belief; as with other fantasies, its psychic standing is much more than hypothetical. It is perhaps this last feature which interferes most with the way we treat our data and present our findings.

A Defense Against Skepticism

Schafer (1976), Messer and Winokur (1980), and more recently Stein (1985) have all drawn attention to the ironic voice in the psychoanalytic process. Defined as a "readiness to seek out internal contradictions, ambiguities, and paradoxes" (Messer and Winokur, p. 823), irony is a familiar stance of Freud's. He stressed what might be called the ambiguity of everyday life, the fact that things are almost never what they seem, that surface is always deceptive, and that true understanding must always go beneath the surface. Irony shows itself in the method of approaching each piece of the patient's behavior with the idea that it may represent something else: Memories may be screens for obscure childhood events, dreams can be translated into latent dream thoughts, symptoms may conceal wishes, and the like. Although Schafer (1976) originally presented irony as one of four "visions of reality" which together constitute the psychoanalytic world view, it can be argued that irony is the quintessential Freudian voice.

Taking an ironic stance, we begin with the assumption that any given piece of behavior represents more than meets the eye. We set aside the surface meaning in favor of the latent intent; or more technically, we see the surface meaning as a derivative of some piece of the patient's unconscious. Irony is frequently used in the service of gaining access to the unconscious; our initial skepticism about a piece of behavior prepares the way for discovery of the more abiding, underlying motives. In this way, the psychoanalyst differs from the traditional philosophical skeptic (who believes in nothing).

But where the psychoanalyst is properly skeptical of the surface, he may be too easily convinced about what lies below and therefore prone to many kinds of logical errors in drawing up his map of the patient's unconscious. We have seen how tempting it is to settle for soft rather than hard pattern matches, to be insensitive to the need for cross-validation, and to be insensitive to the idea that the construct of the unconscious is still only a hypothesis about which the verdict is still out (after almost one hundred years). Thus the psychoanalyst may be initially ironic, but he may not continue this stance as far as he might.

Viewed in this light, the belief in the unconscious can be seen as a kind of refuge against pure (philosophical) skepticism. External reality may be apparently random and discontinuous, but there is a bedrock of psychic reality to fall back on; if a certain content is assigned to the patient's unconscious, then we have an explanation for unrelated bits of behavior. The question at stake is the following: Does such a move do anything more than improve on the narrative truth of our explanation?

Is there some functional advantage in assigning a particular content to the unconscious as opposed to saying something like, "It looks as if you might have done what you did for the following reasons . . . "?

At least four advantages can be suggested. First, in calling the unconscious into account and in finding derivatives of the unconscious in the patient's external behavior, we seem to be making a more lawful statement than if we talk in terms of hypothetical reasons. We have advanced from reason to cause. If we are right in being able to read the patient's unconscious as we claim, then we have accounted for much of the mystery in his behavior because the contents of this unconscious, when subjected to certain transformation rules, will emerge as pieces of the patient's waking behavior.

Second, in discovering the known cause of apparently random behavior, we are spared the burden of the pure skeptic who must claim that nothing is known and that the problem of other minds is essentially insoluble. The uncertainty of visible behavior is replaced by the presumed certainty of discovering the form and substance of the patient's unconscious. Even if not all parts are known, we trust that successive approximations will bring us nearer to its actual shape. Future pieces of the contents of consciousness will be sifted over for what they reveal about this underlying shape, and the suppositions validated on future pieces of behavior. Even if the final answer is always in doubt, the presumption that we can identify an independent variable — the unconscious — which results in certain kinds of dependent responses is significantly different (and thousands of times more reassuring) than the presumption that behavior is essentially discontinuous, fragmented, and unknowable.

Third, we have the well-known benefits which stem from finding an explanation where none existed before. To provide a plausible story for a set of facts is enormously reassuring, particularly when the story changes a random set of happenings into a neatly packaged account with a beginning, middle, and end. Our need for explanation is such that we may often settle for the plausible in favor of the knowable and settle for possible myth instead of apparent randomness. To link our explanation with a potentially knowable unconscious is to give it even more plausibility because it holds out the hope that some day, when all is known, a truly complete explanation will be discovered. Our explanation, instead of being ad hoc and for that reason logically suspect, becomes theoretically perfectible and therefore more persuasive.

Fourth, we may be overly impressed by the metaphor of going below the surface. To the extent that the unconscious is "deeper" and to the extent that a dynamic explanation invokes "depth" psychology, we may fool ourselves into thinking that we have made contact with more fundamental issues and have come closer to the "true" explanation.

But in the last analysis, by pointing to the unconscious as the ultimate source of the behavior to be explained, we have merely exchanged one kind of uncertainty for another. The burden of skepticism and the problem of other minds is exchanged for the more tolerable expectation that eventually we will discover the final solution to the *Ucs.* code. The second stance gives us a chance to look for clues, to try out different formulations, and to be on the lookout for hidden themes; it lets us approach future data in a spirit of discovery and entertain new problems because they always hold out the hope of solution. But it should be realized that their solution may be mainly promissory and conjectural and that our fund of definite knowledge has not actually been enlarged.

Thus, the system unconscious and a belief in its influence would seem to significantly soften the ironic picture. The danger that things are truly as fragmented as they seem is answered by the premise that their meaning is ultimately continuous and knowable and by the corollary that a large number of unexplained events — the patient's life — can be reduced to a finite set of factors — the contents of his unconscious. We now must look at how this task is carried out. We will come back to the problem of meaninglessness in the last chapter.

Features of the System Ucs.

Freud made clear in his definitional monograph that to call an idea unconscious was to say much more than that it was not available to awareness. In the section on special characteristics, he argued that the processes of the system *Ucs.* have the following features: "Exemption from mutual contradiction, primary process (mobility of cathexes), timelessness, and replacement of external by psychical reality" (1915b, p. 187). In another section, he states that the "*Ucs.* is alive and capable of development" (p. 190). What needs to be pointed out is the fact that some of these characteristics make it almost impossible to verify our assumptions about a particular patient's unconscious. If it is true that we can neither confirm nor disconfirm the hypothesis that the unconscious exists in a particular form, then we must ask (following Popper, 1963) whether the hypothesis is not essentially empty. We may hold it for various reasons, influenced in particular by the fact that it protects us from unblinking skepticism, but we should realize that the benefits are primarily metaphorical.

Consider first the assumption that unconscious ideas are "exempt from mutual contradiction." This principle would seem to imply that a complete account of a particular unconscious would not necessarily show any logical sequence or hierarchy of ideas; conversely, it would follow that contradiction cannot be taken as evidence that our construction is faulty. In other words, there are no internal checks which we can apply to determine whether we have identified all critical features of the system unconscious, much less to determine whether we are right in some parts and wrong in others. If contradiction is assumed to one of the organizing rules, then errors of either commission or omission can *never*, by definition, be discovered.

The assumption that the unconscious is "alive and capable of development" introduces a related complication. If the unknown is always changing, then it may be impossible to apply the principles of convergence and cross-validation identified earlier in this chapter. If the unknown is different from one moment to the next, then we can never distinguish between valid description and ad hoc formulation because the former can be as varying as the latter. Lack of reliability over time in our descriptions of the unconscious can either be a mark of error or a sign that we are tracking actual changes, but there is nothing in our description to indicate which is which.

A third difficulty emerges in the section of the monograph titled "Communication Between the Two Systems" (*Pcs.* and *Ucs.*), where Freud describes the nature of unconscious derivatives. He sets forth the general rule that ease of passage from one system to the other varies directly with degree of distortion; thus the *Ucs.* ideas which are subsequently transformed are more likely to come into consciousness than the ideas which are more literally reproduced. It follows that the clues we understand literally do not (by definition) belong to the unconscious. A literal reading of the manifest content will almost surely *not* give us its unconscious meaning because, first, if there is no transformation, it does not belong to the system unconscious, and second, if there is a transformation, we cannot, by definition, use the literal meaning. But if we lack a grammar of transformations, we have no systematic way of going beyond the literal meaning. We can, to be sure, always make guesses about possible transformations, but because the unconscious is always a matter of speculation and because it is always developing, we have no way of validating these guesses.

The force of these three difficulties seems clear. Even though we postulate a knowable unconscious in theory, we may find that it is largely unknowable in practice. If that is the case, we come back to the position of the skeptic who claims that other minds are opaque. We may not take the skeptical position (that minds are unknowable), but we have no way to counter his argument.

What then is the function of the dynamic unconscious? Freud originally proposed it as a way of accounting for gaps in the conscious record; we can now view this problem in a new light. A discontinuity between A' and B' in a patient's stream of associations can mean (1) that the linking idea, A/B, is prevented from entering consciousness because it was not sufficiently disguised; (2) that either A' or B' is a distortion of an unconscious idea, allowed to enter awareness, and that a proper decoding of the distortion would bring us back to the logical sequence AB; (3) that both A' and B' are distortions of A, B; or (4) that his thought had actually been interrupted by an intrusive idea.

To complicate matters further, we have no way of knowing whether a particular idea is to be taken literally or is a transformation of something else. To make the dynamic hypothesis work, we need at least two kinds of information: First, we need to know which parts of the contents of consciousness need to be transformed; and second, we need to have a grammar of distortions which will allow us to apply the proper transformation rules. It should be obvious that the answer to the first question is rarely clear from the clinical context; but until the first question is answered, we have no way of isolating clear text from code and applying our grammar to the proper unknowns.

Since we have no workable method for uncovering the contents of a particular unconscious, we run a serious risk of generating make-believe approximations. But these will never be detected because we can never distinguish clear text from code and because of the absence of a transformational grammar. Thus the hypothesis of the dynamic unconscious may leave us in a worse position than the pure skeptic, because where he is content with knowing nothing about other minds, we pretend to know something but may quite often be wrong. Ignorance may, in the long run, be preferable to error.

We have seen that because we have no procedure for separating clear text from code and no systematic procedure for transforming the code (should it be found) back into its unconscious meaning, we are left with a construct but little in the way of rules of application. We have also seen (in the example from Langs) how an interpretation of the patient's unconscious could equally well be represented as a particular "reading" of the manifest content with no necessary assumptions about the particular underlying structure. But when given the choice between a surface reading and an unconscious construction, we always seem to prefer the latter, and this preference is worth further consideration. Because if the construct is largely metaphorical and we still continue to pursue it, then it must be serving some other purpose which has its own significance and its own set of rules.

Consider first the position of the literary critic who believes only in a descriptive unconscious. He may make a number of assumptions about a particular text but he makes no claim to their validity because he does not assume that he has discovered the true cause. He may prefer his reading to yours or mine, but he is usually willing to listen to alternatives. The reasons for his preference can almost always be defended in terms of the *surface* nature of the text, and the best reading of a text is usually the one which takes maximal advantage of all of its properties (see Hirsch, 1967). The reasoning, furthermore, is usually transparent; the persuasive critic does not invoke vague ideas about transformations or distortions, nor does he appeal to hidden motives which are not available to the general reader.

Because he is restricted to the known text, his explanation must necessarily be more parsimonious than one which involves the substantive unconscious. This consequence follows from the fact that the unconscious can be assumed to take many sizes and shapes and these assumptions can be only partially checked. The very reason that led Freud to postulate its existence in the first place becomes a disadvantage in assessing an interpretation; because the undefined unconscious can explain almost anything, we have no way of checking any particular interpretation. To invoke the dynamic unconscious is to take advantage of unlimited degrees of freedom and thus to produce an explanation which cannot be falsified.

This opportunity to take refuge in an uncheckable construction may be part of the appeal of the "deeper" explanation. By definition, it is out of sight and thus can never be challenged. It could be argued that some of our scorn for the more transparent, literary reading of a clinical "text" may be a rationalization for a procedure that lets us hide our mistakes. Too superficial, we may call the literary reading, implying that deeper is more fundamental; but what is based on surface reasoning is also more open to challenge and counterargument, whereas what is based on the unconscious can never be proved wrong because the unconscious is always changing and never open to inspection.

Unconscious explanations may also have an appeal for another reason. As we have seen, to invoke a particular unconscious motivation allows us to explain gaps in the record. To claim that this kind of explanation has been found wanting is to say that conscious behavior may be more chaotic than we like to think. The randomness of everyday life may be a part of the natural order of things and therefore beyond explanation—a deeply troubling conclusion. By invoking a make-believe unconscious, we can *always* find order in any given piece of behavior—but isn't this (again) simply using a very sophisticated piece of rationalization to avoid the unthinkable?

It seems clear that even if the unconscious were an empty construct, it is far more than an innocent metaphor. By protecting our explanations from falsification and by preserving the apparent continuity of everyday behavior, it functions in a special way to guard our underlying belief in the lawfulness of events. Could it be that these irrational reasons have kept the hypothesis alive for so long, in the face of repeated failures to validate and confirm Freud's original proposal? If psychoanalysis speaks with an ironic voice, we could hardly ask for a more appropriate question.

This line of argument can be sharpened in the following way. The faith in a knowable unconscious is a faith in the premise that all behavior can be ultimately reduced to a set of principles and that what is seemingly random or chaotic can be ultimately explained as lawful and determined. Both assumptions play a central role in keeping alive one part of the Freudian metaphor. The belief in a substantive unconscious can also be seen as one kind of answer to the nomothetic-idiographic debate. Seemingly diverse behaviors, given the hypothesis of a determinant unconscious, can be seen as the logical result of a finite set of transformations, and by use of this hypothesis, it becomes possible to take a nomothetic position. The particular laws remain to be determined, but the principle that variability of behavior can be reduced to a finite set of forces holds out the hope that some day we will have a scheme for explaining all behavior. Take away the hypothesis of the unconscious and we are faced with the dismaying task of finding some other solution to the problem of behavioral complexity and reopening the attack on the nomothetic position, which is currently the one in favor (see Holt, 1962).

We have seen that the substantive unconscious is not only never directly observed but that the rules of transformation are such that we have no systematic way of reading its contents. As a result, we are always putting off the day when its contents are made explicit and brought into comparison with its presumptive derivatives. So long as this day never comes, we are left with a hypothesis that will never be tested and thus with a nomothetic position that is significantly nonfalsifiable. Seen in this light, the hypothesis of a substantive unconscious is a kind of promissory note which will never be cashed.

On the other hand, if the unconscious turns out to be more a metaphor than anything else, it removes the hope of a particular nomothetic solution and increases the chances that only an idiographic explanation will do justice to the human condition. This position is now being echoed by workers in the neurosciences. After many years of assuming that the brain will one day be reduced to a set of finite laws, a number of scientists are now beginning to believe that there is enough indeterminancy to rule out that possibility in either the near or distant future (see Harth, 1982). Trillions of synapses, constantly changing, make each brain at any moment unique and force us to adopt an idiographic position in any attempt at explanation. General laws may be found which will account for some of the variance, but an explanation of the rich texture of any momentary state of mind may be beyond their reach.

Thus a belief in the substantive unconscious — always postulated, never uncovered — may have, among its other functions, the important effect of preserving the nomothetic tradition in personality research and making us feel that some day, when the necessary transformation laws are worked out and we catch a glimpse of this central operator, we will have an explanation for all states of mind, no matter how varied, and for all levels of feeling, no matter how layered. To an extent that is not generally recognized, the hypothesis of a substantive unconscious enables us to function *as if* things were much more lawful than they really are. Each time we construe a particular dream as being the outcome of a specific set of unconscious wishes, we feel as if we are adding evidence to this hypothesis and rediscovering the lawfulness of behavior; we never stop to realize that our constructs are often unsystematic, do not account for all the data, and are frequently little more than ad hoc formulations which will not stand up to careful study. But of course the saving condition is the fact that the search is never complete; the unconscious in question is never more than partially uncovered and therefore the hypothesis is never more than partially tested. And with disconfirmation out of the question, the hope will always remain alive.

The Seething Cauldron

Now we turn to another feature of the metaphorical unconscious which deserves particular attention. We touched on it
briefly in Chapter I when we visited the seething cauldron; now
it needs further elaboration. Here is a description from Freud's
paper on repression:

> . . . the instinctual representative develops with less interfer-
> ence and more profusely if it is withdrawn by repression from
> conscious influence. It *proliferates in the dark*, as it were, and takes
> on extreme forms of expression, which when they are translated
> and presented to the neurotic are not only bound to seem alien
> to him, but frighten him by giving him the picture of an ex-
> traordinary and dangerous strength of instinct. (Freud, 1915b,
> p. 149; my italics)

We are introduced to an autonomous unconscious which has
a life of its own and the capacity to assume a wide range of
terrifying forms. We next learn that it is capable of unremitting
influence. "We may suppose [Freud writes somewhat later] that
the repressed exercises a *continuous pressure* in the direction of the
unconscious, so that this pressure must be balanced by an
unceasing counter-pressure" (1915b, p. 151; my italics). The
sense of a knowledgeable force constantly at work is extended
in the paper on the unconscious: "The nucleus of the *Ucs.*
consists of instinctual representatives which *seek* to *discharge*
their cathexis; that is to say, it consists of wishful *impulses*"
(1915c, p. 186; my italics). Finally, in *The Ego and the Id*, Freud
transforms this mysterious force into a clearly separate organ-
ism in the famous metaphor of horse and rider: The relation of
ego to id "is like a man on horseback, who has to hold in check
the superior strength of the horse. . . . Often a rider, if he is
not to be parted from his horse, is obliged to guide it where it
wants to go; so in the same way the ego is in the habit of
transforming the id's will into action as if it were its own"
(1923a, p. 25).

A richly elaborated metaphor has been developed which assigns the unconscious a life of its own, the ability to assume a wide range of different disguises, and puts it constantly at work putting "pressure" on the ego. It should be noted that this metaphor goes far beyond the nominal definition that there are "determinants of thought and action that are not noticed or appreciated as such" (see Bowers, 1984, p. 228). Freud's metaphor gives the unconscious a life and will of its own — witness the horse — but goes far beyond just a horse. It invokes mystery and a sense of the uncanny and creates the idea of an enemy in our midst whose mischief must be constantly checked. Are these notions all required by the clinical evidence, or do they go somewhat beyond the data? If they do, we have another example of a free-floating metaphor which (like the unconscious) has a life and will of its own and which brings about a particular reading of the clinical evidence which is not justified by the facts.

It is important to realize just how far the idea of an autonomous, willful, and combative unconscious goes beyond the minimal requirements of theory. It is a commonplace observation that we are all the time being influenced by processes outside of awareness (the descriptive unconscious). There are any number of versions of what form this influence may take, and the history of interest in the descriptive unconscious starts well before Freud (see Whyte, 1960). But there is, as Bowers has recently pointed out, "a distinct tendency for the ordinary person to link 'the unconscious' with psychoanalytic formulations of it" (Bowers, 1984, p. 227) and, as part of this confusion, to assume that what is unconscious necessarily takes the form of the substantive unconscious. But this last step is largely metaphorical, fanciful, and more of a good story than any kind of systematic theory. It may be appealing to project the struggle between Good and Evil into the middle of the brain, but this kind of dramatic reading probably belongs more properly in the theatre.

Not only is there little data to support the idea that the unconscious is an autonomous something always pressing for discharge, always ready to take on a wide variety of frightening forms, but there is also reason to believe that this kind of processing in the brain is more the exception than the rule. It has become fashionable to think of the mind as some species of computer; it is a much bolder leap to assume that parallel processing may also be taking place. To speak of an autonomous unconscious is to make a strong assertion about parallel processing in the brain — the unconscious is "doing" one thing while we assume we are "doing" something else.

The metaphor of the autonomous unconscious has, in addition, many parallels with the modular model of the mind. While there have been several strong voices in its favor (see Gardner, 1983), there has also emerged some support for the other side. Fodor (1983), while arguing for modularity to a certain extent, also sees the need for a central processor (an "unencapsulated" region) which ties together the information from each module. An even stronger argument is based on brain studies of animals engaged in a simple discrimination task. John et al. write as follows:

> Our results also do not fit well with a general computer-like model of the brain, with information stored in discrete registers, no matter how many in number. Our data . . . better support notions of cooperative processes, in which the non-random behavior of huge ensembles of neural elements mediates the integration and processing of information and the retrieval of memories. In view of the large number of neurons involved, the question of how the information represented in these neurons can be evaluated and appreciated by the brain becomes of critical theoretical interest. No conceivable neuron or set of neurons, no matter how diffuse its synaptic inputs, can evaluate the enormous amount of neural activity here shown to be involved in retrieval of even a simple form discrimination. Memory and awareness in complex neural systems may depend upon pres-

ently unrecognized properties of the system as a while, and not upon any of the elements that constitute the system. (1986, p. 1174)

This is not the place to enlarge on the problems of a modular model of the mind; we merely point out how Freud's autonomous unconscious must insist on modularity and parallel processing as basic features. To the extent that this model is not supported by current findings, we need to be all the more skeptical of the "horse-and-rider" metaphor and see it as primarily a figure of speech rather than as a blueprint for the way the mind works. To remain aware of the metaphor gives us the freedom to indulge in Freud's fanciful language without taking it seriously and — more important — allows us to develop other models of the unconscious which may lie closer to the clinical findings (we come back to this theme in the last chapter). Once we lose sight of its metaphorical nature, however, and treat it as a piece of theory fully supported by the clinical findings, we have moved from fact to fiction.

We have seen how the model of an autonomous and combative unconscious goes far beyond clinical data and coexists uneasily with recent thinking about cooperative processes in the brain. Nevertheless, it is extraordinarily difficult to relinquish. The mysterious ghost in the machine which forces us to do things against our will harks back to the demons of the Middle Ages; the uncanny something which "proliferates in the dark . . . and takes on extreme forms" carries overtones of evolutionary theory and the survival of the fittest. The unconscious, screened off from direct observation, fills whatever niche it finds available; the underlying thesis of the survival of the fittest supplies the necessary motivation for this kind of internal combat. Because the metaphor resonates with other theories and with earlier ways of looking at the world, it readily acquires an immediate respectability; it sounds as if it *might* be true, and from there it is only a short step to assume it *is* true.

Because of its narrative appeal, the theory becomes more interesting than the facts; failures of confirmation are ignored because they cannot compete with what is really a rather marvelous metaphor. But to the extent that the metaphor has taken over, it has become a serious obstacle to clinical wisdom.

. _____

CHAPTER III

The Myth of the
Innocent Analyst

In the volley of critical attacks on metapsychology and on the theoretical underpinnings of psychoanalysis, the standing of the psychoanalytic *method* has survived largely unscathed. Freud was so fond of his clinical invention that he referred to it as "an impartial instrument, like the infinitesimal calculus," and subsequent generations of psychoanalysts have taken a similar position. Both free association and evenly suspended attention have been taken to be above reproach, and the assumptions which lie behind these procedures are treated as if they were axiomatic and beyond discussion.

In this chapter, I want to look more carefully at what exactly happens and what exactly we mean when we listen with evenly suspended attention. I will look with particular interest at the distinction between neutral and committed listening, asking whether the second kind is perhaps the more common and whether commitment is perhaps a necessary condition for understanding. If that conclusion should turn out to be the case, then we must re-examine the nature of evenly suspended attention; perhaps we will find it more of an evasion of responsibility and influence than a valid description of what we do when we listen to patients. If understanding requires commitment, and if we decide that there is no such thing as evenly suspended attention, then we must conclude that it is more metaphor than "impartial calculus."

Concern about context brings me logically to the issue of projection. If I can show that contextless listening is an impossibility, then it follows that an enabling context is always being projected onto the material. I will distinguish between unwitting projection, a necessary part of understanding, and self-conscious projection in the service of empathy or identification, and make the claim that unwitting projection is a constant ingredient in successful listening but extraordinarily hard to identify or pin down. Partly because of its invisible nature, we have found it easy to buy into the notion of the neutral observer and the protected model of evenly suspended attention. Indeed, the tradition is so persuasive that the only exceptions to this model are treated as gross errors—instances of countertransference intrusions—which is to say that, aside from these mistakes, the rest of us hear only what the patient is saying. I will attempt to show that we very likely *never* hear what the patient is saying in a form that is untouched by our own private accompaniment, and that this subjective coloring is a necessary part of understanding. Thus, it could be argued that countertransference is a commonplace and needs to be seen as a necessary part of any therapeutic conversation. (Abend goes even further—countertransference, he claims, is empathy gone wrong [1986, p. 569].)

In the third section, I will make some remarks about the nature of empathy and how it compares with witting and unwitting projection. It has become fashionable nowadays to speak of empathy as another kind of instrument, equally as precise as Freud's calculus, a psychological X-ray which allows us to read the inside of someone else's mind. I will argue that such a notion is a dangerous oversimplification which obscures the fact that empathy is often confused with unwitting projection and which leaves out of account the role of context and how that operates, in silent but powerful fashion, to color what we think we acquire through this remarkable instrument. You will notice that empathy, seen as a kind of immaculate perception, is closely akin to the neutral model of evenly suspended attention — no one is taking responsibility for anything! The real truth, I am afraid, lies elsewhere. Abend takes a similar position: "I think we have failed to assimilate fully our current state of knowledge about the nature of mental activity into our views of empathy and countertransference" (1986, p. 567).

Many a therapist has experienced the severely obsessive patient who is always quibbling with his words, always correcting his sentences, and claiming that he is always being misunderstood — "That's not quite what I meant to say," is a common refrain. Words and phrases are taken literally; his ear for unintended meaning is so acute that it is often impossible to carry out an extended conversation. This situation represents a kind of caricature of normal understanding and illustrates what can happen to all of us if we give up a certain tolerance for imprecision and conceptual slippage. Conversations are possible because we are usually listening between the lines for what is intended or left unsaid; we take language as a kind of approximation which is open to correction and emendation. Conversation, then, becomes the marketplace for this kind of exchange of ideas. Misunderstanding is a normal occurrence because of the fact that each of us is speaking from a private context of understanding and investing each of our words with a private store of meanings. This tendency is particularly obvious in children, where it is referred to as egocentricism. As we get older, we become gradually aware of this solipsistic danger and take more and more pains to include the other in our frame of reference, but we can only do so much to make this happen.

Some trivial examples will make the point. One of the common hazards of sightseeing is the danger of getting lost, and one of the common consequences of getting lost is asking for directions. Here is a perfect opportunity for egocentricism to rear its head. When the native tells us to go three miles down the road and turn at the red barn—"You can't miss it!"—he is asserting his egocentric world view in dramatic fashion because he is saying, in effect, that the barn carries marked standing for him. In fact, of course, he projects onto it a certain kind of significance. He is unaware of this silent projection and assumes that its significance lies in the barn—hence, "You can't miss it." But of course we do miss it because, for us, one barn is like all other barns and we're ten miles down the road before we realize our mistake.

The mistake comes about not only because the native was projecting his own significance onto the barn, but because, at the moment we heard the word, we formed our own image of the landmark. We set off down the road, looking for a particular barn and matching each of our impressions with this image in our head. But of course this private image of ours bears no correspondence to the image in the mind of the native or to the actual barns along the road.

Now we might ask, Did I understand the native? Clearly not—as shown by the fact that I missed the turn. But also yes, in the sense that I heard his words and parsed his sentence; my understanding went far beyond that of an Albanian tourist who spoke no English. My focus at the moment is the distinction between the two kinds of understanding, and I will claim that whereas we can understand the words of a sentence with evenly suspended attention, we can only understand the meaning, in the sense of making the right turn, by identifying the presuppositions underlying the statement. To take such a step means to go far beyond free-floating attention.

Some further examples may be useful to clarify this distinction. Suppose I am reading a difficult text in philosophy in my role as copy-editor. I can raise questions about the syntax of various sentences and I can certainly spot some of the more common grammatical errors, but I would have great difficulty answering questions about the text or carrying on a conversation with the author. In my role as copy-editor, I am assimilating the text to my own context of understanding, building a bridge between the author's words and my own view of the world. I am completely unaware of the extent to which his world view is different from mine; this difference remains invisible until we enter into the fateful conversation where I find myself unable to enter into a dialogue. (I am indebted to Habermas for suggesting the role of context in this connection.)

Now we can be more explicit about the nature of understanding. Gadamer tells us that

> a person who is trying to understand a text is always performing an act of projecting. He projects before himself a meaning for the text as a whole as soon as some initial meaning emerges in the text. . . . The working out of this fore-project, which is constantly revised in terms of what emerges as he penetrates into the meaning, is understanding what is there. (1975, p. 236)

For *text*, we can read *therapeutic hour*. The meaning is not out there but within us, in our sense of what the author or patient is trying to say and trying to tell us. The books in our library are, from this point of view, not a series of messages waiting to be read, with reading and rereading seen as merely variations on a single theme; no, the books are a potentially infinite set of experiences, and two readings of the same book, widely spaced in time, may be sensed as the discovery of two quite separate messages. We are misled by the physical entity *book* into thinking that repeated encounters are more repetitious than otherwise; I would argue that the physical fact of its book-like state is largely irrelevant to our experience.

From this it follows that the act of reading or listening is significantly creative, that the task being performed is one of constructing, with the author's or patient's help, a set of meanings which belong largely to us, begin with where we are, and are seen as continuous with our experience. It may seem *as if* we are simply registering what is on the page or what the patient "had in mind," but we learn quite quickly that this is not the case when we ask other readers or other therapists about their experience. We are often surprised at the discrepancies and find many ways of coping with the lack of uniformity; the simplest is to assume that I am right and everyone else is wrong. Once again, we are taken in by the physical facts and assume that a single object—a book or a patient— yields a single response, much as a given rose will always be red or white. (Even color constancy does not always hold, as I will show in a moment.)

Let me return to the experience of familiarity. Even though the text or patient will introduce us to a series of new words and new ideas, we always have the sense that they are continuous with past knowledge; indeed, this sense of continuity is a significant part of what we call understanding. Being confronted with a totally foreign landscape, with the feeling that we have stumbled onto an alien planet described by an alien intelligence, will produce a sense of shock but not insight, and we will keep reading or listening in the hope that sooner or later we will find something familiar, something that will serve as the bridge between our state of being and that of the author's or patient's. Our need for continuity and familiarity is a clue, I think, to the fact that the reader or listener is the one who is spinning the tale, taking the active part in choosing what he can use among the words in front of him, in deciding which meanings to favor and which to ignore.

Continuity entails commitment. This is a key aspect of understanding. If we feel that the story is partly our own because it grows out of something familiar, then we are already investing it with our private values. Because it belongs to our world, we see nothing strange in accepting the participants into our home, as it were, granting them (the good ones, anyway) our friendship and trust. We hear them speaking in our voice or the voice of our friends; we read their sentences as we are used to reading our reality; and we assume that their motives are continuous with ours. Commitment allows us to decipher and assign meanings. The author or patient cannot explain everything, but so long as the scene is familiar and we are full-fledged participants, that does not matter; we *know* what is meant just as we know, in each day's reality, what is intended without being told.

But you will notice that this hearing is also a mishearing, and we see the makings of a paradox. The more we feel that we truly understand the text or patient and the more it becomes part of our own world view, the more likely it will happen that significant misunderstanding is taking place and that what might be called our context of discovery is significantly different from the author's or patient's context of creation. I will speak at more length in the next section about the perils of projection, but here I need only remind you that it happens ubiquitously and silently, that it convinces us of many things that are simply not true, and that it leaps into any vacuum of meaning. We project in order to understand, and if the text or dialogue is ambiguous or incomplete, we shamelessly project onto it our own thoughts and feelings in order to make it our own.

True understanding, on the other hand, represents quite a different process. For true understanding to take place, we need to hold our own projections in disciplined abeyance and to make explicit the author's position on the issues being discussed. As Habermas makes clear, we must also investigate very thoroughly the underlying validity claims of the text. And finally, the interpreter must learn to

> differentiate his own understanding of the context — which he at first believed to be shared by the author but in fact falsely imputed to him — from the author's understanding of the context. His task consists in gaining access to the definitions of the

situation presupposed by the transmitted text through the life-world of its author and his audience. (Habermas, 1983, pp. 20–21)

Let me quote something from Samuel Morison's biography of Columbus to make the point. He is describing the landfall in the Bahamas and the events of the following day.

> The Admiral [he writes] was busy gathering such information as he could from signs and gestures; his Arabic interpreter was of no use in this neck of the Indies. On Saturday night he decided that no time must be lost, he must press on to Japan. . . . So it was in quest of Japan that the fleet sailed SW from San Salvador on the afternoon of October 14. Columbus was a bit puzzled what course to take, for the six Indians whom he had detained as guides and future interpreters swept their arms in a wide arc around the western and southern horizon, "and called by their names more than a hundred" islands. (Morison, 1942, p. 238)

Here is a fragment from Columbus's log:

> I here propose to leave to circumnavigate this island until I may have speech with this king and see if I can obtain from him the gold that I heard he has, and afterwards to depart for another much larger island which I believe must be Japan according to the descriptions of those Indians whom I carry . . . and according as I shall find a collection of gold or spicery, I shall decide what I have to do. But in any case I am determined to go to the mainland and to the city of Quinsay, and to present your Highnesses' letters of the Grand Kahn, and to beg a reply and come home with it. (Morison, p. 250)

How do we understand this passage? From our current knowledge of world geography, we would have to read this log as the wild musings of a mad sailor too long at sea — how could he speak of sailing from the Bahamas to Japan when we know that the two islands lie on opposite sides of the globe? But to read the passage in this context is, of course, to misunderstand. Only by fully appreciating the world view of the time and the belief that the Orient lay on the other side of the ocean from Spain can we truly understand either the log or Columbus's movements after the first landfall. Given this world view, we can then come to appreciate how many of the sightings could be interpreted as signs that Japan was indeed only a short sail away and understand why Columbus (in Morison's words) "prepared with pathetic punctilio an embassy to visit the Emperor of China."

> The official interpreter, Luis de Torres, a converted Jew "who knew Hebrew and Aramaic and even some Arabic," was made head of it; and to him were intrusted all the diplomatic paraphernalia: Latin passport, Latin letter of credence from Ferdinand and Isabella, and a royal gift. . . . (Morison, pp. 257–258)

Unfortunately the expedition returned empty-handed.

To truly understand Columbus's log, we must go back in time to the Spain of the fifteenth century and to the widespread interest in the Orient as a treasure trove of gold, pearls, and spices. Knowing nothing about America and enlarging the continent of Asia by various navigational sleights of hand, Columbus ended up by fixing the position of Japan as somewhere close to the Virgin Islands. Now the goal became a possibility, given the ships and crews of his day, and he set sail with high hopes; when he sighted land close to his estimated position of Japan, it was only natural that he would organize an official expedition to meet the Emperor.

What I am illustrating with this example is the way in which a commitment to the fifteenth century world view changes our reading of the Columbus adventure. His pride in having almost found Japan and the decision to send out carefully chosen emissaries can be understood only if we commit ourselves to the same set of beliefs and assumptions as were held by Columbus. Without this commitment, we see only the mistakes and conclude that he was a poor navigator, a foolish but lucky sailor who discovered America only by accident and who probably doesn't deserve the October holiday. We cannot help but trivialize his accomplishment. Indeed, there was a school of historians at the turn of the century who were embarrassed by the log for some of these very reasons. They took the position that Columbus had secret information about some unknown Atlantic islands, that he had no idea of sailing to China but when he missed his objective, he falsified his journal to cover his tracks. These accounts are now discredited, but they provide us with an interesting example of bad history in which the historian imposes his own values onto the material and makes no attempt to understand the context of discovery.

Now turn from reading Columbus's log to listening to a patient. Following the usual model, we listen with evenly suspended attention, which Freud described as the complement of free association. But the listener cannot remain long on the sidelines, so to speak, without a serious loss of understanding. As I have written elsewhere, understanding can only take place if the

> words spoken by one speaker are invested with private meanings by the other. Unless some kind of internal elaboration takes place, the listener hears only words . . . and communication fails. To listen with understanding and involvement requires the listener to be constantly forming hypotheses about the next word, the next sentence, the reference for a recent pronoun, or the color of the bride's eyes, because it is only in the midst of this kind of activity that words take on some kind of meaning. We might even argue that to carry out Freud's recommendation to the letter is to run the risk of losing the meaning and hearing only the words. (Spence, 1982a, p. 116)

If you agree that understanding always takes place in a specific context, we can appreciate the perils of the traditional model. First, it puts the therapist into the position of the partial listener who is hearing words and sentences but rather less in the way of meanings. But it leads to the more serious error of minimizing the role of private context, because to the extent that we begin to understand the patient, we must assume that we are supplying a set of assumptions and committing ourselves to a set of beliefs.

> In response to most utterances [I have written] some kind of internal picture will begin to form in the analyst's mind which only partly corresponds to what is being said, and once this happens, the listener has shifted from registration to interpretation. Perhaps a name is mentioned — one of the patient's friends; some kind of image will very likely come to mind. Perhaps the patient mentions a movie; if the analyst has seen it too, it has already acquired a cluster of private associations that are now aroused and help to color what the patient is saying. This gradually emerging, unwitting interpretation is necessarily different from what is in the patient's mind as he is describing the movie; and even if the analyst has never seen the movie, his picture of what the patient is telling is necessarily colored by his own associations. As his elaboration becomes more fully developed, it takes on its own organization with figure and ground which are necessarily different from the figure and ground assumed by the patient. (Spence, 1982a, pp. 115–116)

The Role of Projection

This line of thinking brings us quite naturally to the role of projection in listening and understanding, for to say that understanding always takes place within a specific context is also to say that, many times, this context is unwittingly projected onto the utterance. Let me begin with some humorous examples from Kosinski's novel *Being There*.

This is the story of an illiterate gardener named Chance who, through a series of coincidences, finds himself in a position of influence and authority. In one of the most striking scenes of the novel, the President is asking him for his opinion about the current season on Wall Street. Chance answers as follows:

> In a garden, growth has its season. There are spring and summer, but there are also fall and winter. And then spring and summer again. As long as the roots are not severed, all is well and all will be well.

The President answers:

> I must admit, Mr. Gardener, that what you've just said is one of the most refreshing and optimistic statements I've heard in a very, very long time. (Kosinski, 1970, p. 54)

Somewhat later in the book, Chance finds himself on a talk show where he is asked a similar question.

> I know the garden very well said Chance firmly. . . . The garden needs a lot of care. I do agree with the President: everything in it will grow strong in due course. And there is still plenty of room in it for new trees and new flowers of all kinds.

The reaction was immediate.

> Chance's last words were partly lost in the excited murmuring of the audience. Behind him, members of the band tapped their instruments; a few cried out loud bravos. . . . The applause mounted to uproar. (Kosinski, p. 66)

One last example. At a dinner party, Chance was asked about the dangers of certain kinds of industrial byproducts.

> "I have seen ashes and I have seen powders," said Chance. "I know that both are bad for growth in a garden." One of the women at the table said in a loud whisper: "Mr. Gardener has the uncanny ability of reducing complex matters to the simplest of human terms . . . by bringing this down to earth, to our own home, I can see the priority and urgency which Mr. Gardener . . . gives to this matter." (Kosinski, p. 106)

In each of these examples, unparalleled wisdom and understanding are being read into the chance remarks of the gardener; they are invested with knowledge and authority by his listeners, who have a need to find him a sage and have no trouble projecting eternal truths into his utterances. Speaking in gardening metaphors, Chance found himself making statements which could be applied to a wide range of affairs, and their very metaphorical nature gave the listener the feeling that he was hearing something profound and was on the verge of discovering some important truth. Their failure to make perfect sense added to this sense of profundity and to the feeling that here was a very wise man who was speaking in parables and perhaps was gifted with something holy and Godlike. The less he made sense, the more people would lend an ear.

For my second example, I turn to the transcribed analysis by Paul Dewald. The patient is talking about a dream in which she was in a playpen with other girls, dressed up in frilly dresses but wearing no pants. A group of men were looking down at them. In her associations, the patient turns to thoughts of the analyst and says, "You are capable of loving me and of not caring what I look like, and for you it wouldn't make any difference about the . . . " There is a sixty-second silence and the analyst says, "You cut someting short there." P: "The surface things." A: "I think you mean the presence or absence of a penis" (Dewald, 1972, p. 175).

Was that what the patient meant? Other possibilities come to mind—frilly clothes or the fact that she was wearing no pants—but Dewald seems bent on one reading of the material, and the thrust of his standard interpretation is anticipated by his comment, "You cut something short there." (If castration is on his mind, then the phrase "cut something short" already alerts us to the specific meanings which will be projected onto the material.)

In the minds of some analysts, this interchange would be an example of evenly suspended attention. Because the analyst is in a state of evenly suspended attention, they would say, he is able to detect the latent castration theme and make the interpretation. I would argue that something much less mystical is going on: namely, that the analyst projected a standard interpretative model onto the material; that this projection operated outside of awareness; and that it made it possible to understand it in a particular manner. But it should also be noted that the castration model forecloses other kinds of understanding. More seriously, the mataphor of evenly suspended attention perpetuates the myth that the analyst is only hearing what is "there" and is in no sense participating in the construction of meaning. This is the myth of the innocent analyst which I think must be re-examined.

Why has the myth survived so long? For at least three important reasons. First, it protects us from the charge that therapeutic work is heavily influenced by suggestion. If all we do is listen with the "third ear," we are simply registering what is "there" and cannot be accused of any kind of undue influence. Once the door is open to the possibility that the analyst selects (even unconsciously) which meanings he will hear and which themes he will develop, we are then playing a new game with quite different rules.

In the second place, the myth of the innocent analyst supports the claim that there is a single meaning in any piece of behavior. To a significant degree, the method of listening with evenly suspended attention was thought to be the solution to the problem of ambiguity in the material. Things are seldom what they seem, Freud warned us again and again; the surface appearance is always deceiving; but what is latent can always be inferred from what is manifest. But after building up a convincing case for ambiguity and multiple meanings, he provided us with very little in the way of methods by which we can decide which meaning to emphasize; as a result, the ambiguity of process has never been properly addressed by the analytic method. Taking refuge in the myth of the innocent analyst is one way out, because this model implies that the meaning he hears is identical to the meaning that matters. We are reminded of Freud's famous jigsaw puzzle analogy: "If one succeeds in arranging the confused heap of fragments . . . then one knows that one has solved the puzzle and that there is no alternative solution" (Freud, 1923b, p. 116). We will come back to this model in the next chapter, where we will study it in more detail.

The idea of multiple interpretations is surprisingly absent in Freud and we sense a kind of double standard in his thinking. Once we assume that meanings are multiple, it hardly follows that the one we discover will be the most significant. Freud's familiar metaphor of analyst as archeologist tended to discount the possibility of multiple interpretations; by comparing thought fragments to archeological ruins, he put the enterprise on a much more concrete and unambiguous footing. The archeological analogy might be called the third reason why the myth of the innocent analyst has survived so long: if all we do is to put together pieces of the past, then we are simply technicians playing mainly technical roles and we can let the meanings take care of themselves.

To summarize the argument, we can say that the archeological metaphor together with the jigsaw puzzle analogy support what might be called the axiom of the singular solution. This axiom is deeply embedded in our psychoanalytic folklore; it assumes that there is a single meaning which is uppermost in any clinical fragment, that the context of the listener is irrelevant (because personal needs and wishes can be set aside), and that the meaning of the protocol lies entirely "out there," equivalent to a set of pointer readings on a temperature gauge. By extension, this axiom assumes that once a tape recorder has been brought into the consulting room, we will have collected all the data necessary to understand the session, that archives of these tapes will constitute a complete (and therefore sufficient) record of the therapeutic process, and that research on these tapes will uncover important truths about the nature of therapy. Assuming the axiom of singularity, we begin to understand why our literature contains fragments of what was said but next to nothing about who is listening; the *who* is unimportant because the meaning is in the material.

The axiom of the singular solution is, on closer examination, discontinuous with many of our working assumptions. Consider the concept of transference. We take for granted the idea that what happens in the "here-and-now" will be heard one way by the analyst and one way by the patient, that his reading of a cancellation or a reminder to speak louder will always take place against the background of personal events, and that our reading of his silence or his coming late will change depending on our specific hopes and fears.

We have listed three reasons why the idea of the innocent analyst, listening with evenly suspended attention and coming up with the singular reading of the material, became so deeply embedded in our tradition. But it is important to go beyond issues of technique in this discussion and point out that this model is also contradicted by another important strain in Freud's thinking. Consider, once again, the well-known paragraph cited in Chapter I:

> The true beginning of scientific activity consists rather in describing phenomena and then in proceeding to group, classify and correlate them. Even at the stage of description it is not possible to avoid applying certain abstract ideas to the materials at hand, ideas derived from somewhere or other but certainly not from the new observations alone . . . we come to an understanding about their meaning by making repeated references to the material of observation from which they appear to have been derived, but upon which, in fact, they have been imposed. (Freud, 1915a, p. 117)

Thus the material of observation is not primary but is always being shaped by "ideas derived from somewhere or other"; in today's language, we would say that observations are always theory-laden. This position agrees nicely with the current hermeneutic argument that context determines content. Freud seemed well aware that there is no bedrock of observation from which we generate our data; to group, classify and correlate phenomena, as he puts it, will always raise issues of what underlying assumptions are being used. Clearly, the same reasoning should apply to the material in an analytic session, and there are scattered places where we can read Freud in this light. Thus, in the discussion of little Hans, he states that

> it is true that during the analysis Hans had to be told many things that he could not say himself, that he had to be presented with thoughts which he had so far shown no signs of possessing. . . . This detracts from the evidential value of the analysis; but the procedure is the same in every case. For a psychoanalysis is not an impartial scientific investigation, but a therapeutic measure. Its essence is not to prove anything, but merely to alter something. (Freud, 1909, p. 104)

In this example, he is clearly departing from the model of the neutral observer. But as the issue of suggestion assumed more prominence in his struggles with Jung and Adler, he tended to retreat to the more immaculate position we have been describing, and unfortunately for the field, the myth of the innocent analyst has become the reigning stereotype.

If we turn away from the myth and look seriously at the need for projection in the service of understanding, we begin to ask quite different questions of the analytic process. We no longer look for ways to cancel out countertransference or ways to create the model analyst, free of projection and other impurities; rather, we try to identify *which* models are being projected in order to bring about such-and-such understandings. If projection is assumed, the question becomes, not how much, but which kinds, out of what frameworks, and for what reasons?

To take seriously the role of projection in our clinical experience is to suggest a new way to look at our case reports. You may have had the experience of being mystified by an interpretation or an intervention; its links to the material seem arbitrary and its motivation idiosyncratic. We are tempted to skip over such accidents or write them off as faulty transcriptions. But if we pay more attention to the role of projection, we can often make sense out of these parapraxes. Consider the patient who begins to describe a time in her kitchen: "I was cutting some liverwurst, and I noticed that the thick skin around it and all made me think of a penis or something like a snake." The analyst replies: "And you were eating it." On quick reading this seems like a non-sequitur and a good example of leading the witness, but a little further thought suggests that the analyst was working with a particular metaphor in mind — the popular fantasy of incorporating the phallus — and in the context of this model, his reply makes perfect sense. But notice the difference from the standard formulation: We are not saying that the meaning of the kitchen incident was contained in the material but, rather, that it became clear when it was heard within the bounds of a particular metaphor. Whether or not this was true or even relevant becomes a separate issue; at this point, we only mention its relevance for understanding the patient's utterance.

So far I have been talking about unwitting interpretations — the projections which we supply outside of awareness and which allow us to understand without knowing exactly why. I have spoken of the way in which our tradition of the innocent analyst tends to minimize this awareness and treat understanding as a normal happening rather than the outcome of a set of specific metaphors. Understanding is needlessly oversimplified and ascribed to the wisdom or experience of the analyst and not to the influence of a particular context.

Now let me turn to some of the specific metaphors which are used in the service of understanding. What form do they take? If we think of the treatment situation within a developmental model, will that sensitize us to ways in which the course of treatment recapitulates the life of the patient and allows us to clarify his accounts of early childhood experience? We might become aware of the ways in which our role as analyst moves between father and mother, mother and big brother, or whatever combination of metaphors that particular family history might allow. Using a quite different model, we might see treatment as a recapitulation of a piece of *our* past and find that our dealings with the patient may repeat a period when we were the main caretaker of a younger sibling, or a period when we began our first clinical experience in internship or medical school. Discoveries of this kind would not necessarily be communicated to the patient, but they would sensitize us to new themes in the patient's material.

To reason in this manner is not to assume that these feelings are necessarily being projected onto the material; rather, it allows us to approach the material from different points of view in an effort to gain understanding of a relevant dimension. This line of reasoning also gives us a way to accommodate different schools of therapy in our approach to the patient; we might learn more about mastery and inferiority and striving for achievement if we listen from an Adlerian point of view, just as we will learn something about time pressure and vicissitudes of termination if we listen à la James Mann, and hear something about disclaimed action if we listen à la Roy Schafer. But bear in mind two important conditions: the projections are always conscious and tentative, tried on for size and clarification; and second, they influence our understanding but not necessarily our interpretations.

A third kind of projection to be considered in this connection comes from the patient. I need not discuss the familiar topic of transference and how the patient's past history and present concerns will inevitably color his hearing of what we say and what we mean. Rather, I would like to focus on the way in which patient projections bear on the nature of cure. Neu (1976), in discussing the question of why interpretations work, makes the interesting distinction between the theory behind an interpretation (the axioms and hypotheses of psychoanalysis and metapsychology) and the theory it provides the patient. Must each theory be true? We may find that the truth value of the latter is the more important. The projections of the patient bear on the second because they color his hearing of our interpretations and thus affect his sense of whether or not they are true. If we are in a state of positive transference and he dotes on our every word, he is gratified merely to hear us speak, and the most banal statement can produce remarkable results. We have become the all-wise Chance the Gardener who can speak in metaphor and make everyone believe him. This influence comes about through projection. The patient imbues us with the air of a prophet and shaman. But take this projection away, or change its mode from positive to negative, and a different picture emerges; the silk purse becomes a sow's ear and we feel helpless and ignored.

Empathy or Pathetic Fallacy?

It has become fashionable in some quarters to call on the empathic instrument as the key to understanding the patient, and empathy is invoked as if it were some kind of final explanation. The term was first coined in the context of the philosophy of aesthetics and was defined as "an act of sympathetic projection into objects or persons distinct from the agent." Four types could be described: general apperceptive empathy, which allows the viewer to animate common objects; empirical empathy, which allows me to see a storm as angry; mood empathy, which allows me to see yellow as joyful; and a fourth type which was called empathy for appearances and which allows me to take others' gestures as symptomatic of their inner lives. The tradition was German, the original term was *Einfühlung*, and it was first given an English translation by Titchener in 1909.

A rather similar concept was identified by Ruskin in his work on painters in the nineteenth century, but from quite a different position. Ruskin was keenly sensitive to the mischief produced when we use our feelings to make decisions about the object of interest, and called the phenomenon the pathetic fallacy. For Ruskin, it was fallacious because it did not describe the true appearance of things but rather the "extraordinary, or false appearances, when we are under the influence of emotion or contemplative fancy" (quoted in Cuddon, *A Dictionary of Literary Terms*, 1977, p. 483). It is easy to see the application of this fallacy to problems of aesthetics, and the history of art criticism can be seen as an attempt to move the basis of criticism away from the subjective and place it on a less personal foundation. And we might ask, in the context of today's excitement about empathy as the ultimate analyzing instrument, whether it would merit its present position if we had called it the pathetic fallacy. It is noteworthy that it was an artist who first took the scornful stance because artists, as you know, spend a good part of their professional lives trying to see the world as it "really is" and separate the appearances of objects from confounding factors such as personal likes or dislikes. An example of this dedication can be found in the way in which Monet would make a painting. He trained himself to be so exquisitely sensitive to the influence of sunlight on color that he would paint by the clock, going back to the scene only during the ten-minute period when the light was the same as the previous attempt. He knew that to wait too long would turn the scene into something with quite different visual properties.

If empathy is an act of sympathetic projection onto the object, it may help us *at times* to understand and anticipate certain behaviors in certain contexts, but it is clearly an act of selection and identification and is certainly not an impartial instrument. Because it is personal and partial, it can easily become pathetic, and I think Ruskin's description can be applied to many case histories in which the author's reactions to the material are mistakenly confused with the patient's meanings. Ruskin's label applies with particular force to the current fashion of deliberately using our personal response as a gauge to something hidden in the patient. Here is another variant of the "innocent" analyst.

Far from being the ultimate analyzing instrument, empathy should be seen as an easy way out of the problem of understanding.

> The interpreter [writes Habermas] appears at first to understand the sentences of the author [read patient]; in going on, he then has the unsettling experience that he does not really understand the text so well that he could, if need be, respond to questions of the author. The interpreter takes this to be a sign that he is wrongly embedding the text in another context than did the author himself, that he is starting with other questions. (1983, p. 20)

At this point, the interpreter may often respond to the lack of understanding by projecting assumptions onto the material in an effort to make it more transparent, using his own reactions — which are undeniably subjective and idiosyncratic — to naturalize the patient's material — the unknown text — and turn it into something familiar. We saw something of this phenomenon in the quote from Dewald. When the patient referred to "the surface things," an ambiguous phrase at best and particularly vulnerable to misunderstanding, Dewald resolved the difficulty by saying, "I think you mean the presence or absence of a penis." Undoubtedly this was *his* association, but to use it as an explanation of what is in the patient's mind comes very close to Ruskin's pathetic fallacy.

By using subjective associations to clarify an ambiguity, we not only take a risk of supplying the wrong interpretation, but we also, to a significant degree, push out of awareness any sense that an ambiguity has occurred. The meaning is in the material; the ambiguity has been swallowed up in our subjective reaction; we might even guess that the analyst's *memory* of the incident has also been altered in favor of his interpretation.

This kind of narrative smoothing prevents us from going back to look at the original text because that text has disappeared forever in the haze of projective readings. We will have more to say on this topic in Chapter V.

If empathy has not stepped in prematurely, the interpreter is confronted with a set of extraordinarily difficult decisions. To return to Habermas:

> The task of interpretation can now be specified as follows: the interpreter learns to differentiate his own understanding of the context — which he at first believed to be shared by the author but in fact falsely imputed to him — from the author's understanding of the context. His task consists in gaining access to the definitions of the situation presupposed by the transmitted text through the lifeworld of its author and his audience. . . . Thus the interpreter understands the meaning of a text only to the extent that he sees why the author felt himself entitled to put forward (as true) certain assertions, to recognize (as right) certain values and norms, to express (as sincere) certain experiences. (Habermas, 1983, pp. 20–21)

In the very first stage of this process, we have departed significantly from traditional empathy. The interpreter's or analyst's understanding of the material is *not* used as a guide to what is happening with the patient, but is instead recognized as being different and thereby differentiated from the unknown we are still trying to discover. To assimilate the patient's understanding to our own is to lose the vital difference and project our meanings into the void. To appreciate the difference is to delay a resolution of the ambiguity, to admit that we are perhaps more uncertain than we were yesterday or the week before, and to recognize once again how much our context of understanding differs from the patient's. To assimilate the patient's understanding to our own is the easy way out, but falls short of extracting full meaning; to inhibit this assimilation, as

Gadamer has pointed out with respect to the reading of classical texts, is more difficult but potentially more rewarding.

> Every encounter with tradition that takes place within historical consciousness involves the experience of the tension between the text and the present. The hermeneutic task consists in not covering up this tension by attempting a naive assimilation but consciously bringing it out. (Gadamer, 1975, p. 273)

The nature of these hidden meanings is further clarified by Ricoeur when he describes the hermeneutic task as one of

> uncovering within the text — and especially within classical texts — *potentialities* of meaning which had been prevented from being actualized, or which had been marginalized, if not repressed, thanks to the interference of power structures with the semantic richness of past texts. (Ricoeur, 1983, p. 14; author's italics)

A similar argument applies, I think, to the way we listen to patients. Truly respectful listening endeavors to uncover the potentialities of meaning implied by what the patient is saying, latent contents of which even he is unaware. Truly respectful listening acknowledges from the outset that our context of understanding is significantly different from the patient's and therefore to use our associations as a guide to understanding is the worst kind of naiveté — you can think of it as a kind of psychoanalytic imperialism which tries to expand its sphere of influence by exporting its most cherished beliefs and assumptions. Ricoeur (1983) is quite right to talk about power structures and how they corrupt understanding, and you can find other examples for yourself by merely looking through the literature.

It is frequently said that the richness, subtlety, and interlocking complexity of the clinical material experienced during the life of an analyst can never be appreciated by an outsider; this argument is used to justify the failure to convince the outsider of the truth of a particular interpretation. Perhaps so. But it is also true that the richness of the material which is, after all, the source of our clinical wisdom and our future theory — this richness is in danger of being reduced to a set of standard formulations, swallowed up in a cloud of "empathic" interpretations which are grounded in current fashions and received metaphors. Here is another danger of the too-quick "empathic" response: It tends to substitute dogma for observation. We have seen in the clinical excerpt from Dewald how a standard formulation was projected onto the material, and this standard reading cannot help but diminish the true nature of what the patient was saying and reduce its unique form and content to a stereotype. Add to this danger the fact that we have very few transcripts of recorded sessions and you will see why psychoanalysis is in a poor position to learn from experience. You might even ask whether we are in a position to learn from patients.

I have argued that some kind of commitment is necessary for responsible listening and this claim casts serious doubt on the credibility of evenly suspended attention. If some kind of commitment is necessary, then we must ask: Where does it come from and what are its credentials? In this context, the role of empathy plays a particularly mischievous part. Both standard dogma and private idiosyncrasies can be dignified by the label and presented — either to the patient or to the outside observer — as explanation and diagnosis. But as I have tried to make clear, they are much more often neither of these but, rather, one of many ways of building a bridge between the analyst's and the patient's contexts of understanding. By building bridges, they enable meaningful listening to continue, but it should be made quite clear that the meaning is being supplied by the listener and does not stem from the patient.

Thus, we can see how the so-called empathic response is the necessary complement of evenly suspended attention. Only by projecting a set of assumptions onto the material can we listen to meaning rather than words. These assumptions take the form of specific metaphors. If I assume that the patient is preoccupied with penis envy, then I can hear the reference to "something missing" as a meaningful statement which, *mirabile dictu*, jibes with a well-known piece of psychoanalytic theory. But if it is my assumption, it confirms nothing and may actually interfere with my ability to carry out Habermas' mandate and discover why certain assertions are put forward (as true), why certain values and norms are recognized (as right), and why certain experiences are expressed (as sincere). To project either dogma or subjective conjecture under the guise of empathy can only stereotype the patient and lead to a misreading of the data — the worst kind of psychoanalytic imperialism.

Truly respectful listening falls somewhere between the Scylla of evenly suspended attention and the Charybdis of unwitting projection. A certain amount of projection is a necessary part of enhanced listening, but the analyst must identify his assumptions as they come into play, label them as tentative, and by all means, avoid giving them the dignity of empathy. Most of them are probably little more than pathetic fallacies which say more about the analyst's subjective state than about the patient's. They may be necessary to provide temporary scaffolding to the bits and pieces of free associations, particularly if the flow is more free than controlled, and they may be necessary to involve the listener in the assumptions behind the associations and in the world view which they express. But they represent, first and foremost, the context of the analyst and should not be confused with the context of the patient, and it is the latter that he must learn to capture.

Truly respectful listening requires a continual making and breaking of tentative assumptions and underlying metaphors in an effort to hear what the patient is "really" saying; as such, it represents an active process which seems quite different from the neutrality of evenly suspended attention.

How much simpler to adopt the metaphor of evenly suspended attention and let the meaning somehow mystically emerge from the material, to glorify our associations as insights and explanations, and—most pathetic of all—to take a reassuring "yes" from the patient as meaning confirmation of our "analyzing instrument." Simpler for us, but I wonder, of what help for the patient? Doesn't he or she deserve much more?

Uncoupled Metaphor

If the substantive unconscious is largely unfalsifiable and if evenly suspended attention confuses projection with empathy, we have reason to wonder whether these concepts may hinder more than they help. There is, moreover, little evidence that either metaphor has been enriched or elaborated by subsequent observation, and every reason to think that remaining with these models has prevented us from adopting others. What is more, the conventional belief in evenly suspended attention as an "impartial instrument" also tempts us to believe that the world is waiting "out there" to be observed, that context almost never colors observation, and that the world of objects corresponds to representations inside the head of the patient. If any of these beliefs is unwarranted, then the method of listening with evenly suspended attention is hardly an impartial calculus.

If the central concepts are more metaphoric than anything else, they are essentially uncoupled from the clinical data base; they can be neither confirmed nor falsified because they are set forth in language that is more literary than scientific. At the same time, psychoanalysis continues to see itself as a science and to search for a traditional scientific identity—despite the fact that it is heavily (some might say fatally) grounded in metaphor. We now examine the standing of this search.

．——————————————

CHAPTER IV

The Metaphor of Psychoanalysis as Science

Nearly one hundred years after its inception, psychoanalysis is still searching for an identity. It would like to call itself a science and, in so doing, claim membership in the reigning Zeitgeist of the twentieth century. The unceasing quest for scientific status and the right to join the better half of C. P. Snow's two cultures is reflected in a variety of pronouncements, some more tempered than others. One of the foremost spokesmen, Charles Brenner, finds no reason for doubt.

> Like every other scientist [he writes] a psychoanalyst is an empiricist, who imaginatively infers functional and causal relations among his data, avoiding, if possible, generalizations that are inherently inconsistent with one another as well as those that are incompatible with well-supported conclusions from other branches of science.

Although its data are different from such sciences as biology and physics, that it is a branch of science . . . there can be no doubt. (1982, p. 5)

Holt, somewhat more tentative, writes about psychoanalysis as a "fledgling science," a field that is struggling to become a science, despite the fact that "it is hard to admit how little *proof* there is for any psychoanalytic hypothesis after all these years of use," despite the fact that the validity of the theory is "quite murky," and despite the fact that "the foundations of our house are tottering . . . there are a few sound timbers under there, no doubt, but we have very little idea which ones they are; and we know that there is deep trouble in the philosophical footings themselves" (1984, pp. 26–27).

Grünbaum appeals to what Freud himself believed.

> Throughout his long career, Freud insisted that the psycho-analytic enterprise has the status of a natural science. As he told us at the very end of his life, the explanatory gains from positing unconscious mental processes "enabled psychology to take its place as a natural science like any other." (1984, p. 2)

But there is a significant difference between the hopes of the creator and the product of his endeavor; even though Freud wanted very much to be considered a scientist and to be the founder of a scientific approach to the study of the mind, the actual standing of his handiwork must be settled on its own merits. Grünbaum fails to distinguish the artist from his art.

Science is both method and metaphor. The search for scientific status and the need to surround the profession of psychoanalysis with the trappings of science may have as much to do with its metaphorical nature as with a need to systematically develop a field of knowledge. The metaphor is seductive because to become a science is automatically to acquire certain rights and privileges and, in this way, achieve instant respectability. Freud was appealing to this metaphor when he wrote that "the intellect and the mind are objects for scientific research in exactly the same way as any non-human things. Psycho-analysis has a special right to speak for the scientific *Weltanschauung*" (1933, p. 159). He was appealing to the metaphor when he expressed his regret that the scientific standing of psychoanalysis was not obvious to others: "I have always felt it as a gross injustice that people have refused to treat psychoanalysis like any other science" (1925, p. 58). It should be clear that the claim to science is, in Freud as well as Brenner, a partly rhetorical move and should not be taken as a necessary description of the product being described.

The metaphor is seductive for other reasons. If we accept Freud's claim that psychoanalysis is part of science, we automatically assign a certain respectability to words like *data* and *theory* and *hypothesis*; we find ourselves believing that presently ambiguous concepts will become refined as more observations are gathered; in short, we can believe in the possibility of systematic progress. When Brenner writes that "psychoanalytic hypotheses, like all scientific hypotheses, are subject to revision as relevant new data become available" (p. 5), we are charmed into thinking that our data are no different from data in physics or chemistry and that our hypotheses are sensitive to data in just the way that hypotheses in the physical sciences are responsive to new observations. The magic word *data* automatically transforms the description of what we are doing into something that is subject to the usual constraints of the scientific method.

What does it mean to call a field of inquiry a science? First of all, it suggests that there is a widespread respect for data and that these data, furthermore, are in the public domain and available to all interested parties. Second, it suggests that theory is data-determined, that it changes in response to new observations, and that these observations are given priority over unfounded assumptions. Third, it suggests that progress is cumulative and that earlier models provide the building blocks for later theory. Fourth, it suggests that argument is grounded on evidence and not on authority and that the basis for a given conclusion is accessible to any interested party and does not depend on who is speaking. Science, by this account, is fanatically democratic. Fifth, it suggests that all theory is tentative and subject to revision, but that revision should be based on evidence rather than fashion.

Psychoanalysis fails on every count. Data, to begin with, are in short supply; they are clearly outside the public domain, for a variety of reasons which we will shortly examine, and as a result, scandalously unavailable (see Cooper's recent critique of the "data-free" field [1986]). Theory is data-determined only in a very narrow sense. Progress is not cumulative; we know very little more about the unconscious today than we did in 1915; the grammar of the primary process, so confidently sketched in the seventh chapter of *The Interpretation of Dreams*, is still a matter of conjecture and speculation; and the rules by which latent content is transformed into manifest content are little more than metaphors and no less metaphorical today than when Freud made his original distinction. Respect for data is rarely observed in coming to public conclusions; published statements are, more often than not, *ex cathedra* rather than closely reasoned; and published argument is founded more on authority than on appeal to the evidence. There is no precedent for an adversarial tradition, either within the psychoanalytic institutes or within the literature. Theory is largely taken as settled, and although lip service is given to the idea that certain concepts are still hypothetical, there is only limited interest in testing these hypotheses. "To my knowledge [writes Cooper] . . . we are without reliable data indicating that any one theory is superior to another" (1986, p. 587). There is still less interest in negative instances. How many unsuccessful cases have been published? How many failures to confirm a particular formulation have been recorded?

In the light of this record, Brenner can only be speaking metaphorically when he writes that the generalizations which constitute psychoanalytic theory "are all empirically based hypotheses which are wholly comparable with those in every other branch of science" (1982, p. 5). Read uncritically, such a statement is enormously comforting; what analyst does not sit up straighter when he reads that our theory is data-based? In our need to believe, we fail to hear the metaphor behind this statement; in our rush to join the ranks of science, we fail to notice the absence of qualifiers (*all* generalizations are empirically based; all are *wholly comparable* with those in other sciences); we fail to notice the lack of specifics. Some of the generalizations, writes Brenner, "are well substantiated by abundant data, some are less well substantiated," but he fails to name names and, in the absence of detail, he opens up enormous room for doubt. Holt is equally nonspecific; when he writes about the "few sound timbers" in our theoretical foundation, he also fails to give the necessary referents and thus raises the question whether the sentence has any real meaning.

To a large degree, the key concepts in psychoanalytic theory are neither confirmable nor falsifiable. Perhaps the most familiar and most flagrant example, as we have seen, is the substantive unconscious. Screened off from observation by its very definition, the unconscious can only be known by its effect on other aspects of behavior. But so long as the rules governing these effects are not specified, so long as we do not understand the precise ways in which latent content is transformed into manifest content or the way in which unconscious ideas are expressed in derivative associations, then the appeal to the unconscious as a form of explanation is logically empty. It may be a useful metaphor, a way of speaking about cause which takes it out of the conscious domain, but as a hypothesis it is unfalsifiable until we have a grammar of transformations. Much the same argument applies to the role of childhood experience in adult pathology. So long as the rules are unknown by which early events are transmuted into later behaviors, we will always be appealing to an empty concept. It may be — in fact, most certainly is — a useful metaphor, but it should not be confused with a testable hypothesis.

We are back to metaphor once again. Any number of central psychoanalytic concepts are more metaphorical than substantive, and their metaphorical strength has diminished little since they were first proposed by Freud. It would seem to be their metaphorical base which provides the fascination to such concepts as the Oedipus Complex (see Simon, 1983) and the primal scene. Their very lack of specificity and absence of an underlying data base give these metaphors their widespread usefulness in all aspects of our Zeitgeist. We have seen how the unconscious draws added strength from its use of the metaphor of depth (as in "deep" interpretations), and we will see shortly the enormous appeal of the archeological metaphor in all branches of psychoanalytic work.

But even though metaphor is everywhere, there is great reluctance to accept the fact that the theory itself is largely metaphorical and therefore lies outside of science. Part of this reluctance stems from an unwillingness to accept membership in C. P. Snow's less-favored culture; part from negative associations to the name of hermeneutics and all that it implies. Grünbaum writes scornfully of the "so-called hermeneutic version of psychoanalytic theory . . . [which rests] on a mythic exegesis of Freud's writings . . . based on profound misunderstandings of the very content and methods of the natural sciences" (1984, p. 1). Holt is equally dismissive in describing the hermeneutic approach as a

warmed-over version of [a position] promulgated by Dilthey and a group of south German late romantic philosophers just about a century ago. During all the subsequent years, it has been rediscovered periodically by those who wish to find some way to be intellectually respectable without having to exert themselves as strenuously as scientific method demands. And surely, for the last fifteen years, many a psychoanalyst has come under the influence of this misleading doctrine. (1984, p. 23)

Not only romantic and misleading, it is unchanging, periodically warmed over, and connotes laziness and lack of moral fiber; is that why it emerged from *south* Germany?

The issue in recent years has become more and more polarized (see Blight's "Must Psychoanalysis Retreat to Hermeneutics?" [1981]) in a way that is directly reminiscent of C. P. Snow's attempt to dichotomize the two cultures of science and humanities. The choice, it appears, must be either/or; thus, to assume a hermeneutic or metaphorical emphasis is to renounce science and to give up the hope of joining the preferred establishment. This desperate rearguard action against the warmed-over theory of a few misguided Germans helps explain the ringing statements by Brenner about the undoubted scientific standing of psychoanalysis. The horror of accepting the hermeneutic position helps account for the never-ending search to show that Freud's system is truly data-based, ruled exclusively by the laws of evidence (see Edelson, 1984), and evolving implacably in the best scientific tradition. The rearguard action can be called the search for historical truth.

The Search for Historical Truth

The search takes many forms and appears in both clinical and theoretical domains. When working with patients, psychoanalysts feel a constant need to reconstruct a significant past event which can be used to fill in a missing piece of the clinical picture and to explain a significant part of the patient's distress, to find a childhood encounter which will provide a reasonable way to understand a later fixation, and to uncover the particular setting which permitted certain ideas to be naturally assumed and develop into current beliefs. In the domain of theory, a search for historical truth is a search for the brute facts in the clinical material, in the accumulated record of case reports across the years, which are supposed, as in any good science, to form the basis of the theory.

To search for historical truth is to live out the metaphor of analyst as archeologist and to believe, along with Freud, that pieces of the past lie buried somewhere in the person's unconscious. The metaphor can be enlarged to the view of analysis as a science, built up on a foundation of discrete findings which make up the evidential data base and which can be recovered from the past. Consider one of Freud's earliest formulations of this model:

> In face of the incompleteness of my analytic results, I had no choice but to follow the example of those discoverers whose good fortune it is to bring to the light of day after their long burial the priceless though mutilated relics of antiquity. I have restored what is missing, taking the best models known to me from other analyses; but, like a conscientious archeologist, I have not omitted to mention in each case where the authentic parts end and my constructions begin. (1905, p. 12)

The archeological metaphor is surely one of Freud's master plots (see Brooks, 1984), one of the more convincing story lines (see Schafer, 1983) in the corpus. As metaphor, it functions as a kind of literary figure by which we might choose to represent the course of development and by which we are guided in the course of treatment. If convincing evidence could be found by which we could establish, once and for all, that certain kinds of early experiences stayed with the patient and did indeed bring about later changes, then we have grounds for changing the concept from metaphor to hypothesis. We are no longer dealing with a literary figure which has mainly a rhetorical appeal; we now have the beginnings of a truly explanatory system. If historical specimens could be found, and if the analytic community found them convincing, then we could think confidently about moving, in Max Black's words, from metaphor to algebra.

It is one of the main themes of this book that no signs of this algebra exist and that there are no clinical specimens which convincingly support the archeological metaphor. The search for this kind of historical truth has, to date, come up empty. But the failure to find evidence will never be taken as a sign that the metaphor is incorrect, just as the failure to find the Titanic on the bottom of the North Atlantic was, prior to 1985, never seen as grounds for calling off the search. The search for historical truth will continue — but the lack of evidence should be noted.

The search for historical truth continues because a successful outcome would establish the lawfulness that is a necessary part of science. To say that early events have a necessary, lawful, and predictable influence on later developments and to collect evidence for these impingements prepares the way for an understanding of the forms of influence and their classification. This leads, in turn, to a still deeper understanding. Once this step is taken, we would have a framework within which observations could be fitted, and we would be on our way toward building a nomothetic science. Once this step was taken, individual observation could be fitted into an overall pattern and evidence would become cumulative.

It is important to realize how far we are from this fortunate position. We are still searching for historical specimens which can be fitted into a web of belief (see Quine and Ullian, 1978). While our literature is bursting with clinical vignettes which seem to support the archeological metaphor, they are not true data for at least two reasons: With only a few exceptions — and the exceptions are usually the more trivial observations — the so-called data are significantly incomplete — anecdotal rather than archival; even if reasonably complete, they tend to be either theory-laden or context-laden. What is more, we have no grammar of early development, no clearly defined system by which early experience is transformed into later behavior. We can say that a given event, A, after time t, may reveal itself as A'; but because we have no calculus of transformation, we have no way of combining observations or of validating or falsifying previous findings. Instead of an archive, we have a literature of anecdotes, a dumping ground of observations which have little more evidential value than a 30-year-old collection of flying saucer reports.

It seems very likely that our lack of cumulative progress and our awareness of this lack help to accelerate and broaden the search for historical truth. Wearing our clinical hat, we search for developmental precursors of later symptoms; wearing our investigator hat, we search for the raw data of the session which will explain the therapeutic effect. What "really happens" within the session? What are the brute facts of the session and how can they be related to the usual kind of case report? Can we somehow unpack the clinical narrative and decompose it into its raw ingredients, giving us a true account of the clinical encounter and putting our usual vignette on a more solid footing? Can some sort of bedrock be established which would somehow be more genuine than our partly literary accounts?

The quest for historical truth within the session or across sessions is just as uncertain as the quest within the patient's past. The cry for unpacking was met by the discovery that there are very few brute facts and that the "story" represented in the case report is only one of many stories, which all have a family resemblance. No one of these stories carries a one-to-one correspondence with the "facts" of the clinical encounter; these "facts" merely represent another, perhaps a more disconnected, account. Thus the end result of a careful unpacking would be the exchange of one account for another; neither would have standing as a specimen in an archival sense, and neither would be free of the hidden influence of theory and context.

For an example of how observation cannot be divorced from theory, consider the following anecdote from Brenner concerning a patient who, he felt, had been "overwhelmed by penis envy since childhood."

As another illustration of how she felt about being without a penis, she came into my office one day indignant because, when she had gone to use the lavatory just before, she had found the toilet seat up.

"No one," she said, "has any right to leave a toilet seat in that position."

"Why not?" I asked.

"Because," she said, "it looks so ugly that way."

She explained that she had always felt one of the ugliest things in the world is a toilet with the seat up. If the lid or the seat were down, it looked presentable, but she could never stand the way it looked with the seat up. (1982, p. 172)

Does the unpleasant sight of open toilet seats stem from an envy of men and all their rights and privileges (including the right to urinate while standing), or does it stem from a much more complicated set of considerations? Interior decorators who design matching covers for toilet seats would be affronted by the sight of an open seat — for purely aesthetic reasons. From another point of view, an open seat brings into view the contents of the bowl, and under certain conditions, that is better left unseen. From the standpoint of pure form, a lifted seat spoils the symmetry of design and detracts from its overall appearance, much as an automobile is uglier with its hood up or its trunk open.

With these considerations in mind, it seems apparent that the interchange with the patient has more than one meaning. It is no longer a transparent piece of data (similar to a meter reading) whose significance is immediately clear to all observers and whose meaning can be readily detached from its context. Brenner may be entirely right in his interpretation, but the outside reader will not be convinced unless he is given a vast amount of additional data about this particular patient — and these data are not supplied.

The anecdote is also weakened by the absence of alternative explanation. If Brenner had recognized the insufficiency of his argument or the possibility that other explanations might also be considered, his capacity to persuade would have been significantly increased; the reader might have felt uneasy about the evidence but willing, at least, to be convinced. But to be told that this example is an illustration of penis envy when no effort is made, in the material, to suggest (and then demolish) other alternatives is to sharply reduce its capacity to persuade, as well as to call into question its standing as a specimen of anything.

It seems likely that Brenner feels no need to supply alternatives; in his eyes, the specimen is complete and entirely transparent. From the context of his clinical experience, his understanding of the theory, and most important of all, his understanding of the patient, this specimen is entirely self-evident — it *signifies* penis envy just as a falling barometer signifies a change in the weather. Projected onto the specimen is an aggregation of theoretical assumptions that the outside reader may not share; and even if partly shared, they may not be operative at the time of reading the example.

For a similar example of how theory supplies meaning, consider a recent study by Dahl (1983). A group of analysts listened to the early sessions from an analytic case and interrupted the reading whenever any one of them decided that enough evidence had accumulated to support one among a set of possible hypotheses. Each interruption was defined as a call, and many single calls were heard — indeed, it was unusual for the group to decide in unison that any given hypothesis could be supported at any given time. Confidence ratings were given to each call by all members of the group. Dahl found that a judge's confidence for his own calls was significantly higher than that for those of his colleagues. This finding suggests that each clinician heard the material in his own preferred manner, influenced by his theoretical bias. If this finding can be generalized to the domain of all clinical specimens, then it seems clear that they do not function as data in the ordinary sense. Any given anecdote carries a variety of meanings, depending on the reader and his particular internal state at the moment of reading. Although Brenner has argued that "what a psychoanalyst does with the data which derive from applying the analytic method is no different from what any scientist does with his or her data" (1982, p. 5), we are beginning to recognize at least two important differences: Clinical data are far less transparent, and second, the lack of transparency usually goes unrecognized.

For a detailed example of how meaning may be influenced by context—the unspoken assumptions of patient and analyst—consider the following interchange, which took place on the day after a Labor Day cancellation.

Patient	Analyst
Described in glowing terms the fine parties he had attended over the holiday weekend.	(Sounds like he can get along very well without me.)
Mentioned the fact that he was somewhat late. "You will think it is a resistance but it was nothing of the kind."	
His lateness (barely noticeable) was caused by difficulty in getting a cab. He had one hailed but someone else got there first. Very angry— yelled "Fuck you" at the driver.	(Cabbie, who passed him by, stands for me, who cancelled a session.)
"Fuck you" (to the analyst).	
More thoughts about the parties over the weekend.	

Then, thinking ahead, he announced that he and his wife had decided to accompany their son to college. He might have to miss a session, but the son was more important.

The theme of losing a session is still continuing and is obviously very charged with feeling. The decision to accompany your son to college shows that you are a good father, unlike me. At the same time, it returns the affront caused by me in dropping a session.

(Angrily) "Who are you that I should care about missing a session?"

[Parenthetical material occurred to the analyst but was never put into words; direct quotes represent near-verbatim utterances. Other wordings are approximate.]
[Taken from Kanzer, 1981, pp. 79-80]

Where are the facts in this interchange? The analyst begins by deciding that the patient was not affected by the Monday cancellation, partly as a result of hearing the report of the "fine parties" over the holidays. But somewhat later in the hour, he makes the interpretation that he was affected and that he wants to cancel a session in turn. What caused the change in interpretation? It seemed to partly hinge on the incident with the taxi and the fact that the same curse was directed at both cabbie and analyst. The analyst assumes that missing the cab reminded the patient of the Monday cancellation and that cursing the analyst (in the same language) relieved him of his anger at the cabbie (and perhaps of his anger at the Monday cancellation). The equivalence of cabbie and analyst is confirmed by using the same curse on both.

Once the equivalence is established to the analyst's satisfaction, he listens to the material in a somewhat different way. When he next hears of the impending cancellation (linked to the trip to accompany the son to college), he decides that the patient was in fact hurt by the Monday cancellation and frames an interpretation along these lines. The patient responds with an angry outburst.

Was the interpretation right or wrong? It leans heavily on the incident with the cab driver and the assumption (never made explicit) that the cabbie became a substitute for the analyst. Against this context, it seems quite natural to hear the trip to college as a quid pro quo — a response to the Monday cancellation.

But the equivalence is less than compelling, and it is also true that the interpretation is somewhat unfairly circumstantial. To add to our doubts, there is also the early evidence (noted by the analyst) that the patient was unaffected by the cancellation (unless his report of the "fine parties" is an example of protesting too much).

What stands out most of all is the way in which context controls understanding. The early reference to the weekend parties can be heard as both (a) a claim that the patient never missed the analyst over the holiday weekend; and (b) a claim that he missed him keenly but is pretending the opposite. The plan to take his son to college can be heard as (a) the carrying-out of a longstanding intention that is unrelated to the transference; (b) as a sign that he, the patient, is free to come and go as he chooses; and (c) a sign that he was hurt by the skipped session on Monday and chooses to pay the analyst back in the same coin. (If the hour falls on a holiday, does its absence have the standing of a cancellation? Would any patient — regardless of how needy — really expect the holiday not to be observed?)

The analyst chooses the third option, as we have seen, but does not mention the other two possibilities. The failure to include alternative accounts in his interpretation may have been responsible for the patient's sudden anger. The truth value of the interpretation may have been unnecessarily colored by its authoritarian form, and the patient's feelings about authority may have generated some of the anger. What is more, the interpretation may have been quite simply wrong. To be unfairly accused in a rather didactic manner might easily make a patient angry.

What should be noticed is the way in which meaning is constantly being projected onto the material — by both patient and analyst. What disturbs the dialogue is the fact that assumptions held by both parties are never made explicit and therefore never get analyzed. To complicate matters further, surface meaning is always suspect. The patient's first statement is not taken at face value but as evidence that he does not miss the analyst. The patient's lateness — no matter how slight — is assumed (by the patient) to indicate (to the analyst) that he (the patient) chose not to come on time. The parallel between missing the taxi and missing a Monday session (regardless of the holiday) sensitizes the analyst to the parallel in curses; these parallels prompt the transference thought (it was never expressed in words) that the patient is still reacting to the missed session. It therefore follows, given this line of reasoning, that the trip to take his son to college is a response in kind to the Monday cancellation.

As meanings — whatever their truth value — are projected onto the clinical material, there is a tendency to lose sight of what exactly was said. Once the trip to the college is heard as a response to the cancellation, it becomes difficult to hear it as simply a trip; once the patient responds angrily to the interpretation, it is tempting to look for deeper reasons for the anger and not consider the possibility that he expressed outrage at being misunderstood. Perhaps most telling of all is the way the meaning of the missed hour is never brought into the center of the discussion, despite the fact that its assumed significance colors a good part of the interaction. We wonder to what extent this focus is more a concern of the analyst than the patient. It did happen, after all, on an official holiday.

The way in which context influences understanding and the way in which the analyst chooses quite deliberately to focus on certain meanings and not others shows up, once again, the extent to which the analyst is far from innocent. There is another feature of the interchange which should also be considered — how different it is from a normal conversation. We have already noted the extent to which both parties subscribe to the rule, "surface is deceptive" — what you say is not what you mean, whereas in normal conversation, the opposite rule tends to obtain. But to an impressive extent, other rules are *not* broken, and to bring them into focus, we need to study the normal assumptions we bring to any dialogue.

The strong need to believe that a normal conversation is going on beneath the surface is an ever-present feature in human interchange. This need represents one of the four Conversational Implicatures described by Grice (1967); it is firmly rooted in our approach to conversation and may easily generalize to the analytic situation. Thus it comes about that minor misinterpretations by the analyst are frequently overlooked by the patient, and even significant mistakes may either be ignored or rationalized away. The extent of this misunderstanding is not known because of the difficulty in getting access to the critical data (the dialogue just presented is one of the few attempts to represent both sides of an analytic dialogue); but the chances are good that its frequency is much greater than we like to believe. Notice that this issue cannot be evaluated from the transcript alone because the patient's recognition of the problem is never put into words.

> Our talk exchanges [states Grice in an analysis of ordinary
> conversation] do not normally consist of a succession of discon-
> nected remarks, and would not be rational if they did. They
> are, characteristically, to some degree at least cooperative ef-
> forts; and each participant recognizes in them, to some extent, a
> common purpose or set of purposes, or at least a mutually
> accepted direction. This purpose or direction may be fixed from
> the start (e.g., by an initial proposal of a question for discus-
> sion), or it may evolve during the exchange; it may be fairly
> definite, or it may be so indefinite as to leave very considerable
> latitude to the participants (as in a casual conversation). But at
> each stage, *some* possible conversational moves would be exclud-
> ed as conversationally unsuitable. We might then formulate a
> rough general principle which participants will be expected (ce-
> teris paribus) to observe, viz: "Make your conversational contri-
> bution, such as is required, at the stage at which it occurs, by
> the accepted purpose or direction of the talk-exchange in which
> you are engaged." One might label this the Cooperative Princi-
> ple. (Grice, 1967, Part II, pp. 6–7)

This paragraph refers to normal conversations, but it applies
almost as well to psychoanalytic dialogue. Because of the in-
struction to the patient to say whatever comes to mind, we
might rule out the possibility that some remarks would be unacceptable. Nevertheless, as we noted above, the Cooperative
Principle is probably still active much of the time and must
continue to exert an influence on understanding, if not on
utterance. Gadamer's analysis of the way we go about learning
ancient languages also applies to the way we listen to the patient's free associations:

> We learn that we must "construe" a sentence before we at-
> tempt to understand the individual parts of the sentence in their
> linguistic meaning. But this process of construing is itself al-
> ready governed by an expectation of meaning that follows from
> the context of what has gone before. It is also necessary for this
> expected meaning to be adjusted if the text calls for it. This
> means, then, that the expectation changes and that the text

acquires the unit of a meaning from another expected meaning. (Gadamer, 1975, p. 259)

Combining the arguments from Grice and Gadamer, we might say that the two partners in a psychoanalytic "conversation" are implicitly, if not explicitly, obeying the Cooperative Principle, and that this collaboration comes in part from practice in everyday discourse and in part from the underlying therapeutic alliance. The search for a common meaning not only puts a limit on both free association and evenly suspended attention (the two principles explicitly governing utterances from patient and analyst), but supplies an initial hypothesis which is applied to incoming utterances and forms the initial, overall construal which precedes more detailed understanding.

Because of its asymmetrical nature, however, the psychoanalytic dialogue also tends to subvert the Cooperative Principle. Because the analyst tends to remain silent and does not always feel the need to correct obvious misunderstandings, the two strands of the dialogue may often diverge without notice. Under these conditions, the differing foreunderstandings can make for quite separate construals and because silence is the rule (at least for the analyst), the full extent of this mischief may never be known. Even when a misunderstanding is put into words, it is not necessarily detected. Even if pieces of the interchange are not misunderstood, they can be overlooked or even misheard. Mishearings are not always caught in time, and when caught, are not always corrected; the analyst might ask for repetition, but not necessarily the patient, whose response would depend on the state of the transference and similar complicating factors.

It should be realized that the possibility for this kind of misunderstanding tends to limit the use of both free association and evenly suspended attention. There is a clear contradiction between the conventional idea of the latter, in which meanings are transparently registered without ambiguity, and the argument by Gadamer that understanding is a complicated under-taking which never begins with a clean slate and which is al-ways overlaid by foreunderstanding or prejudice (in the nonpejorative sense of prejudgment). The contradiction is still in force when countertransference is removed from the picture; even the most neutral psychoanalyst will still encounter prob-lems of understanding language and will always be making tentative construals of the patient's utterance before full recog-nition takes place. It would be folly to assume, in the absence of countertransference interference, that perfect understanding is always present.

The ways in which context influences meaning present us with serious obstacles to understanding therapeutic process. The facts of the matter are rarely transparent or equally acces-sible to all interested parties; in almost no therapeutic inter-change is the subject under discussion a clearly bounded idea which stands alone in time and space.

> Context [writes Jonathan Culler] is boundless in two senses. First, any given context is open to further description. There is no limit in principle to what might be shown to be relevant to the performance of a given speech act. This structural openness of context is essential to all disciplines: the scientist discovers that factors previously disregarded are relevant to the behavior of a certain object; the historian brings new or reinterpreted data to bear on a particular event; the critic relates a passage of a text to a context that makes it appear in a new light. . . . Con-text is also unmasterable in a second sense: any attempt to codify context can always be grafted onto the context it sought to describe, yielding a new context which escapes the previous formulation. (1982, pp. 123–124)

As new commentary is grafted onto old evidence, changing the data base and prompting new interpretations, we have a classic recursive spiral which can only get larger, not smaller. Seen as an ever-expanding text, the psychoanalytic literature of case reports is a boundless source of material for partial construction, and because it is anecdotal and episodic, it lends itself to new readings by each new theorist who comes along. But the readings are noncumulative because they are incomplete: either anecdotal or ambiguous. Because we have no specimens which are publicly accessible, we have no opportunity to extend and refine past interpretation or to compare current practice with the way in which analysts once behaved.

The search for historical truth becomes the victim of this ever-expanding context. We now begin to see more clearly why specimen interpretations can never be frozen: what is a specimen for one generation becomes problematic for another. The very sensitivity which Freud trained us to develop — the distinctly psychoanalytic capacity to find links between apparently separate domains of meaning — precludes a fixed set of archival documents in which the past resides forever. All understanding, we are taught, is partial at best; new context will necessarily alter the best reconstruction; no guidelines exist which can tell us which reading is primary or which reading is privileged.

One lesson seems clear: No interpretation is sacred. If context is boundless and ever-expanding, the grounds for reaching a conclusion about this or that meaning are forever shifting. An archive can be constructed, but its contents will always be open to interpretation and elaboration.

Explication de Texte

For another illustration of the way in which context influences meaning, for another illustration of why it is necessary to empathize and identify with the motives of patient and therapist in order to understand the clinical material, I turn to a recent clinical interchange reported by Schwaber (1981). The patient (Mr. R) was a young photographer in his early twenties who complained of such somatic symptoms as stomach distress, headaches, and dizziness, coupled with a feeling of detachment and a frightened sense of being far removed from things in his life. He was particularly uneasy about reflecting on the early years of his life. Whenever he looked at early pictures or listened to tapes of himself as a child, he would experience some of the symptoms listed above. In the hour in question, the patient was speaking of the importance of photography in his life; toward the end of the session, he was speaking about the experience of elation in his work. It is important to remember one crucial fact about the analyst while reading this material: She (Dr. S) was about to go off on vacation and was particularly sensitive to this theme as the session was unfolding.

I will now present a partial transcript of the hour in question, taken from the paper by Schwaber (1981, p. 359). It is not clear whether this fragment is the verbatim dialogue or reconstructed by the analyst at some later time, but for our purposes the difference is not important because my emphasis will be on the nature of the important details of the interchange, on the way in which these details change in importance and even visibility as we learn more about the interchange, and on the way in which context can influence understanding. Even a near-veridical transcript would be subject to the same transformations of detail and the same subtle change in meaning and we would still be left, at the end of the reading, with no final sense that we had uncovered what "really" happened.

MR. R: I can remember even way back having the experience of elation. I can remember it being triggered by how it might look photographically, as in a beautiful scene or in music. When I see something that looks good, there is a very strong desire to take a picture and kind of freeze it there, as with a beautiful sunset. It's an experience all of a sudden of my sensibilities becoming really heightened, like I'll notice the pores of someone's skin and it looks great, and I want to take a picture and catch it. . . . I know a psychiatrist who became interested in photography and took it up more and more . . . on his vacation . . . finally giving up psychiatry . . .

DR. S: I wonder if my vacation may have been stirring such thoughts, of my waning interest in my profession.

MR. R: I'm not sure how to understand what you mean. I'm thinking of the joke of the two psychiatrists meeting in an elevator. I wonder if you know the joke, and if you do, will you answer. . . . I think you responded defensively to the idea of a psychiatrist switching to photography. . . . I didn't mean to be critical . . .

At this point it would be useful to ask both analyst and patient to provide a fully unpacked gloss of the interchange so that we would be in a position to know the associational and referential context of each of the key terms and a summary of their history in the analysis and in the patient's life. We must do without a complete unpacking for the present, but we do have certain clues which can be listed here before we undertake a more complete reconstruction. Mr. R was particularly sensitive to being ignored and could remember instances when both his mother and his girl friend showed a significant lack of interest in his work. He was also fond of music (as was his father) and remembers turning to music to ease feelings of isolation and insignificance. Thus, both experiences of looking and listening have particular significance for him as a child (and prove exceptions to his complaint that the early years of life were significantly distressing). We might also assume that the experience of looking has a particular relation to his profession as a photographer and that the experience of listening has a complementary relation to his role as analysand; thus, looking refers (by extension) to his life "outside" and listening to his life "inside" the analytic hour. We also know that experience of not being listened to (and presumably, looked at) was particularly painful and might give rise to some of the symptoms mentioned.

With this material as background, we can return to the text of the hour. I will take up each sentence in turn, followed by whatever underlying meanings we can discover.

Mr. R: *I can remember even way back having the experience of elation*. Knowing that he felt great trepidation about remembering the first 13 years of his life, we might choose to place particular emphasis on the word *even*; read with that added emphasis, the sentence seems to be saying that this original concern no longer applies quite as strongly, perhaps because the analysis is moving forward and/or because at this particular moment he feels a sense of trust in the analyst and feels brave enough to look at his early life. What we do not know, of course, is how the sentence was *said*—that is, was he talking *about* elation or was he also *feeling* elated as he spoke? Hearing the tape (if there was one) would help answer part of that question; we could also learn from both patient's and analyst's recollection because, while not necessarily veridical, they would give us an experiential context for understanding the text.

The locution "having the experience" has the ring of detachment; the patient could have said "when I feel elated" or something more active and direct. If our impression is correct, we might choose to score this expression as an example of what Schafer (1976) has called "disclaimed action." In this case, the emphasis on the experience rather than on the subject who was experiencing it may also reflect Mr. R's interest in photography and his need to "capture" the moment (see below, next statement) and see himself as a camera making a record rather than a person who is always part of his experience.

I can remember it being triggered by how it might look photographically, as in a beautiful scene or in music. We first notice that the punctuation seems wrong—the comma should come after *scene*—and we might speculate that the error gives us some clue as to how the analyst was listening because she is not making a distinction between *looking* and *listening*. As we have seen, this distinction is vital for the patient. Does this oversight also reflect the fact that perhaps she was listening to the patient less than she should have, either because she was thinking about her upcoming vacation or because of some other recent intrusion? Whatever the reason, we will shortly discover that her next comment seems to be less than perfectly attuned to the material.

The word *trigger* has a particular meaning in photography (as in triggering a flash) and suggests that perhaps the patient has some particular incident in mind (a specific sunset, perhaps — see the next sentence).

When I see something that looks good, there is a very strong desire to take a picture and kind of freeze it there, as with a beautiful sunset. Here is another example of what Schafer would call disclaimed action. The patient begins with the pronoun *I* and then shifts to the passive voice ("there is a very strong desire . . . "), distancing himself from the responsibility of taking the picture. We are also separated from the scene in question — what sunset, when and where? Does this partial and abstract form of retelling reflect the patient's conflict about looking, sensing it both as pleasurable and also distressing? Going further, we might speculate that this style of passive and abstract reporting may lead directly to loss of interest on the part of the listener, which gives us a clue as to why his friends and family seem preoccupied and unavailable. Similar forces may be acting on the analyst during this hour; if she becomes frustrated with Mr. R's half-telling, she may turn to thoughts of vacation.

It's an experience all of a sudden of my sensibilities becoming really heightened, like I'll notice the pores of someone's skin and it looks great, and I want to take a picture and catch it. . . . Again the passive voice intrudes, only to be (surprisingly) interrupted by the active voice and a striking image. Surely this memory refers to a specific person and scene — a face, perhaps, or a nude — with specific associations for the patient. Once again, he is telling but not telling — is he now experiencing some specific somatic distress? The pictures being described are never shown (never fully "developed") and we can appreciate once again the analyst's likely sense of frustration. To add to the problem, time is running out — the hour is coming to an end.

I know a psychiatrist who became interested in photography and took

it up more and more . . on his vacation . . . finally giving up psychiatry.
. . . The patient has changed the subject, moving away from
the close-up image and whatever feelings it aroused and turned
to what is perhaps a safer topic. But is it? Has he turned toward
his friend or toward the analyst? The story about the psychiatrist may be meant for the analyst's ears; properly decoded, it
might be taken to mean that he wishes the analyst to become
more appreciative of his imagery and to learn to look (with her
mind's eye) as well as listen. Mr. R's complaint that people pay
him less attention than they might may have to do with his
feeling that they do not show the right kind of *visual* appreciation of his conversation, do not appreciate his choice of images,
and that, even while listening, they are not seeing what he sees.
Because this would require a special gift, it becomes clear that
most of his listeners would disappoint him and reinforce the
feeling that he was being ignored.

Thus, the point of the remark is not the reference to vacations—that seems almost incidental—but the fact that he was
able to influence the psychiatrist to become more like him (Mr.
R). Perhaps he is less worried about the analyst leaving than he
is trying to bring the analyst closer, more like him, and perhaps
less critical and forbidding. If the analyst could look rather
than listen, he might feel less misunderstood and more certain
that the "pictures" he was seeing during his associations were
seen by someone else.

Dr. S: *I wonder if my vacation may have been stirring such thoughts, of
my waning interest in my profession.* She responds to the transference note being struck but chooses to pick up on the reference
to vacations. This move may come about because of what I
have called the projective fallacy (see Spence, 1982, p. 229).
The vacation is uppermost in the analyst's mind and she assumes that it must also be just as significant for the patient.
Making this assumption, she hears the thought about the psychiatrist giving up psychiatry as necessarily referring to her;
the added word *vacations* probably tripped the balance. Focusing

on the vacation and its implied separation, she may be less aware of the more abstract theme developed in the preceding paragraph, which has to do with the transition from listening to looking. Her paying it no attention may be one reason why Mr. R responds as we are about to hear.

Not only does she fail to comment on the transition from listening to looking, but she repeats the error in failing to reflect on the images of sunsets and pores, images which undoubtedly have great significance for the patient. Once again the analyst is listening without looking, perhaps repeating the behavior of Mr. R's friends and family and adding to his feeling of being misunderstood.

Mr. R: *I'm not sure how to understand what you mean.* This remark can be heard on several levels. Does he really not understand the analyst, or does he simply *choose* not to understand? His later remarks make it sound more like the second, and if that is the case, it is another candidate for Schafer's category of disclaimed actions. The patient has already formed a judgment, but he is wording it in such a way that we think he is only puzzled. The fact of his having reached a decision is borne out by the next comment.

I'm thinking of the joke of the two psychiatrists meeting in an elevator. By introducing the idea of two psychiatrists, he may be speaking of his wish to put himself on a more equal footing with the analyst and vice versa; if she were more like him, perhaps she would begin to look rather than listen. Unfortunately the joke is never told and we can never learn the details of what the patient had in mind. Here is another example of telling but not telling.

I wonder if you know the joke, and if you do, will you answer. . . . An interesting example of the projective fallacy. The joke is clear to the patient and he assumes that from the brief description of two psychiatrists in an elevator that it will be clear to the analyst as well. But as Schwaber points out in her discussion of this episode, there are several such jokes and thus the reference is ambiguous. Yet despite this knowledge, she *assumed* that it was the joke about the psychiatrist who, on being told "Good morning," wondered what his colleague may have meant (Schwaber, 1981, p. 360). Here is another projective response because there are no grounds for assuming anything—or rather, no unambiguous grounds.

The patient's assumption that he has given the analyst enough information may also relate to his predominantly visual mode of experiencing. If he "sees" the two psychiatrists in the elevator, he may also visualize the remainder of the scene, including the punch line; since the image is clear, he also assumes that the analyst has the same picture and therefore knows what he is talking about. Here again, the patient's emphasis on the visual mode may contribute to his being misunderstood.

The remark can also be heard as a kind of test. If the analyst is "looking with her mind's eye," then she will see the joke clearly; if she knows the joke, she passes the test and is proving her empathic skills. But if she stumbles and does not guess the right joke, then the patient has further proof that he is being misunderstood. Again, we have cause to wonder just how much he contributes to the constant misunderstanding about which we hear so much. His first remark after the intervention can be heard in this light; to say that he does not understand may indicate that he takes this opportunity to misunderstand and not that the analyst was being unclear or off the point. Given this tendency to look for misunderstanding, then *any* remark by the analyst would be questioned, there being no way in which she could respond "correctly."

I think you responded defensively to the idea of a psychiatrist switching to photography. . . . We can read this statement as both a further extension of the theme of being misunderstood and as one containing a certain amount of truth—the fact that the analyst, sensitized to the upcoming vacation, may have jumped at the chance to pick up a reference to it and was, in fact, hearing the patient. Keen followers of Gill and Hoffman (1982) might want to argue that the response was technically correct because every chance should be taken to interpret the transference: The analyst was about to go on vacation; the patient undoubtedly had thoughts about it; and here was a likely opening. They might also argue that the significant fact may be that the patient has made *no* explicit reference to the vacation and that the resistance to this awareness should be interpreted before the derivative.

From what we know about the patient, neither of these moves, although perhaps technically correct, would be altogether applauded because of his history of being misunderstood, from which we can deduce a rather strong need to be misunderstood. We might also suspect that he is fairly skilled at picking up defensive responses in others as part of his campaign to maintain his misunderstood state. Here the fact that he may be right is less important than making him aware of his sensitivity to such misunderstanding and to his tendency to magnify its importance. From the patient's point of view (and using what was for him a relevant metaphor), the analyst may have always seemed slightly "out of focus." One would suspect that unless and until this resistance were clarified and worked through, *no* interpretation or intervention, no matter how "correct," would be accepted.

I didn't mean to be critical. . . . We wonder if in fact he did, and if his critical stance is again being used in the service of maintaining his air of being misunderstood. We can also hear the patient making a discovery about himself, an observation about his response. As he listens to himself replying to the analyst's intervention, he may begin to hear for perhaps the first time a critical note in his association to the joke and in his choice of words. Thus the remark can be heard as marking the beginning of insight into his role of maintaining himself as being misunderstood.

The hour is over and the patient leaves. "I noticed," Schwaber writes, "that he completely avoided looking at me and his body seemed rather strikingly shrunken in its stance" (1981, p. 360).

We have now completed our partial unpacking of the Schwaber vignette. It is clearly only one of many possible reconstructions (a choice of different readings can be found in Davison et al., 1986, pp. 286–288). It could also be extended in depth by asking both patient and analyst to provide an extended gloss of (a) their memory of the hour and the private meanings of each of the key words; (b) the significant surround, which might include the analyst's sense of her upcoming vacation and the patient's prevailing expectations about being misunderstood; and (c) their current experience while rereading the transcript, the associations it brought to mind, and their memory of what they thought and might have said at key moments in the interchange. Further insights into the linguistic properties of the dialogue might be gained by putting the transcript through the kind of analysis illustrated in Dahl et al. (1978), which looks at the semantic and syntactic properties of each statement with particular reference to ways in which the intended meaning (or the presumptive intended meaning) is distorted and transformed as it is being expressed. Many of these distortions in the original work by Dahl et al. seemed to be in the service of countertransference. A similar effort might be applied to the present dialogue. To be maximally effective, however, this approach must begin with the verbatim transcription of the session, and it is not altogether clear whether this dialogue is verbatim or reconstructed.

Once we have unpacked the dialogue from different theoretical perspectives and from the different vantage points of participants and observers, we then face the task of reassembling the pieces of the experience in a way that will optimally recover the event for the outside reader. Faithful reconstruction would not only provide him with what was said but also with the sense of the larger context experienced by each speaker. Thus we would want to somehow illustrate or dramatize the patient's sense of being interrupted by the intervention and try to capture the extent to which this was felt to be a significant intrusion, as opposed to the quite different sense that the analyst was not necessarily following his chain of associations and thus providing him with an opportunity to be misunderstood. We would also want to capture the sense of concern in the analyst that time is running out on the hour, that she needs to make a reference to her vacation, and the possible sense of discovery and relief when the opportunity presented itself in a reference to vacations.

It is also clear that the word *vacation* is hardly sufficient to represent what the analyst had in mind during this session. A proper reconstruction would need to explore the subject in depth. What were her plans and whom did they include? Where was she headed? Was there a possibility for sunsets and perhaps sunbathing? If so, the patient's references to sunsets and skin would take on new significance, perhaps adding to the analyst's conviction that her *own* vacation was being described. If this were her experience, it should also become part of the reader's; as the overlap between patient's associations and the analyst's preoccupation becomes more compelling, we see the inevitability of her intervention and we understand it in both a theoretical and an experiential sense.

But now suppose that her vacation is long overdue and carries associations of urgency and even desperation; then the patient's comment about the psychiatrist turning photographer carries somewhat different overtones. To the extent that the analyst feels the need to find satisfaction elsewhere, the patient's comment becomes even more pertinent; if the overlap were sufficiently compelling, the analyst might even feel that the patient was reading her mind and "find herself" making the interpretation before she feels it is necessary. To the extent that countertransference feelings are pertinent, the intervention was partly defensive — and yet the patient, in labeling it as such, is being defensive in return because he is taking advantage of the analyst's error to maintain his favorite stance. Here is why we need to know the meaning of the vacation. If it was felt as long overdue, we see more clearly how and why the intervention came about, and even more important, we understand how difficult it would have been for the analyst to step back and see the patient's response as being defensive in its own right.

I have been arguing in a linear fashion about the relevance of various contexts on our understanding of this segment, but this may not be the best way to enhance understanding. Pertinent contexts cannot be presented seriatim because of our tendency to strive for closure at the earliest possible moment; once we have sensed the meaning of a given interchange, it tends to become the *only* meaning, and subsequent qualifications are likely to have minimal effect. Thus it would be a mistake in a finished reconstruction to present the reader with the bare dialogue, as I did in the earlier part of the chapter, because by the time he has read that section he has already formed his own impression of what analyst and patient were saying and trying to say, and any further attempts at reconstruction will necessarily fall under this shadow. The finished reconstruction must be a creative product which establishes the initial setting with as much care as a playwright shows in describing his first scene and introducing his characters. Context must be carefully provided. At certain times this context might well contain significant amounts of uncertainty; at other times, certain themes might be brought into focus so sharply that other issues are necessarily pushed to the background.

It becomes clear that no two reconstructions will be alike. My choice of context, pacing of details, and balance between discussion and text can significantly affect the reader's sense of coherence and necessity. If I present Dr. S's vacation thoughts in just the right way, highlighting the details which overlap with the patient's associations, I can easily justify her intervention and make it seem inevitable and necessary. A less friendly

reconstruction might choose to emphasize the technical problems of interpreting the transference; given this kind of unpacking, the analyst might seem to be largely grasping at
straws by taking a distant reference to her vacation as sufficient
warrant for an interpretation. The picture of hastiness and
impatience would then be "validated" by the patient's sense of
being interrupted, and his remark that the analyst was being
defensive would be heard as just rather than symptomatic. By
building too strong a case in favor of the patient, we would miss
the sense in which he may have *chosen* to be misunderstood and
needed to put the analyst on the defensive.

Reconstruction, in short, is clearly a creative enterprise
whose form depends on the goals in question. What "really
happened" has many different faces and can be told from many
points of view. Because unpacking can be extended indefinitely
in a variety of different directions, some selection is necessary
in the final product, and we can assume that the motives and
goals of the unpacker are playing a significant part in what is
selected. We also notice that the nature of the "facts" is constantly changing. As we learn more about Mr. R's history, of
his interest in looking and his concern about being misunderstood, we begin to see even the more casual parts of the dialogue as assuming new importance. The "fact" of the joke of the
two psychiatrists has one referent for the analyst, quite possibly
a second for the patient, and undoubtedly a third for the reader. Many of the significant facts in this vignette are invisible at
first reading and become clarified only by seeing them from
different sides and from within different contexts. And the discovery depends, in large part, on our standing as members of
the psychoanalytic community who share the same culture with
analyst and patient; without this membership, no context, no
matter how artfully crafted, would have much effect.

The conviction that follows from this kind of reconstruction
deserves a few words of discussion. If we are brought closer to
understanding the events of an hour, it is because they are

accommodated within our experience as analysts and our experience in general; understanding rests on

> recognition of a given piece of behavior as being part and parcel of a pattern of activity which we can follow, which we can remember or imagine, and which we describe in terms of the general laws which cannot possibly all be rendered explicit (still less organized into a system), but without which the texture of normal human life — social or personal — is not conceivable. (Berlin, 1981, p. 128)

A satisfactory reconstruction of the Schwaber vignette depends on making the outside reader privy to the experience and background of the original participants, bringing him or her inside the lives of analyst and patient at that particular time and place, and providing the essential context of what was thought and said. The pluralistic nature of the facts and the multiplicity of possible contexts make it clear that no one version will be sufficient. Until that final version is achieved, we are dealing with trial accounts, possible *constructions* of a complicated event that are always open to new arrangements, depending on the skill of the presenter and the range of new horizons which can be laid before the reader. The final version might be called a true reconstruction, but since that final version will always elude us, it seems safer to speak of better and better approximations to this version, all called *constructions*.

What is the truth value of the Schwaber reconstruction — what is its evidential status? Did Dr. S make a tactical mistake in raising the issue of her vacation? Was it actually a defensive response which interrupted the patient's stream of associations? Did Mr. R truly feel interrupted, or did he merely choose to emphasize that feeling in the interests of putting the analyst on the defensive, of demonstrating how he was always misunderstood, and perhaps as a way of taking revenge on Dr. S for going away? The truth is everywhere and nowhere; it resides, to a certain extent, in each of these possibilities, but it is hard to see how they can be arranged in some final hierarchy of certainty. Nor do we come any closer to the truth by appealing to the reconstructions of patient and therapist because their memories are also influenced by context and by subsequent experience. Suppose we listened to Mr. R's recollections and then proposed an alternative which he found unacceptable; are we any more convinced that this alternative is less true, knowing his characteristic style of choosing to be detached and misunderstood?

In looking at the same problem from a different context, Gaylin had this to say:

> Truth like beauty may be only in the eye of the beholder. There may be many truths and there may be no truth. Or absolute truth may exist but only in an unknowable state. Psychoanalysis is aware of this. It draws a distinction between "actuality" and "reality," truth and perceived truth. It reserves the term "actuality" for the world of events as they actually are; in doing so, it assumes an essential truth about things, existence, and events. "Reality" is our subjective perception of that actual world. Each of us perceives a different reality. All of us take the actual events and interpret them according to the biases of a lifetime of experiences. So that while all of us may occupy the same space and the same time and be exposed to the same actual events, we are living in different real worlds. . . . We do not perceive that we are constructing images and stories that are uniquely ours; we will not see them as mere foci of our elaboration. We will define *the* truth in terms of *our* reality, not the actuality. We will, therefore, "see" different things without lying or any attempt at distortion; we will build from the same raw ingredients different structures. (1982, pp. 111–112)

To what extent can this tendency be reversed? To what extent can the reader be made aware of multiple and overlapping readings of the same sentence; to what extent can he be weaned away from his naive absolutism and trained to see multiple meanings, multiply arranged? To carry out this mission is only to emphasize Freud's insistence on the ambiguity of everyday life and to admit that what goes for patients goes for us as well, that to insist on a single case history or a single correct interpretation is to impose the worst kind of double standard on our patients and to preach what we should not practice. Because in the final examination, to be multiply aware of multiple meanings is the true test of what Isakower called the "analyzing instrument" and of what Schafer calls the "analytic attitude" (see Schafer, 1983).

What, then, is being reconstructed and where is it? The more pessimistic reading of this question is given by Jacobsen and Steele (1979), who argue that the triggering event is always being pushed back farther in time so that we are always approaching but never discovering it. Clues given by the patient allow us to approximate its possible shape, but its existence always remains in doubt, to be inferred from its consequences. Thus reconstructive reasoning is always circular, problematic, and based on rather weak evidential grounds. The few exceptions to this rule become famous as anecdotes with an almost mythical power and tend to substitute for general documentation; because they are often dramatic and obey our expectations, they tend to be persuasive and blind us to the lack of general documentation.

A more complex answer to the problem is provided by Derrida in his discussion of deferred action (*Nachträglichkeit*; see Culler, 1982, pp. 162–164). This formulation allows us to locate the determining event (reconstruction) in no particular space and time, as having no historical truth, but still possessed of psychical reality and what might be called narrative truth. The determining event in the patient's psychic reality "never occurs as such, is never present as an event, but is constructed afterwards by what can only be described as a textual mechanism of the unconscious" (Culler, 1982, p. 163).

Because it is not fixed in space and time, it can always be constructed anew, and here we see the fragile claim of historical fact. A given happening is given meaning by what happened in the patient's mind at the time; these happenings are out of reach of contemporary witnesses and perhaps equally unavailable to the patient himself; nevertheless, we can construct a plausible context and a reasonable explanation. As more facts are known and as the question is examined from different angles, the meanings may deepen and the given event is transformed from a simple scene to one of multiple levels. Since there is no clear dividing line between fact and interpretation, we have no way of seeing the event "by itself" and comparing it to the event enriched by the additional context.

Something like this seems to happen with the Schwaber vignette. Was Mr. R's reference to the psychiatrist turning photographer a reference to the analyst's vacation? Yes and no. Yes, from the standpoint of the listening analyst with vacation uppermost on her mind; no, perhaps, from the standpoint of the patient who was caught up in a specific scene and remembering (perhaps with heightened sensitivity, even elation) an experience in which he successfully convinced someone else to stop listening to the world and start seeing it — an exception to the rule that no one understands his way of living. We can speculate that perhaps the analyst's intervention, showing her partial understanding, was wrong because it was right — wrong because it violated the patient's sense of being always misunderstood, and right because her upcoming vacation may have been a partial cause of the manifest, if not the latent, content of the patient's remark. But here another distinction becomes clear. The intervention may have possessed its own technical quality (correct or incorrect), but this aspect may be quite unrelated to the way in which the patient *chose* to hear it, for reasons of his own preferred style of seeing the world. This "fact" can hardly be read from the transcript; it may not even be gathered from Mr. R's recollections because the patient now is possibly quite different from the patient then. In similar fashion, we may accept such a reading because we *choose* to hear the evidence that way, not because the conclusion is inescapable.

Thus the evidence for any interpretation or reconstruction is not exhausted by the words, although the words certainly contain significant clues to the final meaning. Because so much depends on context, we cannot locate the "grounds" for an explanation in either time or space, but that does not mean that they do not exist and do not carry significant evidential weight. Nor does the shifting influence of context on utterance mean that awareness of different shadings cannot be taught and that our sensitivity to multiple meanings cannot be heightened. It does mean, however, that no final answer is likely to be forthcoming, that any "reconstruction" so stated is partly wrong, and — what is even worse — that a "final" reconstruction closes off the possibility of other readings of the same data, much as an inexact interpretation works in service of the resistance (see Glover, 1931). The ambiguity of everyday life will always elude us and can never be completely described; for this reason, a final reconstruction is always just beyond our reach.

The question may be wrongly put. Rather than ask "What happened?" the more sensitive reader might wonder, "In how many ways can this text be experienced?" much as we might respond to a poem or a work of art. Can the tension in Mr. R between wanting and not wanting to be understood be experienced as real? Can we empathize with his preference for looking over listening while also bearing in mind his fear of seeing too much? Can we share the analyst's sense of the hour coming to an end with unfinished business (her vacation) still unmentioned, her appreciation (perhaps even her excitement) at hearing a convenient point of entry in the patient's associations, and finally, her complex reactions to his defensive reply? Can we separate the technical rightness or wrongness of the intervention from the sense in which Mr. R *chose* not to understand, and can we separate his choosing from his possible later awareness, as he was speaking, that he was contributing to the confusion? If we are sensitive to these different layers of resistance, then we are better able to speak to their resolution.

To train readers to experience a vignette in this kind of depth is to illustrate the analytic attitude in action (see Schafer, 1983). Good examples of this kind of multiple reading would tend to make the analyzing instrument more of a learnable reality and less of a mystery, to make it more accessible and visible and less vague and privileged. As finer distinctions are made between levels of intention and awareness, between changing states of awareness and changing styles of resistance, a new vocabulary should emerge which should make these distinctions more reliable and more widely shared. New methods of explication will come into play and these methods, in turn, can be applied directly to the analytic process. For the first time, we will begin to recognize and appreciate the ambiguity in everyday life and perhaps come a little closer to seeing things as they really are.

Why History Cannot Be Science

The quest for repeatable structure in the patient's life parallels the nineteenth century search for reliable patterns in history, a search which has been well described by Isaiah Berlin (1981). Both quests are probably rooted in the same search for certainty and the desire to put all reasoning on a strict logical basis. The appeal seems quite natural. History, as Berlin makes clear,

> purports to deal with facts. The most successful method of identifying, discovering and inferring facts is that of the natural sciences. This is the only region of human experience, at any rate in modern times, in which progress has indubitably been made. It is natural to wish to apply methods successful and authoritative in one sphere to another, where there is far less agreement among specialists. (1981, p. 104)

He goes on to underscore two particular reasons for wanting to make history a natural science: first, our sense of the "inevitable logic" of past events, moving in a river of time; and second, our sense that the order of events is an objective order which follows certain laws and that prolonged study of many orders will give us insight into their general nature.

Yet despite the high hopes for a scientific history during the nineteenth century, the end result was disappointing.

No general laws were formulated—not even moderately reliable maxims—from which historians could deduce (together with knowledge of the initial conditions) either what would happen next, or what had happened in the past. The great machine which was to rescue them from the tedious labors of adding fact to fact and of attempting to construct a coherent account out of their hand-picked material seemed like a plan in the head of a cracked inventor. The immense labor-saving instrument which, when fed with information, would itself order it, deduce the right conclusions, and offer the proper explanations, removing the need for the uncertain, old-fashioned, hand-operated tools with which historians had fumbled their way in the unregenerate past, remained a bogus prospectus, the child of an extravagant imagination, like designs for a perpetual motion machine. (p. 110)

Berlin goes on to argue that the objective order of events is largely illusory and that any explanation of the past depends heavily on the subjective arrangement and rearrangement of *some* of the facts (not necessarily all); this arrangement is not dictated by events but is significantly imposed on the material by the historian, guiding his selection of facts and even guiding his sense of what a fact may be.

Historical explanation is to a large degree arrangement of the discovered facts in patterns which satisfy us because they accord with life—the variety of human experience and activity—as we know it and can imagine it. . . . When these [patterns] are of wide scope, permanent, familiar, common to many men and many civilizations, we experience a sense of reality and dependability that derives from this very fact, and regard the explanation as well-founded, serious, satisfactory. (p. 132)

Empathizing with the key figures in the account, we "understand" through identification and projection why they acted as they did, but this understanding is not based on a logical sequence of observations organized by general laws but based on our sense of kinship with others of our species. The "because" of science, as Berlin makes clear, is quite different from the "because" of human affairs and the appeal to cause assumes quite a different form in the two cases.

One further difference must be stressed. The natural science — nomothetic — account takes an outside, objective stance which makes a clear separation between observer and observed. The rate of fall of a stone is a repeatable and observable "fact" which can be predicted within very narrow limits. Analysis and prediction make no demands on the "who" of the observer or on his knowledge of the human condition. To understand a historical (and, by extension, a clinical) event, on the other hand, requires an "inside" stance and on our being able to identify with the motives of the actor or patient. It is this inside stance which allows us to make a judgment as to what are the "facts" of the case, where one ends and another begins; this state of affairs comes about because not all the "facts" are visible, because many do not emerge until we put ourselves into the shoes of the figure in question, and because the final meaning is always colored by both theory and context.

If our view of the clinical data is always colored by both theory and context, what is apparently transparent to one observer may be quite meaningless to another; the specimen sufficient for the first may be ambiguous to the second. This fact alone helps explain why the search for historical truth has failed and why we should probably abandon the archeological metaphor. The belief in an archeology of the mind or of the session carries with it the idea that pieces of the past remain intact and can be recovered unchanged. The metaphor encourages us to look for tracings of the past, variously disguised but somehow recoverable, which could be used to validate the theory — both within the patient and within the session. But such a belief entails a kind of positivism which simply does not apply to the clinical material. The search for historical truth fails once we realize that the observer is always part of what is observed. The search for data within the session to confirm this or that interpretation also rests on the assumptions that the clinical material exists independently of the observer, and that what was compelling or transparent for him will necessarily be the same for an outside judge. If our hermeneutic position is correct, then it must follow that the meaning of the material is highly dependent on who is listening to it, and that what was true for the treating analyst, at a particular time and place in the treatment, will never be true again.

But what is bad news in some quarters is good news in others. The fact that the clinical data are theory-laden and context-dependent is no barrier to building them into a readable narrative; indeed, a narrative thrives on surplus meaning, and the richer the network of associations, the greater its aesthetic appeal. It could be argued that the very reasons that prevent us from uncovering reliable evidence and thus systematically validating the theory smooth the way toward constructing a plausible narrative. Narrative thrives on a mixture of fact and fiction; theory does not. Narrative benefits by rhetorical elaboration; theory does not. The credentials of the observer are critical for writing theory but almost irrelevant to writing narrative; aesthetic fit is always more important than justification. Theory building is discontinuous, episodic, and often marked by critical reevaluation; narrative tends to be seamless, continuous, and tends to smooth over what is unknown.

CHAPTER V

· ──────────────────────

The Sherlock Holmes Tradition: The Narrative Metaphor

In place of transparent data, in place of specimen interpretations, in place of an accumulating archival account, there has emerged a literature which represents a compromise between observation and speculation. The word *literature* is particularly apt because it is modeled as much on fiction as on fact. Rather than aspire to accurate approximations of the therapeutic experience, we have tended to favor a series of compromise renderings which conform to a certain genre—a genre I will call the Sherlock Holmes tradition. This genre was originated by Freud, and we continue to mistake it for the real thing right up to the present. Cases written in the Sherlock Holmes tradition provide us with a tour guide to the country in question, listing the high spots and the more famous sights along the way, but not with a detailed look at either the natives or their customs. The tour guide must, of course, be distinguished from a serious travel book, which would take us behind the false fronts of the

Potemkin villages and give us a more detailed account. The compromise functions more as a kind of entertainment, a detective or mystery story, than as a serious archival account which can be studied with renewed understanding by future generations of therapists. Even though it presents itself as an accumulation of clinical evidence, this accumulation is a poor approximation of the real thing.

The genre is familiar to all. It features a master sleuth (therapist) who is confronted by a series of bizarre and disconnected events (symptoms) reported by a somewhat desperate and disorganized client (patient). The sleuth listens, watches, and ponders, never prejudging, never despairing, almost never surprised, always confident that when all the facts are in, the mystery will disappear and the truth will emerge. In the typical Sherlock Holmes adventure, the eccentric client makes a dramatic appearance, often arrriving on a dark and stormy night, and presents an account which seems partly fantastic and somehow familiar. The events seem to have no logical connection with one another or with pieces of his past; frequently he seems close to despair and may have come to Holmes only as a last resort. Holmes, by contrast, listens calmly and dispassionately, serene in the knowledge that the patient sifting of all the evidence will always yield the singular solution. And it does. When the explanation is finally revealed, all the once baffling clues become obvious and integrated into a continuous account which leads inevitably to its conclusion; what was once disconnected and bizarre becomes understandable and almost commonplace.

At times the master sleuth cannot be distinguished from the therapist; listen to Watson set the scene:

> It had been a close, rainy day in October . . . Finding that Holmes was too absorbed for conversation, I had tossed aside the barren paper and, leaning back in my chair, I fell into a

brown study. Suddenly my companion's voice broke in upon my thoughts.

"You are right, Watson," said he. "It does seem a very preposterous way of settling a dispute."

"Most preposterous!" I exclaimed, and then, suddenly realizing how he had echoed the innermost thought of my soul, I sat up in my chair and stared at him in blank amazement.

Holmes goes on to explain how this piece of mind-reading was accomplished:

> "After throwing down your paper, which was the action which drew my attention to you, you sat for half a minute with a vacant expression. Then your eyes fixed themselves upon your newly framed picture of General Gordon, and I saw by the alteration in your face that a train of thought had been started. But it did not lead very far. Your eyes turned across the un-framed portrait of Henry Ward Beecher, which stands upon the top of your books. . . . Your face was thoughtful. You were recalling the incidents of Beecher's career. . . . You could not do this without thinking of the . . . Civil War. . . . [When] I observed that your lips set, your eyes sparkled, and your hands clinched, I was positive that you were indeed thinking of the gallantry which was shown by both sides in that desperate struggle. But then, again, your face grew sadder; you shook your head. You were dwelling upon the sadness and horror and useless waste of life. Your hand stole towards your old wound, and a smile quavered on your lips . . . At this point, I agreed with you that it was preposterous, and was glad to find that all my deductions had been correct." (The Resident Patient. From *The Complete Sherlock Holmes*, Vol. I., pp. 423–424)

Holmes' deductions are confirmed by the fact that they *exactly* match the thoughts that were running through Watson's mind, thoughts which leave behind revealing clues in the expression on his face and the direction of his gaze. In story after story, the master-mind Holmes attests to the idea that nature can be read like any other book so long as one pays attention to the smallest detail and is careful to organize his observations in the most logical fashion. Inspector Dupin, in Poe's *Murders on the Rue Morgue*, shows a similar ability — he also broke in on a chain of associations in a most remarkable manner. And Henry James was fond of referring to the figure in the carpet which the practiced eye might discern. If nature were a book, we could learn to read it; the patterns, if not immediately obvious, are waiting all around us to be discovered; truth is simply a matter of finding the pattern. Freud extended the model to include psychic reality and the discovery of patterns in the unconscious. The logic had become much more complicated because he no longer believed in the transparency of motives, a crucial assumption for Holmes, but the search for pattern continued along with the belief that there are a set of givens out there, only waiting to be discovered.

Peter Brooks has noticed a similar parallel between Freud and Sherlock Holmes; he places particular emphasis on the narrative thread.

> The urgency of narrative explanation in modern times is . . . well represented in the nineteenth-century invention, the detective story, which claims that all action is motivated, causally enchained, and eventually comprehensible as such to the perceptive observer. . . . Freud apparently was fully aware of the analogies between psychoanalytic investigation and detective work. Faced with fragmentary evidence, clues scattered within present reality, he who would explain must reach back to a story in the past which accounts for how the present took on its configuration. The detective story exhibits a reality structured as a set of ambiguous signs which gain their meaning from a past history which must be uncovered so as to order the production of these signs as a chain of events, eventually with a clear origin, intention and solution, and with strong causal connections between each link. The figure of the detective may be seen as an inevitable product not only of the nineteenth century's concern with criminal deviance, but also, more simply, of its

pervasive historicism, its privileging of narrative explanation, accounting for what we are through the reconstruction of how we got that way. (1984, pp. 269–270)

What is the evidence in the typical case report for suspecting the influence of the Sherlock Holmes tradition? First of all, I want to put particular emphasis on the singular solution. It is our first clue that we are dealing with narrative rather than archival accounts. Where an accumulation of archival reports is typically open to a multiplicity of interpretations, some building on one set of facts and some building on another, a narrative functions best when *all* the evidence is accounted for and where no other explanation is possible. In the Sherlock Holmes tradition, the facts, patiently gathered and cunningly arranged, build up a pattern which is compelling and necessary; they lead directly to the culprit. Consider Holmes' advice to Watson: "How often have I said to you that when you have eliminated the impossible, whatever remains, however improbable, must be the truth" (Conan Doyle, *A Study in Scarlet*, 1938). The Sherlock Holmes tradition has no adversary tradition, no interest in alternative explanations, because the force of the narrative is significantly diminished when more than one ending is proposed.

Now compare Freud's jigsaw puzzle analogy:

> If one succeeds in arranging the confused heap of fragments, each of which bears upon it an unintelligible piece of drawing, so that the picture acquires a meaning, so that there is no gap anywhere in the design, and so that the whole fits into the frame — if all these conditions are fulfilled, then one knows that one has solved the puzzle and that there is no alternative solution. (Freud, 1923b, p. 116)

The singular solution has become an expected part of our clinical tradition. Case reports are almost always presented as if the interpretation proposed is the only interpretation possible. The final formulation seems to be dictated inexorably by the clinical material. This tradition makes for enjoyable, even fascinating reading, but seriously interferes with anyone, either from our time or from the future, who chooses to use the data in ways other than those chosen by the author.

Second, it should be noted that facts in the Sherlock Holmes tradition are always seen within a positivistic frame. The observer is always separated from the object being studied; the reader is always peering down at the faint footprints across the moor. The image of Sherlock Holmes and his magnifying glass becomes emblematic of the positivistic world view. Facts are knowable pieces of the reality "out there," distinct as to size, shape, and smell, guiding us inevitably in one direction or another. Where the clinical reality is ambiguous and multiply determined, in the Sherlock Holmes tradition the facts are signposts which lead us unerringly to the solution. The magnifying glass metaphor blinds us to the more hermeneutic perspective developed in the previous chapter. Many of the so-called "facts" are only being created by us: They never exist until we choose to see or hear the clinical encounter in a particular way, and without the perspective of the treating therapist, they can be easily misinterpreted.

Third, we come to argument by authority, which is closely connected with the fact that the evidence is usually incomplete. Impressed, perhaps even awed, by the master sleuth and his uncanny ability to see beyond the obvious, we willingly give way to spectacular feats of deduction within the Sherlock Holmes tradition, perhaps shaking our head at the missing links in the reasoning but eager to get on with the story. This particular narrative genre clearly supports the tradition of privileged withholding—and it was eagerly supported by Freud. Early in his career, he argued that if the reader was not inclined to agree with his formulation, additional data would scarcely change his mind (see Freud, 1912, p. 114).

The unspoken allegiance to the Sherlock Holmes tradition helps to make clear why our literature has no adversary tradition; once a case is solved, who would be interested in an alternative explanation? It helps explain why we have no archive of unsuccessful cases or mistaken interpretations — these could never compete with our more exciting successes. It helps to explain why our literature is highly readable but epistemologically useless; under the sway of the Sherlock Holmes tradition, we are always tempted to turn partial data and partial understanding into a continuous story that has balance, structure, and just the right amount of plot. Such a story becomes a satisfying aesthetic experience and a worthy member of the Sherlock Holmes tradition. It goes without saying that it has no value as evidence. To the extent that the narrative tradition has been substituted for more traditional data collection, we have significantly compromised our respect for the evidence and our role as keeper of the psychoanalytic tradition.

Is the usual case report fact or fiction? Brooks raises this question in connection with Freud's Wolf Man case and its well-known primal scene.

> When Freud has uncovered — or more accurately reconstructed — this primal scene, which would appear to be crucial to the narrative of the Wolf Man's case, he proceeds to erase it. In the two long bracketed passages added to chapters five and eight . . . he questions whether the primal scene, the observation of parental coitus, ever has any reality as an *event*. It might rather be a phantasy concocted from the observation of animals copulating, then referred back to the parents. Thus in the place of a primal scene we would have a primal phantasy, operating *as* event by deferred action. . . . This "solution" might appear irresponsible, an abandonment of all distinction between the fictional and the nonfictional. . . .(1984, p. 276)

Does the case method give us an embellished account which is designed to delight as much as inform the reader? We have seen that data are virtually nonexistent; we are now raising the question whether (following Freud) the material is further smoothed over to reinforce the expectation of a continuous story with a singular outcome. If this is true, case reports would qualify as poetry, with poetry defined as "truth which has been ornamented by fiction and figures in order to delight and move the reader" (Abrams, 1958, p. 298).

What are these delights? First, the satisfaction of finding a logical and coherent solution to a puzzling problem, coupled with the added pleasure of finding the solution familiar. If the story line takes advantage of one of the more important metaphors in psychoanalytic theory, the reader comes away with his trust in the theory upheld once again. The narrative construction, an uncertain mixture of fact and fiction, is taken as data and therefore read as evidence supporting the theory.

Second, we have the delight of the onlooker in gaining access to private lives and private thoughts. We exchange the commonplace truth of public affairs for the unique truth of privileged accounts. Notice that the reader cannot distinguish between fact and fiction — but this does not matter. The pleasure of being an insider, if only for a brief period, and a participant in an otherwise secret interchange makes up for the lack of adequate documentation, the absence of verbatim dialogues, and the lack of validating evidence.

Third, the reader shares the usual delight of any listener at the beginning of a tale. "Place yourself in my hands," says the narrator, "and I will take you to faraway places which you have never seen and show you things you would never believe." Can the clinical account be our modern-day equivalent of the Tales of the Arabian Nights? We see the seductive power of the unseen narrator; we see how narrative persuasion, in contrast to archival persuasion, depends on *not* showing all the evidence. We see how the arbitrary authority of the narrator works to compel a belief that his story is the *only* story, and finally, we see how it reinforces the suspension of disbelief.

The last is particularly important and is brought about by several features of the usual case report. Consider first its factual trappings. Represented as a faithful account of an actual happening, authored by a real person with recognized (and confirmable) credentials, the report is expressly designed to command respect. Next comes the need on the part of the reader to read the story and discover its ending—what Brooks would call his narrative desire (see 1984, Chapter 2). Third, we have the temptation to give way to authority and to endow the privileged account with a greater veracity than perhaps it deserves. Suspension of disbelief follows. Who would want to break off an exciting and suspenseful account only because some detail seemed out of place or some sequence seemed unlikely? Even if these thoughts occur to the reader, we can always take refuge in the author's need to protect his sources; any suspected alteration in the facts can be put down to the requirement to protect the patient.

Once the forward momentum of the narrative has been established, we are reading horizontally rather than vertically. We look forward to see how the story will come out; we look back to see where it started; but we are far less interested in what the story is about, in either reference or referents. The thing talked about—the subject of the story—fades in comparison to the story itself; in the language of the Russian Formalists, *fabula*—the tale as told—replaces *sujet*—the basis for the tale—and as *sujet* disappears, so does the evidence.

This is not to say that specific events, persons, and places do not take on maximal significance; they do. But held in the grip of a compelling story, the reader is much more inclined to let the author define his terms as he chooses and to participate (with him) in the quest for meaning. To stand back and ask evidential questions, to challenge the moment as it appeared to the only living witness, or to second guess the author before the final die is cast is to break one of the central rules of the narrative tradition.

Nor is it clear that challenge is possible. Once the reader has committed himself to the role of listener, believer, and participant, once he is caught up in the narrative suspense of the opening moment, once he has felt the full force of what Brooks would call his narrative desire, it becomes all but impossible to find grounds for disbelief and to challenge either the facticity of the evidence or the authority of the narrator. The pleasures of readership far outweigh the discomfort of criticism.

Evidence that the Sherlock Holmes tradition is still flourishing today comes from Wallerstein's recent report on the Menninger Foundation Psychotherapy Research Project (1986). Each of the 42 cases described in this book is given a brief descriptive title such as Bitter Spinster, Rebellious Coed, Masochistic Editor, and so forth. These "descriptive sobriquets" (Wallerstein's phrase) attempt to capture some central truth about each patient (see Wallerstein, 1986, p. 28); at the same time, they cannot help but carry forward the spirit of the Sherlock Holmes tradition and reinforce the narrative character of the clinical account. By turning life histories into short stories, they run the risk of minimizing the details which do not agree with the case titles. Clearly superior to such standard labels as the Wolf Man and the Rat Man, they nevertheless take us back to the days of Sherlock Holmes and such stories as The Adventure of the Noble Bachelor or The Man with the Twisted Lip.

Narrative Appeal of the Dora Case

In a well-known essay on the Dora case, Marcus (1977) attempts to carry out a traditional *explication de texte* and focus on the strictly literary qualities of Freud's writings. By looking closely at Freud's various rhetorical moves, Marcus helps us to see why the Dora case has remained a landmark of exposition and persuasion which has perhaps never been surpassed in the clinical literature. But in alerting us to Freud's mastery of rhetoric and to his complete command of the narrative voice, Marcus has also called attention to the way in which the context of a well-told tale can significantly influence the truth value of what is told; in other words, how narrative truth may pre-empt historical truth. In this section, I will explore the implications of this practice for its effect on our views of clinical evidence and on the relation between evidence and developing theory.

The Dora case, as Marcus has made clear, is a clinical *tour de force* in which all significant features of the patient's life are presumably explained. The grounds for these explanations are frequently less than convincing, and yet we come away persuaded and impressed by the clinical reasoning. Marcus helps to show that conviction probably lies more in Freud's rhetorical skill, with its mixture of irony, dogmatism, understatement, and dazzling interpretation, than in any evidence that the treatment was succeeding or that one interpretation led inevitably to a particular change in thought or behavior. Indeed, what stands out are the facts that the treatment was abruptly broken off and that the critical symptoms remained unchanged. Nevertheless, as Marcus makes clear, Freud was able to turn a clinical failure into a literary success.

The appeal of the Dora case and its undoubted standing as a literary masterpiece make us aware of the influence of what might be called rhetorical craft and the subtle power of the clinical narrative. Not only does a well-crafted story make us feel that now all the facts are understood but, in addition, the power of the clinical narrative is such that it can easily swallow up the occasional unexplained event or mistaken interpretation and prevent us from seeing that certain things have not been explained at all. Narrative fit is misleading because it cannot be used as a criterion of validity. Narrative smoothing can obviously be applied to both true and false accounts and speaks only to the craft and resourcefulness of the author and his rhetorical skill. From the standpoint of theory, narrative fit is no guide to the truth of an explanation or proposition. Using narrative fit alone, we have no way of distinguishing more fundamental instances of cause and effect from more fanciful interpretations. As any lawyer well knows, a good story may be simply untrue — and yet, at the same time, we cannot assume that what is convincing is necessarily problematic. Good writing is not necessarily suspect.

So far, I have been talking about the persuasive power of the clinical narrative in what might be called its public, explanatory guise, wherein different pieces of clinical material are assembled to support a theoretical proposition. This form of explanation, which depends heavily on narrative persuasion, models itself — for a variety of reasons — on the clinical interpretation. In its typical form, the latter provides us with what *might* be true, not necessarily with what *is* true. It provides us with reasons which are not necessarily causes (see Eagle, 1980). It rarely suggests alternative explanations. Its principal goal is to bring about insight and change *in the patient*, rather than present a reasoned argument which relies on public data and shared rules of evidence and logic.

When the clinical account is transposed to the public domain and presented as a form of explanation, it is no longer designed for the benefit of one individual, tailor-made to the needs of the patient, but must now be accessible to all. I have written elsewhere about the problems of narrative unpacking and of the need to provide the outside reader, having only normative competence, with the same familiarity with the evidence that is possessed by the treating analyst (privileged competence). But not even a complete unpacking of the privileged narrative would necessarily convince the outside reader, and this failure points to the core difficulty in the clinical account.

Consider two examples from the Dora case. In the first, Freud is discussing the significance of Dora's second dream, in which he found

> several clear allusions to transference. At the time she was telling me the dream I was still unaware (and did not learn until two days later) that we had only *two hours* more work before us. This was the same length of time which she has spent in front of

the Sistine Madonna [an association to the second dream] and which (by making a correction and putting "two hours" instead of "two and a half hours") she had taken as the length of the walk which she had not made round the lake [another association]. (Freud, 1905, p. 119)

Freud is claiming a link between dream and analysis, suggesting that the two dream details anticipated the coming termination (only two hours more work). We can read this as a possible interpretation of the dream details, but Freud is suggesting something more — namely, that the facts of the case (that it had only two hours to run) are anticipated by the dream.

The second example concerns Dora's pseudo-appendicitis. Its symptoms appeared nine months after the meeting with Herr K. by the lake when he "had the audacity to make . . . a proposal" (p. 25). Freud finds the nine-month interval "sufficiently characteristic" to conclude without hesitation that the first event triggered the second — that the meeting with Herr K. precipitated the attack of appendicitis which "thus enabled the patient . . . to realize a phantasy of *childbirth*" (p. 103). But speaking more strictly, this line of reasoning, although a plausible interpretation, is only one of many possible explanations. Nevertheless, it is presented without question or comment. If the Dora case were a piece of fiction, we would not think twice about accepting the possible link between the assignation by the lake and appendicitis. By the same token, if this anecdote were part of an extended interpretation to the patient, it would seem entirely natural to present the appendicitis as a derivative of the assignation; we might then wait for subsequent associations from the patient to extend our understanding of the formulation. But in the context of a public, explanatory account which is open to public debate and subject to the usual rules of evidence and logic, something more is needed to supply conviction and to ground the instance in a stronger network of support.

What other explanations could be found? We are told that the attack occurred shortly after the death of Dora's aunt (to whom she had clearly been attached) and during the time when she had been staying with her uncle. Either of these events might have caused the symptom. Moreover, if a pregnancy fantasy had actually been stimulated by the meeting with Herr K., we might expect to see earlier signs of relevant symptomatology before the nine months had run its course — hysterical vomiting, for example, specific food preferences, and the like. Convergent evidence of this kind would add a considerable degree of conviction to the pregnancy hypothesis. This is not to argue that Freud was either right or wrong, but only to point out that what is fitting as a clinical interpretation does not suffice as a public explanation.

What seems to be happening in each of these instances is that the satisfaction of finding a narrative home for the symptom, dream fragment, or piece of behavior completely overshadows any doubt as to the credibility or validity of the explanation. Merely to incorporate all the findings into a single pattern represents a considerable aesthetic achievement, and the reader may be more impressed by the scope of the undertaking than by its inherent validity. Our need to find a home for an unexplained symptom may make us unnecessarily susceptible to the narrative approach, and less inclined to look carefully at the underlying reasons for any given assumption. It seems clear that the truth value of any piece of the Dora case is intimately connected with its place in the total explanation, and when any piece of the puzzle is singled out for careful scrutiny, its grounds seem less convincing.

Freud was well aware of the need to provide a comprehensive account. In the introduction to the Dora case, he tells us that his goal was to restore "what is missing, taking the best models known to me from other analyses" (1905, p. 12). The initial account (provided by the patient)

> may be compared to an unnavigable river whose stream is at one moment choked by masses of rock and at another divided and lost among shallows and sandbanks. . . . The connections — even the ostensible ones — are for the most part incoherent, and the sequence of different events is uncertain. (p. 16)

As treatment proceeds, so the story changes. At the conclusion of the ideal treatment, we should have available a story that is "intelligible, consistent, and unbroken" (p. 18). Marcus expands on this goal:

> A complete story [he writes] . . . is the theoretical, created end story. It is a story, or a fiction, not only because it has narrative structure but also' because the narrative account has been rendered in language, in conscious speech, and no longer exists in the deformed language of symptoms, the untranslated speech of the body. At the end — at the successful end — one has come into possession of one's own story. It is a final act of self-appropriation, the appropriation by oneself of one's own history. This is in part so because one's own story is in so large a measure a phenomenon of language, as psychoanalysis is in turn a demonstration of the degree to which language can go in the reading of all our experience. What we end with, then, is a fictional construction which is at the same time satisfactory to us in the form of the truth, and as the form of the truth. (Marcus, 1977, p. 414)

On one level, then, the expanded clinical account seems to be eminently reasonable as a description of the case and satisfies our need for an "intelligible, consistent and unbroken" story. Why is it unsatisfactory as public explanation?

First, we have no way of participating in the account; we must resign ourselves to our role as spectators. We can appreciate the aesthetic merit of each of the examples listed above, but we have no way of arguing that any given explanation could *not* be true or that another explanation, not provided by the author, is probably more correct. This difficulty stems from the fact that we are not given access to all relevant data; that we are not provided (by the author) with what might be called his rules of inference so that we can evaluate his reasoning; and finally, and of particular relevance to psychoanalytic presentations, because the grounds for relating any two events in the patient's history have largely shifted from secondary to primary process forms of reasoning. As soon as the primary process in invoked as the basis for understanding causal linkages, there is no limit to how distant (in meaning, time, or space) two events can be and still be seen as related. Because the primary process brings into play a wide assortment of transformational devices (many of which have never been catalogued), the author of the public account is in a position to assert a connection which cannot be challenged because we have no independent evidence of the particular device being invoked.

Consider Freud's explanation of Dora's addendum to the first dream — the fact that each time she awoke, she smelled smoke. He first reasons that the latent meaning of this addendum must have been deeply repressed because the account was late in appearing — it was reported on the day after the dream. As such, he reasons that it must be more than usually significant and probably related to the forbidden wish for Herr K. (Just before the "unlucky proposal" by the lake, Herr K. had rolled a cigarette for Dora.) Freud decides (without the benefit of Dora's associations) that the smell of smoke represents a longing for a kiss from Herr K. Because he (Freud) was also a smoker, he assumes that in the treatment context, the addendum represents a wish to be kissed by the analyst.

It seems logically impossible to argue that this interpretation could *not* be true, largely because we are presented with a single equation with two unknowns. We have no direct knowledge of the forbidden wish, and we have no specific information about which mechanism of the primary process has been brought into play. So long as the link between latent and manifest content follows an unknown transformation rule, there is no way to predict from a given piece of latent content, A, to its manifest derivative, A'. Thus it would be impossible to carry out a thought experiment on some part of Freud's reasoning by assuming, for example, that the smell of smoke did not mean the longing for a kiss but something else — say, not-kiss — because the transformations of A, following the rules of the primary process, are essentially infinite and because we have no certain knowledge of the precise nature of the wish.

When a plausible interpretation is presented, usually without comment, as a sufficient explanation, it suffers in particular by its reliance on the primary process. The rules of the primary process which are clearly relevant to the formulation and understanding of the *clinical* narrative (the mutative interpretation) cannot be abstractly invoked in the public, *explanatory* narrative because they preclude the use of the usual rules of inductive and deductive reasoning and the possibility of falsification. A similar objection can be raised about the unconscious, as we have already seen. Whenever unconscious motives are invoked in the explanatory account, the outside reader has no way to critically evaluate the argument for the simple reason that not all the data are available. For each instance of unexplained behavior, one or more unconscious propositions or fantasies could be supplied which would explain the occurrence. Once again, we have too few equations and too many unknowns. Unknown content could be sensibly discussed if it followed a single transformation rule, and many transformation rules could be understood with known unconscious contents, but the presence of *both* unknown contents and unknown transformation rules gives the reader no choice but to accept the public narrative on faith. He may be enlightened (or entertained), but he will never be truly convinced.

It seems clear that the usual clinical narrative in its unvarnished form cannot be used as a theoretical explanation which tries to relate specific data to general propositions. The private narrative is tailored to the patient and is designed for its therapeutic effect; the public explanation is addressed to the outside observer, necessarily accessible to his normative competence, and is intended as a permanent contribution to knowledge. The private account has, as its goal, the formation of an "intelligible, consistent and unbroken" narrative; the public explanation may actually seek to highlight islands of incoherence and unclarity, examples of clinical events which could not be explained. (The fact that such islands seldom appear in our literature is an indication of how frequently the public account has been accommodated to the private.) The first may frequently invoke the unconscious as an explanatory concept, either implicitly or explicitly, and use the full range of primary process mechanisms as a means of supplying continuity to the surface account and as a means of relating material from different states of awareness; the second, as we have seen, must avoid unconscious explanations because they are essentially empty. The first account has access to the unlimited space/time domain of the patient's psychic reality, and the contents of this domain, combined with the wide variety of available primary process mechanisms, can be organized in a near-infinity of ways. The second account has access only to the space/time domain of the reader's external reality, and claims of similiarity or identity between events or ideas must be given some kind of external validation or public justification. Thus I can appeal to the law of gravity to explain the fall of a stone, but I cannot appeal to an unknown primary process mechanism to explain the particular form of a dream image. Freud's account of Dora's addendum fails to convince us because we have no external knowledge—beyond the suggestive oral connection—of the specific mechanisms by which kiss was transformed into smell of smoke. (But notice that this kind of knowledge is not necessary for the clinical interpretation.)

Because the first account aims to further the goals of treatment, it has no need to provide alternative explanations or to critically examine specific hypotheses—indeed, it has no need to frame the issues in a problematic and potentially disprovable manner. But the second account aims at generating some kind of permanent knowledge and to reach this goal greater than average conviction must be achieved. This can only be attained by taking a critical look at each hypothesis and evaluating its standing with relation to other possible explanations. Only when competing possibilities are shown to fail in some systematic manner is the credibility of the surviving explanation significantly enhanced.

The private narrative approaches the contents of the patient's psychic reality as a set of data needing to be accounted for (and perhaps changed), and it adopts an entirely pragmatic attitude toward this task. The engaged therapist is in no position to "study," in any systematic manner, the conditions under which interpretation leads to change (largely for this reason, treatment is never equivalent to research). Runyan (1981) has characterized the setting in everyday practice as the place where "minimal resources are available for inquiry, where investigation ceases once a single plausible explanation is reached, or where inquiry stops once an interpretation consistent with a prevailing theoretical orthodoxy is produced" (p. 1076). But to frame the undertaking as a public explanation and give it more general significance, a crucial change in genre and attitude must take place. The initial symptoms of the patient and their *in vivo* interpretations must be subjected to public scrutiny and evaluation. To make knowledge claims about the significant events in the treatment, they must be further examined, changed from "uncriticized" to "criticized" facts (see Pepper, 1948), and expressed in such a way that they are open to further criticism. Disconfirmation and falsification are two varieties of this further criticism.

When the private narrative is unwittingly substituted for the second—that is, when interpretation is presented as explanation—we have an instance of dogmatic argument, which Pepper has described as the "dictator" of cognition. Dogmatic accounts rely heavily on three kinds of dogma—the dogma of infallible authority, the dogma of self-evident principles, and the dogma of indubitable fact (see Pepper, 1948, pp. 19–26). We can see how any attempt to substitute interpretation for explanation is an appeal to the craft of the analyst and to his privileged (but unknowable) competence—hence, it relies on the dogma of infallible authority. As such, it stands outside the domain of critical discourse and, whether we agree or disagree, it is immune to criticism. Appeals to unconscious contents, unconscious transformations, and other moves of this kind may also belong to this category because in such reasoning, the unconscious is often given the standing of an inscrutable "ghost in the machine" whose ways are wondrous to behold but beyond the reach of counter-argument.

The dogma of self-evident principles may appear whenever clinical success is substituted for explanation. It often happens in clinical accounts which are heavily biased toward the interpretive model that a given event (suppose the therapist raised his fee) is followed by an apparently unrelated event (suppose the frequency of dreams decreased). The dogma of the self-evident principle asserts that because they were contiguous in time, the first *must* be the cause of the second. No attempt is made to critically examine under what conditions the first might cause the second, and under what conditions A might cause not-B or not-A might cause B. The principle of contiguity is inviolate.

The dogma of indubitable fact is less often brought into play because the analytic attitude prides itself on what might be called its benevolent skepticism and its healthy suspicion of surface appearances. But the same thing cannot be said about the content of interpretations. An unsocialized clinical account masquerading as explanation will often present the reader with a series of interpretations in a form that suggests that their rationale is self-evident. I have written elsewhere about the psychoanalytic double standard which applies the principle of multiple meanings to the patient and the principle of privileged competence to the analyst. For interpretations to function as explanations, they must be shaped in a way that makes their rationale accessible to those with only normative competence.

Narrative Smoothing

In an imaginative analysis of Freud and his manner of telling stories, Hertz (1983) uncovers a disturbing parallel between Freud and Dora. They were both reticent; neither told the whole story; and finally, we find a certain vagueness about the source of both Freud's and Dora's knowledge. In the case of the latter, it is often untraceable, whereas Freud often chooses not to reveal because it "would have led to nothing but hopeless confusion" (see Freud, 1905, p. 27). And even granted that Freud's aim is to fill in the gaps in her account and provide us with a story which is "intelligible, consistent, and unbroken" (p. 18), we are still left with a number of rather arbitrary interpretations and puzzling conclusions that do not seem supported by the evidence. Freud frequently tends to assert an interpretation rather than allow the facts to speak for themselves.

To put it bluntly, how much of the Dora case can we believe? The parallel with Sherlock Holmes makes us uncomfortably aware that both accounts are stories of a certain kind, and if narrative appeal explains why we are persuaded by Dora, does it also imply that we are presented with a good story more than a faithful account? If it is true, as Hertz argues, that Dora is at times part Freud, to what extent does Freud project his own problems and issues onto his patient? Where does Dora leave off and Freud begin?

We are confronted with a problem of narrative smoothing, of which it is useful to distinguish two types. One kind — editorial smoothing in the service of justification — is an attempt to bring the clinical account into conformity with some kind of public standard. The resulting genre often takes the form of the Sherlock Holmes tradition. That genre has been represented by such specimens as the Dora, the Wolf Man, and the Rat Man cases. Each of these, in turn, is largely a narrative account which attempts to tell a coherent story by selecting certain facts (and ignoring others), which allows interpretation to masquerade as explanation, and which effectively prevents the reader from making contact with the complete account and thereby prevents him (if he so chooses) from coming up with an alternative explanation.

Smoothing in the service of justification would seem to consist of two kinds of omissions. On the one hand, there is a kind of selective reporting which uses the clinical material to exemplify a particular principle or axiom; anecdote is chosen for its illustrative power and for its ability to further the argument. Quite a different kind of narrative smoothing results from the assumption that what is clear to the treating analyst is clear to the reader — in other words, that privileged competence is equivalent to normative competence (see Spence, 1982a). By failing to provide the background information and context surrounding a particular clinical event, by failing to unpack the event in such a way that all its implications become transparent, the author runs the risk of telling a story that is quite different from the original experience. This kind of narrative smoothing comes about because, as we have already seen, the "facts" are not fixed, the referents are never unambiguous, and each reading will necessarily depend on the preconceptions and prejudices of the reader. This kind of narrative smoothing results from a failure to take into account the hermeneutic properties of the clinical event.

Since Freud's time, it would appear that smoothing in the service of justification has significantly increased. The narrative structure of the average clinical case in a current journal is buttressed by only a handful of anecdotes (in contrast to the very detailed accounts of, for example, Dora's two dreams and their analysis). In the face of such smoothing, we are presented with clinical impressions which must be accepted almost entirely on faith, by conclusions which are discovered by undescribed technical procedures, and by observations so heavily mixed with theory that it is almost impossible to form a second opinion. Transparent clinical specimens are notably lacking.

The second kind of narrative smoothing—in the context of discovery—takes place in the consulting room, long before the case is ever published. This kind of smoothing begins with leading suggestions ("Could you have been jealous of your brother when he came home as an infant from the hospital?") and continues, in more subtle form, in a variety of guises— urging certain interpretations more than others, supporting the patient in certain kinds of explanations, "hearing" one meaning in a tone of voice or a dream as opposed to others. Many other forms could be listed. The scope of the problem is difficult to evaluate. Grünbaum suggests that "each of the seemingly independent clinical data may well be more or less alike confounded by the analyst's suggestion so as to conform to his construction, at the cost of their epistemic reliability or probative value" (1984, p. 277). But despite his concern for such influence and the obvious impact it would have on our view of the theory, Grünbaum can cite only one specific example (pp. 212–214)— which greatly weakens his case. The problem is also complicated by the fact that evidence of smoothing within the hour is clearly tied to smoothing in the service of justification. If the latter looms large, it will be all but impossible to detect the former.

Even if we assume for the moment that both kinds of narrative smoothing take place, it seems clear that smoothing at the moment of publication is much more insidious than smoothing at the moment of discovery. Evidence of suggestion within the hour can often be detected by inspection of the transcript (some examples are provided by Spence, 1982, p. 194, and by Gill and Hoffman, 1982). Pieces of the transcript which are subject to such influence can then be systematically discounted in a further analysis. Merely to claim that such influence *is possible* need not prevent us from taking precautions which guard against their influence; thus Grünbaum's charges must be held in abeyance until more data are in. Second, it would seem as if the psychoanalytic method, with its emphasis on silence, neutrality, and minimal content, would tend to guard against overt suggestion. Third, what looks like suggestion may sometimes be something quite different. Some of the more refined techniques which have been developed for analyzing the transference (see Gill and Hoffman, 1982) can also be used to uncover the grounds for apparent compliance, and it often occurs that what is superficially seen as agreement with the analyst may contain different motives or assumptions. If the analyst is alert to these differences, he is often in a position to clarify the interaction and translate apparent compliance into something more combative — and more complex.

Whether or not they always behave above suspicion, it seems fair to say that analysts as a group are increasingly alert to the dangers of undue influence and the way in which the analyst's thoughts and feelings come to influence the patient. By contrast, we are relatively naive with respect to the dangers of selective reporting, unobtrusive narrative revision, argument by authority, or the use of interpretation for explanation. Because of the esteemed position of Freud's five cases, they still serve as our primary specimens of clinical reporting. As a result, we tend to underestimate their faults and minimize their capacity for mischief. And because of our respect for confidentiality and for the wisdom of the analyst, we have no way of challenging the clinical report. Where the traces of suggestion or leading the patient or other kinds of smoothing within the hour can often (if not always) be found in the transcript, the traces of alteration in the published report are almost always invisible. Once the record has been changed and the case report is published, it is almost impossible to reconstruct what "really happened" and to isolate actual cause and effect from what might be called narrative sequence. Where conventional history has the benefit of different historians trying to analyze the same set of events, psychoanalysis has the rule of one analyst—one case; we never have the benefit of second opinions or alternative explanations.

In both kinds of narrative smoothing we see the heritage of the Sherlock Holmes tradition. Accepted concepts are treated as axioms, stereotype is given precedence over more unexpected observations, and evidence that does not fit the stereotype is usually not reported. The "findings" under these circumstances have nothing new to tell us because they are influenced by an outdated framework which is projected onto the clinical material. Because the raw material of the clinical happening is never exposed to public scrutiny, there is no way for theory to change because disconfirmations are never made visible. As a result of the two levels of narrative smoothing, it would appear as if the reported data are fully in agreement with the received theory. Because of this agreement, there is no reason why theory need ever change, and it may be for this reason that references to Freud tend to dominate the literature even a half century after his death.

The two levels of smoothing just described have important implications for the future of both psychoanalytic theory and clinical practice. The two levels can also significantly influence one another. So long as smoothing in the service of justification is in effect, we will *never* be aware of how much damage is produced by smoothing in the service of discovery. Ignorance of its true nature may lead to unwarranted pessimism about the possibility of ever testing clinical propositions within the clinical session. Grünbaum has taken the position that psychoanalytic truths can only be tested *outside* the clinical setting ("it would seem that the validation of Freud's cardinal hypotheses has to come, if at all, mainly from well-designed *extra*clinical studies, either epidemiologic or even experimental"—Grünbaum, 1984, p. 278)—in other words, that smoothing within the hour is irreversible in its effects. But just because we are not always aware of the original texture of the clinical dialogue and just because it is perfectly possible for this kind of smoothing to take place, it does not follow that it presents us with an impossible methodological obstacle or that its effects cannot be isolated, when and where they occur, and kept separate from the other clinical data.

Turning to smoothing in the interests of justification, what are its consequences? Quite early in the Dora case, Freud addresses himself to the issue of technique and how it should be reported.

> There is another kind of incompleteness which I myself have intentionally introduced. I have as a rule not reproduced the process of interpretation to which the patient's associations and communications had to be subjected, but only the results of that process. Apart from the dreams, therefore, the technique of the analytic work has been revealed in only a very few places. My object in this case history was to demonstrate the intimate structure of a neurotic disorder and the determination of its symptoms; and it would have led to nothing but hopeless confusion if I had tried to complete the other task at the same time. (Freud, 1905, p. 12)

We read these lines today with a certain amount of tolerant skepticism. To reveal technical procedures might have, in fact, clarified some of the more obscure passages in the case and given us ways of understanding how Freud arrived at certain conclusions. We might also suspect that full disclosure might have revealed interpretations which did not produce insight, clarifications which were rejected by the patient, and other examples which would tend to disrupt the flow of the narrative and interfere with the kind of story Freud was trying to tell. Whatever the reasons, failure to report specific technical procedures has plagued the psychoanalytic literature up to the present time, and the tendency to report clinical insights without paying attention to precisely how they were arrived at is one of the more grievous examples of smoothing in the interests of justification. Where Sterba has referred to this omission with the forgiving label of "scientific tact" (see Gray, 1982, p. 622), we have come to see, with the recent disclosures by Gill and Hoffman (1982) and Dahl et al. (1978), that much more than tact is involved.

This type of smoothing has produced what Gray calls a "developmental lag" in technique:

> It has for some time been my conclusion, rightly or wrongly, that the way a considerable proportion of analysts listen to and perceive their data has, in certain significant respects, *not* evolved as I believe it would have if historically important concepts allowed their place in the actual application of psychoanalytic technique. (Gray, 1982, p. 622)

Although he attributes this lag largely to a failure to bring the insights of ego psychology to bear on problems of technique, it can also be argued that the lag would never have developed if technical moves were made public as soon as they happened and were given as prominent a place in the literature as other kinds of clinical material.

The reporting of technical considerations tends to take two forms. On the one hand, there was (and is) heavy reliance on Freud's early papers on technique, and this reliance on tradition has directly influenced the lag in technique, as Gray makes clear. A second factor has to do with level of language. When technical changes were reported, as with Anna Freud's monograph on defense (Freud, A., 1937), or in later papers by Sterba (1953) and Hartmann (1951), they tended to be couched in such abstract (metapsychological) language that it was hard to decide exactly what was being described. Consider Sterba commenting on the need for more attention to defensive processes:

> We are still very much impressed, even fascinated, by the id contents which psychoanalysis enables us to discover. The working of the ego is so inconspicuous and silent that we are hardly

> aware of it. . . . It has been my observation that it is a most difficult task to teach students to pay attention to these mute and subterranean workings of the ego. (Sterba, 1953, pp. 17–18)

How are these id contents discovered — and are they "discovered" correctly? How would they appear in the clinical material? What are the "subterranean workings of the ego" and how are they detected? How does one discriminate, in the clinical material, between id and ego? Almost no paper on technique or changes in technique has concerned itself with the specifics of where attention should be focused, which part of the patient's associations should be addressed, how the meaning of these associations varies with the context of the session, how defense can be recognized, and a host of other technical details. Even Gray's paper, admirable in calling attention to the lag, does not offer any verbatim examples of patient-therapist interchange, examples which proved so edifying in his earlier paper on two contrasting ways of viewing intrapsychic activity (see Gray, 1973).

We are faced with something more than scientific tact. This kind of smoothing might more fairly be called a conspiracy of silence which perpetuates several unwarranted assumptions. First, it seems as if technique is so well understood and sufficiently refined that no discussion is in order. Second, it seems as if all trained analysts are largely in agreement on how to listen and how to interpret. When examples come to light that call this refinement and agreement into question, a common reaction is that these must be bad examples, the exception that "proves" the rule (see Malcolm [1984a] and her review of Gill and Hoffman; she considers the possibility that the bad examples are "merely exceptionally inept" but concludes that there is no way of deciding for sure, given the state of the literature). In other words, the possibility of editorial smoothing raises the question but leaves the answer in doubt.

But the converse should also be noted. Creative, insightful clinical work is also buried behind abstraction and other kinds of editorial smoothing and as a result little of the clinical wisdom generated by experienced analysts in the course of their careers will ever be documented or passed on to younger colleagues. Clear advances over Freud's technical procedures may occur at a much higher frequency than is assumed in general, but these exceptions, or disconfirmations, are never reported and thus disappear as soon as they happen. We are faced by the final irony that the most detailed accounts of patient-doctor interaction appear, not in the psychoanalytic literature but in popular fiction (such as the novel *August*). These accounts naturally mesh perfectly with the Sherlock Holmes tradition.

A further consequence of editorial smoothing concerns the hermeneutic nature of the clinical enterprise. Despite the determined efforts of Grünbaum to "expose the exegetical myth" of hermeneutics (1984, pp. 1–9), there is every reason to believe that hermeneutic principles are used every day in the process of clinical discovery. The precise nature of this process and the particular way in which the analyst listens, conceptualizes, and interprets have remained unexplored, largely because of smoothing in the service of justification. But even though the data are in short supply, it seems clear that the analyst does not function in a hypothetical-deductive fashion to arrive at a specific interpretation. Despite the tendency to present a case history as if it were some kind of detective story, the actual manner of listening—of choosing what to listen for, of deciding how large or how small to make the units and which kinds of pattern matches carry weight and which do not—is much more hermeneutic than deductive.

Hermeneutic in what sense? The task of the analyst, first and foremost, is to understand rather than explain, and to understand meaning above all. But meaning is not necessarily "out there" in any clear and defined sense, and even when the referents are clear, their meaning is quite different whether

viewed by analyst or by patient. We have technical procedures
(of a kind) which tell us that we should interpret resistance
before content or defense before wish, but these states or concepts do not come with labels attached; they must be discovered
in the clinical material and the process of discovery is largely a
hermeneutic endeavor. But the details of this discovery are hidden by narrative smoothing.

Paradigmatic and Narrative Modes

Clinical reports can be read in two quite different ways: as
transparent accounts of a particular patient with particular
symptoms which are treated by a certain technique, or as evo-
cative recoveries of mood and atmosphere, often vague as to
specifics. The first reading corresponds to Bruner's paradigmatic mode of thought (see Bruner, 1984), which is concerned with general causes, general categories, and general
principles, and which attempts to reduce the specific symptom
or complaint to a broader rule and fit the individual details into
a larger pattern. A case account of this kind attempts to minimize ambiguity and emphasize "reference at the expense of
sense. It aspires to the astringent goal of singular definite referring expressions with severe restrictions on alternative senses"
(Bruner, 1984, p. 14). What happened and how it took place is
given first priority; the writing attempts to be as transparent as
possible so that we, the readers, are given ringside seats in the
consulting, examining, or operating room. Language must be
denotative rather than connotative, and precision of reference
and simplicity of style is the sought-after goal. Cases of this
kind are often written in a standard format (see, for example,
the Clinical Pathological Conference — CPC — regularly reported in the *New England Journal of Medicine*), and as a result, similarities and differences among cases can be identified and interpreted.

The second reading corresponds to Bruner's narrative mode of thought. It

> maximizes sense at the expense of definite reference . . . sacrifices denotation to connotation. It is for this reason that the metaphoric richness of a story or a line of poetry is as important as the events to which it refers and why . . . a story cannot be reduced to a set of atomic propositions derived from its particular set of statements. (Bruner, 1984, p. 14)

The narrative account of a case, if done successfully, will give us a feel of what it was like to be Dora and have her dreams interpreted by Freud; it will give us a sense of how he approaches her presenting problem (but not necessarily provide us with the precise manner of treatment); and it will often evoke different reactions in different readers because it tries to evoke a mood or a feeling rather than provide the reader with a flow chart of the ongoing treatment. Such accounts depend heavily on a highly developed style, using a figurative and metaphoric language which goes far beyond the "facts." Since each report bears the stamp of the author, our view of the case is necessarily colored by his particular theoretical and rhetorical stance. As a result, it is almost impossible to consider similarities and differences between cases of the same type or to build up a coherent set of specimen reports; each narrative impression is more or less unique.

Each mode of reporting brings about its own kind of narrative smoothing. If the focus is on reference at the expense of sense, the "facts" in the case will be organized with an eye to logical consistency and coherence and the prejudices of the author/observer will be minimized. Metaphor will be held to a minimum and transparent language will be used where possible. But this objective stance tends to leave out of account the ways in which the "facts" are not completely clear and to minimize the contribution of prejudice, bias, or preconception to understanding. By treating the case as a closed set of "facts" to be reported, the author has committed himself to an impossible position which assumes that all meanings are "out there," ready to be described and put into words, and that all observers would take the same view of the proceedings. A smoothing which maximizes facts over feelings may, ironically, end up by doing an injustice to the facts because they frequently do not speak for themselves, and no amount of transparent, referential description can bring them alive. The paradigmatic account may earn high marks for objectivity but low marks for rhetoric, and the final impression may be much less than the author had hoped, simply because it lacks narrative appeal.

If the focus is on sense at the expense of reference, we come away inspired and even enthralled — but not necessarily informed. Crucial facts may be misrepresented and consensus slighted in favor of rhetoric, but we may be wiser in significant ways. We may not be able to identify the source of this wisdom or test its truth value, but our horizons have been extended — often irreversibly. After reading the Dora case, for example, it is never possible to go back to hearing the reports of a crazy patient as so much nonsense and take up once again the modal stance of the alienist in the middle of the nineteenth century. The revelation of the Dora case lies in a significant shift in mode of listening which Freud illustrates over and over again, showing us how it is possible to "read between the lines" and listen to several contexts at the same time. The truth value of his discoveries matters much less than his demonstration that symptoms can be treated as words, that repetition can be treated as remembering, and that Dora's comments to Freud can also be treated as comments intended for her father or Herr K. Only a narrative account could bring these impressions to life and allow us to enter into the interaction in a way that reveals the possibilities of this new way of listening.

It can be seen that many or all of the heard "voices" in the Freudian conversation can be easily lost if we try to pin them down too soon. When Dora "speaks" with the voice of her governess or addresses Freud as Herr K, the sense evoked by her words is probably more important than the words themselves; thus any attempts to "get the record straight" could easily end up by losing the most important discovery of all — that Dora is speaking in many tongues. Rorty tells us that "we have not *got* a language which will serve as a permanent neutral matrix for formulating all good explanatory hypotheses, and we have not the foggiest notion of how to get one" (1979, p. 348). If all accounts are more or less misleading, then it would seem better to smooth the narrative in favor of what makes it distinctive rather than in favor of what makes it trivial.

Accounts in the narrative mode work best by illustrating rather than by specifying, and we turn to such accounts to find new ways of understanding or accounting for what we already know. The Dora case continues to be read as literature because it allows us to participate in Freud's discovery that patients talk in many tongues and gives the reader a chance to share his surprise at Dora's response — particularly his surprise at her decision to abruptly terminate the treatment. But giving the rhetorical account high marks for evoking this kind of surprise does not mean that we must go on being slaves to metaphor and figurative language. Part of the charm of a favorite narrative lies in the sense it conveys of surprise and wonder. But we can be surprised only so often.

We have noted that the narrative mode conveys a highly personal statement about a specific experience, and it is not designed to categorize this experience or account for it in more general terms. How can its wisdom be extracted and put to more general use? We are faced once again by the Sherlock Holmes dilemma. The narrative cannot be generalized into a set of "findings" because the two modes of thought are not interchangeable (see Bruner, 1986); a generalized statement of narrative findings would be, after all, a contradiction in terms. But to read Freud as literature raises a groundswell of concern in many circles because it implies that we value his narrative appeal more than his respect for the "facts." Neither the narrative nor the paradigmatic mode can completely account for the clinical happening; they explain some of its intricacies but leave a residue unexplored.

> A person trying to understand a text is prepared for it to tell him something. That is why a hermeneutically trained mind must be, from the start, sensitive to the text's quality of newness. But this kind of sensitivity involves neither "neutrality" in the matter of the object nor the extinction of one's self, but the conscious assimilation of one's own fore-meanings and prejudices. The important thing is to be aware of one's own bias, so that the text may present itself in all its newness and thus be able to assert its own truth against one's own fore-meanings. (Gadamer, 1975, p. 238)

Gadamer goes on to explain that prejudice does not necessarily mean "unfounded judgment" but can be understood more broadly to refer to the set of assumptions, witting and unwitting, which we bring to any new experience. Both Gadamer and Heidegger before him have argued that these assumptions will inevitably color our understanding of a new text, that it is, as we have seen, simply impossible to listen with evenly suspended attention, and that we must be constantly on the alert for the effect of prejudice and the way it closes our eyes to the full meaning of the text. One test of this openness is measured by our sensitivity to the "newness" of the text; our awareness of what makes it different and distinctive can only operate when we are not searching for standard meanings or validating favorite hypotheses.

When the analyst tries to capture the "text" of the fifty-minute hour, he tries to listen for newness in a variety of ways. First, he may notice the difference between his reading of an episode and the way it is reported by the patient; disparities of this kind often serve to initiate an interpretation. Second, he may be struck by the way in which the patient's response to him

(as analyst) does not match his sense of what the patient intended to say or do; the newness of this response can be used to
gauge the amount of distortion and may lead to a transference
interpretation. Finally, he may be struck by disparities between
the patient's history and the standard psychoanalytic account,
and if this newness strikes him with enough force, he may try
to publish the discrepancies and what they imply.

In each of these instances, the appreciation of newness must
come after an understanding of meaning, but the meaning is
rarely on the surface. Thus it must follow that to listen clinically is to listen hermeneutically and we need to identify two
senses of the process: vertical and horizontal. The target utterance may contain a hidden message which might be revealed
through association or gesture or slip of the tongue, and in that
case, we look beneath surface appearance and listen with the
"third ear"; we try to decode the utterance by attending to its
surround. Listening in this mode captures the popular image of
the psychoanalyst, but it is only half the story. The target utterance may also be less than it seems, not more; it may simply be
a variation on an old theme, the nth repetition of a familiar
complaint or goal. Listening in this vein demands less suspicion and more déjà vu, an ear for overtones and an eye for
pattern matches, an ability to detect similarity in differences
and a sensitivity to transformations and permutations. Listening in the first vein, we listen vertically because the target
utterance is assumed to take the place of something else; to
listen in the second vein, we listen horizontally because the
target utterance belongs to a family of utterances which have
appeared at some earlier time, and we must keep the old images intact in order to spot a new member. To listen in the first
vein is to listen to the harmony of the hour; to listen in the
second vein is to listen to its melody.

These are some of the lessons of the Dora case which were
elaborated and clarified in Freud's later clinical papers and
amended (slightly) by his followers. But we have seen how

editorial smoothing tends to give us the findings from a session and little of the procedures which produced the findings; as a result, we are still largely in the dark as to how an analyst listens most of the time. Conspicuously lacking is an insider's account which describes the analyst as he listens to the hour, now vertically and now horizontally, an account which would tell us how he goes about choosing how to listen and what to say, and how he amends his response in the face of new clinical material.

The failure to report the details of the listening process is one of the most serious consequences of editorial smoothing and reflects a grievous misreading of Freud's central contribution. As we noted earlier, his revolutionary discovery was less content and more process; as a result, his specific interpretations in the clinical papers should be read more as illustrations of how to proceed than as truthful interpretations which made a significant difference to the patient and which should be slavishly copied. Editorial smoothing reduces the process to a handful of trivial conclusions and leaves out of the record the clinical wisdom of the treating analyst who is always finding new ways of combining horizontal and vertical approaches. Edelson (1983) correctly reminds us that "a psychoanalysis without surprises cannot properly be termed a psychoanalysis at all" (p. 93), but the number of surprises in the average case report tends to approach zero.

The distinction between horizontal and vertical listening makes it clear that evenly suspended attention is only one part of the analytic stance. Decoding manifest into latent content — the popular image of the "mind-reading" psychoanalyst — may take place from time to time, but to focus on the vertical approach to the exclusion of everything else tends to give a mystical flavor to the proceedings which they do not deserve. It also underestimates the sheer lawfulness of the interpretative process, just as the failure to report the complete context of discovery leaves the impression that good psychoanalytic work is essentially ineffable and beyond description, the godchild of genius which cannot be taught.

A full report of the context of discovery would also make us aware of the creative component in good interpretations and the variety of choices which are available at any given time, The standard case report makes it seem as if the interpretations cited are necessarily the right answers; alternative explanations or "readings" of the material are almost never provided. But if we are listening for theme and variations, the number of repetitions we hear will depend on our tolerance for transformation and our choice of unit, and these are clearly individual choices which are rule-governed in a general way but which also contain many degrees of freedom. In the paper cited above (1983), Hertz found a way to map the Dora case onto *What Maisie Knew* and, through this comparison, raised a new series of questions about the relation between author and his central "character." In a somewhat different vein, Peter Brooks (1984), Michael Shepherd (1985), and I have all compared Freud with Sherlock Holmes; each of us looks on the case report as a kind of detective story which begins with mystery and incoherence and ends with many questions answered and a sense of final understanding. Each of these comparisons managed to find points of correspondence between apparently dissimilar texts; each comparison provides a new reading of Freud and helps to enlarge our understanding of his approach.

What is the truth value of these readings? In his critique of the hermeneutic approach, Barratt calls Ricoeur to task for not specifying

> criteria by which rival interpretations within psychoanalysis might be adjudicated. . . . Implicitly and subtly, Ricoeur seems to identify truth and the movement of psychoanalytic interpretation . . . [and] circumvents the question raised by interpretations which are efficacious yet wrong. . . .(1977, p. 462)

Barratt goes on to argue that

> It is wholly unsatisfactory to assume, as Ricoeur seems to do, that truth somehow emerges by necessity within the psychoanalytic situation. It would be equally unsatisfactory to suggest that truth is to be discerned solely on the basis of personal resonance, or to argue that idiographic interpretations are to be validated by reference to certain fixed universal types, which are actually not the concern of the psychoanalytic endeavor. Freud's psychology as a hermeneutic system does imply a set of criteria for the arbitration of conflicting interpretations. (pp. 462–463)

Does it follow that Freud's system implies a set of criteria? It may be closer to the mark to say that if we choose hermeneutics as a mode of understanding, then we also must rule out the idea of a single method. Ricoeur tells us that "there is no general hermeneutics, no universal canon for exegesis, but only disparate and opposed theories concerning the rules of interpretation" (1970, p. 26). Gadamer makes it clear that the hermeneutic approach is distinguished by the fact that it is method-free; truth is not contingent on method but, rather, truth and method complement one another. Barratt's critique seems to assume that the task of interpretation is primarily one of uncovering, that listening is always carried out within a vertical mode. As soon as we consider the horizontal approach, then it would seem as if we can listen to the material on a variety of different levels, using a wide range of transformations. Each new reading of the Dora case will find something new to say; this is a necessary consequence of the fact that understanding always takes place within a certain context, subject to a certain tradition, and that what strikes each reader as "new" and therefore worthy of comment will necessarily vary as a function of his experience and training. And having compared Freud to Henry James and Sherlock Holmes would not seem to limit, in any way, the comparisons still to come; we can confidently expect attempts to find points in common with culture heroes yet unborn.

In a similar way, an attempt to find a particular pattern in a patient's life and uncover a particular theme and variations does not exhaust (or even reduce) the "truth" of the clinical material, leaving less around for the next interpreter. We do not "account for" the variance in a set of data by a coefficient of correlation. It is partly for this reason that questions of method seem out of place and why it is important to appreciate the fact that competent analytic work implies much more than merely decoding a text. If only decoding were involved, then it would be entirely proper to speak of true and false accounts — but this is not the case. There is clearly something more.

How can we extract and preserve the wisdom of the "something more"? It is here that concern with method and criteria most get in the way. Narrative smoothing has the effect of turning a hermeneutic adventure into a staid, pseudoscientific account which gives the impression that all interpretations are overdetermined, that all surprise has been accounted for (if it ever existed), and that the received theory is entirely correct. Narrative smoothing manages to eliminate alternative readings of the material and makes it impossible for the curious reader to participate in the encounter; it thus diminishes his ability to contribute to the final understanding. Narrative smoothing presents us with a finished product; it fails to open up the text for any kind of shared discovery.

In their zeal to prove Freud right in matters of fact and find every possible way of validating his theory in the clinical material, his heirs have produced a literature that says next to nothing about the process of discovery. Gray tells us that perhaps the most important element in the study of technique "lies in identifying, *in more than usual detail*, the manner or choice of the analyst's *forms of attention* during the conduct of the analysis" (1982, p. 621; first italics mine). We have seen how certain kinds of narrative smoothing tend to swallow up these details and present us with case reports which are largely predictable in their findings — and significantly mysterious as to how these findings were discovered. And although popular fiction has attempted to rush into this vacuum with its own gothic fabrication (e.g., the novel *August*), we are still left in the dark as to how analysts really listen and what they do with what they hear.

The answer to Gray's plea for more detail must come from the analyst himself. It cannot be supplied by the transcript, which is mute with respect to the inner process of paying attention, and it cannot be supplied by Freud's classic cases, no matter how slavishly they are copied. Part of the reluctance to unpack the session more fully may come, as Gray suggests, from the fact that the analyst often chooses to protect himself from too detailed an awareness of how he functions — in part for narcissistic reasons. Part of the reluctance may stem from lack of practice (as Freud suggested in another context; see Gray, 1982, p. 651) and part from what Gray calls an "inner tendency to maintain a natural or at least a maturely typical state of virtual ignorance of those functions of the ego that potentially enable it to observe itself" (p. 651). And part may stem from the fact that we have not yet arrived at a model of clinical listening which does justice to the intricacies of the process and which would guide us in the study of the context of discovery.

Such a model, it would seem, must begin at the point where the analyst first "opens himself to the text" (in Gadamer's words) and begins to make distinctions between what has never been said before, what is being repeated, and what is repeated but slightly changed. The model must take into account both horizontal and vertical modes of listening and the conditions under which they occur. A careful study of process might, for example, reveal that an attempt to "decode" the target utterance (that is, to listen vertically) may take place when the utterance does not arouse any kind of historical interest or resonate with earlier fragments of the treatment. Conversely, attempts to listen horizontally may take place when clear parallels appear between different parts of the treatment (as may happen, for example, during the termination phase of treatment when earlier symptoms are revived).

But defining the "newness" of the material is never an easy judgment; it clearly depends on the context brought to bear at that particular time and place, and the model must find some way of defining this context and integrating it into the listening process. First, it must be unpacked in such a way that the outside reader comes closer to understanding the privileged competence of the treating analyst and his reasons for hearing the material in just the way he does.

A faithful account of the listening process and a full description of the context of discovery will very likely have the appearance of a disconnected series of insights, strung together by time. Surprise, bewilderment, and faint glimmers of understanding probably all circle one another during the average hour in much the same way that they appear during a dream state, and here we come to the greatest danger of narrative smoothing. The seamless account of the clinical Sherlock Holmes cannot do justice to the way in which the patient's responses are first vaguely apprehended, then recombined with remembered fragments of earlier sessions or with pieces of theory to arrive at some partial understanding which often proves completely wrong and misdirected. An honest account must document these failures and begin to tell us when an hour ended in complete dismay, when an interpretation was misunderstood and intensified the resistance, and when — because this also happens — associations were properly decoded and the simple meaning of a dream or symptom stood out clearly for the first time. Current narrative accounts tend to focus only on successes and misrepresent the number of false hypotheses which must be discarded or the number of times the treating analyst was just plain wrong. No wonder that Gray warns us of narcissistic injury.

We begin to appreciate how narrative smoothing can be

compared to secondary revision during dreaming. Such revision has the aim of processing the chaotic dream as experienced and turning it into something more "followable" and which conforms more closely to the narrative shapes we like to hear. A similar process seems to overtake our clinical experience and make it more palatable for outside consumption. But the stereotype has dulled our appreciation of the excitement, wonder, and surprise contained in the actual event, and the stereotype will teach us nothing worth knowing. The true discoveries lie ahead.

Alternatives to the Sherlock Holmes Tradition

We are now in a position to look back on the distinctions reviewed in the preceding pages and search for some underlying themes. One contrast stands out immediately. On the one side, we have labels which seem to support the metaphor of psychoanalysis as something quite straightforward and paradigmatic and a view of the case report as a transparent account of a circumscribed set of events. Under this heading we would list such terms as singular solution, positivistic approach, and a view of hermeneutics (if it emerges at all) as a systematic procedure for uncovering the hidden message. Given this view of the function of the case report, it is not surprising to find that Freud saw no need to include specific considerations of technique. We have argued that this omission led directly to what Gray has called the "developmental lag" of technique.

But it should also be clear that the decision to emphasize a generally positivistic point of view carries with it a wish to identify psychoanalysis as science. If case reports are presented as singular accounts of singular events, then the reader need not concern himself with other interpretations of the facts. But if we dwell on the other end of the continuum, then a much different set of conditions appears. In the Dora case, we found reason to wonder whether interpretation might be masquerading as explanation and whether the explanations presented as final might be rather more provisional. If we emphasize the metaphoric mode of thinking which enters into clinical accounts, then we become sensitive to hermeneutics as a form of demystification (see Ricoeur, 1970, p. 27). This view of the matter makes for bad science but exciting hermeneutics because it suggests that there are any number of meanings contained in the clinical encounter and that the responsible author should be concerned with presenting as full a *range* of alternatives as possible.

We begin to see how the need for a scientific psychoanalysis has influenced considerations of narrative presentation and, very likely, played an important role in narrative smoothing. Conflicting accounts of the same incident, while fascinating to a student of *Rashomon*, are clearly an embarrassment to followers of a positivistic tradition. If science is the reigning metaphor, then psychoanalyst as artist must find somewhere else to practice. We can begin to see how Freud's need to legitimize his discoveries had the unfortunate effect of minimizing what is perhaps their greatest strength. The longer that psychoanalysis insists on being a science, the more it will play down one of its main attractions—the search for multiple meanings and the search for decision rules to select among them.

Decision rules are important because not every interpretation is privileged. To say that more than one meaning may be true is *not* to say that all meanings are equally true. Barratt (1977) is correct in his charge (see above) that Ricoeur has not specified criteria for choosing among different interpretations; it is less obvious that Freud provided us with a list. One of the less-noticed advantages of the Sherlock Holmes tradition is related to this problem. If only one explanation is given for any clinical encounter, then we never have to raise the question of choosing among several. To argue by authority and to close the door on the adversary tradition is to evade the difficult problem of what makes one interpretation more persuasive, more comprehensive, or more insightful than another. Clearly, more is involved than whether or not the patient agrees with the formulation, but up to now, very few principles have been suggested which might distinguish between good and bad interpretations.

We begin to see how the promise of narrative truth — the promise, that is, of a singular solution to each clinical problem — has given psychoanalysis the trappings of science without the inner substance. Where the search for historical truth has come up short, frustrated by lack of convincing data, the campaign has continued on other fronts. The presentation and (pseudo)documentation of psychoanalytic work have tended to convey the impression of much more clarity and finality than actually exists. It becomes clear how the Sherlock Holmes tradition is more than just a literary conceit: It operates as an important weapon of persuasion, conveying the impression that clinical conclusions are lawfully arrived at in some (undefined) systematic fashion and that multiple meanings are the exception rather than the rule. And as noted, it has ruled out of court the much-needed discussion of rules for deciding among the different meanings.

The need to present psychoanalysis as a sophisticated form of deduction has misrepresented the nature of the clinical endeavor and simplified the underlying hermeneutic problem. By reaching prematurely for membership in the scientific fraternity, psychoanalysts have been guilty of evading the difficult issues which confront the average practitioner each day of his practice. Issues of meaning cry out for some systematic attention; they get very little. It is not enough to appeal to the analyst's ability to decode conscious thoughts into unconscious antecedents (as in Greenson, 1967) because, as we have seen, the unconscious is more metaphor than a substantive piece of knowledge. It is not enough to rely on free association as the "impartial calculus" for decoding the patient's productions because, as we have seen, we almost never listen with evenly

suspended attention devoid of expectation or unwitting interpretation.

In trying to capture and sort out the elusive meanings of the
clinical encounter, we are following Rorty in his plea for the
hermeneutic position. We are trying

> to make some sense of what is going on at a stage where we are
> still too unsure about it to describe it, and thereby to begin an
> epistemological account of it. . . . We will be epistemological
> where we understand perfectly well what is happening but want
> to codify it in order to extend, or strengthen, or teach, or
> "ground" it. We must be hermeneutical where we do not under-
> stand what is happening but are honest enough to admit
> it. . . . (Rorty, 1979, p. 321)

It can be seen that this definition of hermeneutics as a sophisticated way of coping applies to much of what we do within
the therapeutic hour. We listen to the patient's early associations with a hunch about their meaning; this hunch is often
clarified by a new piece of material, and the clarified hunch,
now given as an interpretation, often produces something quite
tangible in the way of confirming evidence. Patient response is
clearly one of the decision rules we use in our work. But if the
patient is silent, or if the patient objects to a formulation, then
we need some kind of larger theory to fall back on, and this is
where the hermeneutic tradition has the most to offer. And as
Rorty makes clear, being hermeneutic at times does not prevent
other approaches at other times; it is possible to balance one
mode of thinking with another.

The Sherlock Holmes tradition not only stands in the way of
gaining access to the clinical happening, but also interferes
with the way in which evidence contributes to theory. Because
the clinical happening is reduced to stereotype, we tend to treat
dissimilar incidents as alike; because the stereotype is often
modeled on metaphor, we tend to find confirmation where we
should find surprise. By moving too quickly from the clinical

happening to the Sherlock Holmes account of it, we leave behind the particular features of the patient which must also be accounted for and which contain their own kind of wisdom. The Sherlock Holmes tradition, because it is modeled on metaphor, tends to read into the clinical happening what is always true — and never true.

Most damaging of all is the absence of detail. The messiness of a specific encounter never survives the kind of narrative smoothing which turns it into a good story, but it is this very messiness which may contain the greater part of our knowledge. The patient, after all, is the source of psychoanalytic wisdom — not the theory — and we must take pains to let the patient speak freely. The patient, writes Lacan, is not the *object* of psychoanalysis but, rather, its *subject*; it is from the patient that we learn about the workings of repression, the logic of the primary process, and the way in which remembering can be disguised as repetition (see Felman, 1983, p. 1048). Holzman (1985) makes a similar point: "It is not the therapy that is destroying the science, for it is the therapy that has given us the science, and without it the extraordinary hypotheses of psychoanalysis could not have been produced" (p. 765). If the patient is the source of all knowledge, then it follows that his or her sayings must be preserved in a form as close to their original as possible, and not transformed into just another "case."

In the final accounting, the Sherlock Holmes tradition is one of the central metaphors of psychoanalysis and, as such, subject to all the dangers of metaphorical thinking outlined in the first chapter. To the extent that it is transparent and functions automatically, it interferes with good investigation. By fitting all cases into the same format and by placing emphasis on sense instead of reference, it can only interfere with the voice of the patient. Other modes of presentation need to be explored in the interest of preserving what is valid and useful about the clinical encounter; one such mode will be explored in the next chapter.

To an important extent, the Sherlock Holmes metaphor actively interferes with our awareness of other metaphors. It protects them from falsification because it emphasizes stereotype over the specific clinical happening and because it perpetuates a single narrative over a more complicated account. By these means, it makes it easy to conclude that the patient is merely suffering from the standard Oedipus Complex or castration anxiety or long-suppressed grief reaction. What is an embarrassment to the narrative is omitted, but this embarrassment is frequently an important clue to a new formulation. If narrative smoothing always wins over surprise, then the theory will never change; free-floating metaphors will always remain reified and detached because the disconfirming data have already been removed from the account. On the other hand, once we stop telling good stories and find more satisfactory ways of presenting our clinical experience, any number of unexpected happenings will come into view, challenging the accepted metaphor and forcing us into a long overdue revision of the theory.

CHAPTER VI

Rule-Governed But Not Rule-Bound: The Legal Metaphor

In the absence of certified facts and benchmark examples, it is tempting to settle for a seamless narrative account which smooths over any and all uncertainties and gives the feeling that everything is understood. We have seen the seductive appeal of the Sherlock Holmes tradition and how easily it fools us into thinking that we have brought back an honest report of the clinical happening with a minimum of ambiguity and a maximum of certainty. Even when we know that the "facts of the matter" are always hostage to context and theory, it is hard to resist the first good story that comes along; even though we know full well the dangers of narrative persuasion, it is hard not to fall under its spell.

Consider the following clinical anecdote from Brenner:

> At a social gathering the evening before, the patient had been unable to remember the name of an acquaintance, A. He was embarrassed by his lapse of memory at the time and felt unhap-

py about it both then and later, since it was obvious to him that he had hurt A's feelings. He rather liked A, though he knew him only casually. He particularly reproached himself because A was obviously just recovering from a recent neurological illness. His face was still somewhat distorted and one arm was nearly useless. "How cruel," said the patient, "to do such a thing to a man who has been through so much." (1982, p. 183)

The behavior to be explained is a circumscribed parapraxis — forgetting a name that was otherwise available to awareness. The problem to be solved is the question of why, under these particular circumstances, the name was forgotten. Once the answer is arrived at, we can ask whether it is found to be persuasive both to the patient and to the outside reader. Its persuasive power can depend on either a narrative or a paradigmatic form of reasoning. An explanation based on a narrative model will depend, as we have seen, on a singular solution supported by argument by authority, exclusion of other alternatives, and the suspension of disbelief — all features of the Sherlock Holmes tradition. An explanation based on a paradigmatic model will depend on the parsimony of the argument, the logic of the reasoning, the number of alternatives considered (and rejected), and a sense in which the final explanation represents the most reasoned synthesis of the widest range of options. Brenner chooses the first.

It quickly became clear (and Brenner discusses this issue at some length) that forgetting the name is not the only thing that happened; it was followed by an awkward failure to make social contact, a turning away, and a sense (on the part of the patient) that A had been snubbed, had felt snubbed, and that he (the patient) was at fault for snubbing him. To properly explain the forgetting, as Brenner makes clear, we must also explain the actions that followed.

He begins to form an explanation in the classic manner — the patient associates to the name of A (which he now remembers).

It reminded him of the name of a rival of younger days, a man with whom he had competed unsuccessfully for a girl to whom they were both attracted. She had preferred his rival, which had made the patient unhappy and jealous for a time, but it was nothing serious. He had not thought of either the girl or of his successful rival for years. He did not see how that memory could have much to do with what had happened the night before. (p. 194)

We have the beginnings of an explanation, but the patient minimizes its significance and moves on to another chain of associations. Should we accept the disclaimer? Many analysts certainly would not, taking the standard view that this response indicates denial rather than lack of interest and reason that the material about the old girl friend deserves much closer attention — precisely because the patient wished to leave it behind. His reluctance to continue raises a troubling question in the mind of the reader. Perhaps any subsequent explanation is only a clever way of leading the analyst off the track, and therefore has more standing as a piece of resistance than as a final account. The final account, by this reasoning, will always be suspect. Whatever the reasons behind the choice, we are confronted by the decision of the analyst to believe the patient's story; the fact that there is no attempt to justify this belief greatly weakens its credibility.

The patient continues his associations:

Then he began to think how frail and crippled A had looked. It reminded him of the way his father had looked during his last illness. With tears in his eyes, the patient berated himself for his lack of sympathy toward his father during the last years of the latter's life. As the patient, an adolescent, grew taller, stronger, and more manly, his father had become progressively more feeble and childish. At the time, the patient had been secretly scornful of his father's seeming lack of courage and of his babyish demands for care and attention. When, on one occasion, the patient's mother had expressed similar critical thoughts, the patient had joined in and had expressed contempt for his father's weakness in sarcastic, derisive terms. That was, however, the only time the patient had given expression to his thoughts about his father. The latter died, unexpectedly, a few weeks later. (p. 184)

There are some striking parallels between his response to A and his remembered response to his father. Of particular interest is the similarity between the guilt felt by the patient after snubbing A and the remorse he felt after his father's death (described later in the account). Drawing on the parallel, Brenner describes the memory lapse (and the attendant behavior) as

a compromise formation resulting from a conflict of childhood origin. A principal drive derivative in the conflict was the patient's jealous, competitive wish to castrate and be rid of his father, a wish that had been expressed in adolescence by despising and ridiculing him when he was feeble and close to death. The memory of having done so, stimulated by A's appearance and, to a lesser extent, by his name, was repressed and the wish was displaced to A. He insulted A, but silently, not in words. He did not call him bad names; he forgot his name. He felt no satisfaction at having insulted A. He felt, instead, despite the defense of displacement and despite his self-imposed silence, a measure of the guilt and remorse he had experienced after his father's death, an event, it will be recalled, that had occurred soon after the patient had aired his contempt for his father. He castigated himself, he confessed his misdeed in his analysis on the following day, and he wept as he talked of the dead father whom he loved and hated, despised and envied. (pp. 185–186)

How persuaded are we by this account? From the standpoint of the narrative model, it makes a wonderful story, not only accounting for some striking parallels between present and past but also invoking the mystery of the unconscious and the somewhat romantic belief that specific childhood events still cast a spell over present behavior. But notice that the appeal to unconscious content is largely rhetorical; we have (once again) no independent evidence that this particular piece of the past has continued to exert its spell. It could just as well be argued that under the spell of the unhappy meeting with A, the patient chose to remember his father's last days in a way that seemed similar to the meeting. Even though Freud made the assumption that some associations to a recent event or a dream fragment could be interpreted as causal, he never gave us a way of separating those which were from those which were not (see Spence, 1981, and Grünbaum, 1984). We are open to the fallacy of *post hoc, ergo propter hoc*.

If Brenner's explanation succeeds as a piece of narrative, it seems quite unpersuasive as a piece of logic. In the first place, it is grievously unparsimonious. Why go to all the trouble of remembering the former girl friend and the dying father; could we not assume that the mere sight of a recent neurological impairment (useless arm and somewhat distorted face) would arouse anxiety and result in loss of memory and an unwillingness to make social contact? If we decide to look further and explore the patient's associations, why should we not concentrate on the first set of thoughts, the reaction to A? If the shock of meeting a disabled acquaintance is not sufficient, we might add a second line of associations (girl friend and rival). But to then decide (on somewhat dubious grounds) that these are not relevant only adds another layer of incredulity to the argument.

In the second place, the argument fails to be persuasive because alternative explanations are neither identified nor comprehensively discussed and the grounds for choosing one interpretation over another are never explored. We have seen how it is not necessarily obvious why the patient's disclaimer (about the girl friend) should be accepted; it is not obvious why the patient's memory of his father's death should be accepted as memory rather than as fabulation; it is not obvious why the choice to concentrate on the father and ignore the girl friend should be taken at face value and not questioned as a piece of resistance. Most damaging of all, it is not obvious that Brenner's formulation is clinically useful and productive. Assuming he voiced his interpretation to the patient (although this is never stated), did it result in a series of new associations? In greater insight? In the recovery of memories previously unexpressed?

Many of the questions just raised turn on an interpretation of the "facts of the matter" and, as we have seen, this is by no means a simple matter. In the context of the clinical event (as experienced by the analyst), it may have seemed overwhelmingly obvious (to him) that something more was at stake than the fact that friend A was recovering from a serious handicap; this conviction (assuming it was present) might account for the decision to gather further associations. In similar fashion, it might have seemed at the time that thoughts of girl friend and former rival were indeed irrelevant to the issue at hand, and that the final set of memories about the dying father provided such a good pattern match with the interaction with A that it had a particular claim toward being seen as causal. Granting all this, the problem remains that what is evident for the treating analyst is not necessarily obvious to the reader, and that only slight differences in point of view will produce significant obstacles to agreement.

From a narrative perspective, on the other hand, slight differences in point of view are rarely fatal. As we have seen, certain kinds of ambiguity add richness to the narrative account; some authors even try to cultivate unclarity as a way of heightening suspense and uncertainty, and as a way of forcing the reader to place even more reliance on the author. If we cannot unravel the story on our own, we are forced to put ourselves even more in the hands of the author; thus, heightened ambiguity tends to increase the suspension of disbelief.

In the final accounting, it is giving way to the author's authority that makes his account persuasive. Brenner, after all, was there; we were not. If not all the evidence is presented, and if there is room for disagreement because of problems of context and theoretical assumption as to the meaning of the clinical material, then we are in no position to challenge his conclusion. But by the same token, even though we are persuaded on narrative grounds, we are not necessarily truly convinced on paradigmatic grounds, and it is becoming clear that we cannot build theory on narrative truth alone (see Spence, 1982b).

When Brenner explains the parapraxis as a "compromise formation resulting from a conflict of childhood origin," he is not so much offering a formulation as invoking a metaphor — one which is familiar to all psychoanalysts. But it is not presented as a figure of speech — quite the contrary. It is intended as a serious attempt to explain a puzzling piece of behavior. It is not convincing as a piece of explanation, for reasons we have already examined, and in its guise as providing us with a full accounting of the material, it interferes with the use of other metaphors. It also prevents us from realizing that very little has been explained.

Something else happens as well. An uncritical reading of this account would suggest, once again, that we have support for the conventional Freudian proposition that a parapraxis can be understood as a derivative of early childhood conflict. In the face of new clinical evidence, it would appear as if the scientific status of this explanation has been made even stronger. But additional support has not been provided. We have no independent evidence that a childhood conflict is still active, that it has some resemblance to the encounter with A, and that the two patterns are similar enough to account for the memory lapse. All that Brenner has accomplished is to invoke a metaphor in the guise of explanation. Instead of giving us a full and persuasive accounting of the clinical happening, he has fallen under the spell of the Sherlock Holmes tradition.

A close study of this example helps us to see why psychoanalytic theory has remained relatively unchanged for almost one hundred years and why, in this specific instance, the concept invoked by Brenner to explain the parapraxis is very nearly the same concept first proposed by Freud. On the level of metaphor, it would seem as if we have evidence for some kind of confirmation, but the evidence is not sufficient to tell us just how the hypothetical concept of parapraxis needs to be adjusted. Metaphors, in other words, are not open to emendation or elaboration. If we want to invoke the hypothesis of ongoing childhood conflict, we would need a much more detailed model which would (1) specify the necessary grounds for assuming the presence of a childhood conflict; (2) provide the necessary grounds for a positive pattern match between present and past; (3) tell us how to identify instances of retrospective falsification in the clinical material; and (4) tell us how to separate associations which are clues to causal mechanisms from associations which are not.

If the grounds for a general proposition are largely metaphoric, then there is no way for a friendly critic to claim that a particular set of findings did *not* support the underlying concept; from a superficial reading, it would appear as if the proposition had been confirmed. Thus the absence of critical data makes it *always* possible to uphold the received theory; as a result, there is no pressure to change established concepts. If the argument remains at a metaphorical level, no proposition will ever be disconfirmed because metaphors are not falsifiable. What is more, if the data supporting a particular formulation are not available for public scrutiny and discussion, there is no possibility for the gradual refinement and clarification of theory, and it is largely for these reasons that we see so little change in the basic concepts. What tends to happen instead is that the accepted metaphor tends to become substituted for the clinical findings. When metaphor masquerades as explanation, we have lost the sense that the concepts are provisional and tentative, that they can, if necessary, be "replaced and discarded without damaging" the theoretical structure (see Freud, 1914, p. 77), or that we are engaged in a long-term effort to "formulate (our) basic scientific concepts with increased precision, and progressively so to modify them that they become serviceable and consistent over a wide area" (see Freud, 1914, p. 117). Metaphor has become literalized and dead; it has lost its tentative flavor and becomes instead a piece of theory; and the theory, such as it is, has been effectively uncoupled from the clinical findings.

Narrative as Resistance

From the standpoint of the psychoanalytic theory of therapeutic process, the temptation to fall under the Sherlock Holmes tradition can be represented as a form of resistance. This resistance includes an intolerance for ambiguity, a need to get on with the story, and a readiness to leave certain questions unanswered. "Analytic case summaries," writes Schafer, "purport to say what is true of the individual when they should say what is true according to the details of the different investigations that have been carried out within each analysis" (1983, p. 204). In the attempt to generate a set of truths or to confirm a set of accepted propositions, the clinical report invariably simplifies and stereotypes the enormously complicated web of circumstances.

In the process, it parallels the initial attempt of the patient to tell about his life — and this is why it can be defined as a resistance. In both cases, simplification always interferes with understanding. In the clinical situation, we have learned to accept the initial report as only a first approximation of later and more extended accounts (see Schafer, 1983), and to realize that the initial story line will be superseded by an entangling array of criss-crossing plots, some never completed, others overlaid by familiar myths, still others never understood. It is time to apply the same wisdom to the published literature and to realize that reports written in the Sherlock Holmes tradition are just as approximate and just as unfaithful to what is being described as the first account presented by the patient. These case reports are just as much in need of expansion, unpacking, and informed revision in the service of what might be called the benign suspicion that the "facts" are otherwise, the suspicion that we cannot reduce the clinical happening to a set of propositions (see Ricoeur, 1970, for a discussion of psychoanalysis as a school of suspicion).

In one of his papers to a more general audience, Freud stressed his interest in building a general theory of the mind.

> I have told you that psychoanalysis began as a method of treatment; but I did not want to commend it to your interest as a method of treatment but as an account of the truths it contains, an account of the information it gives us about what concerns human beings most of all — their own nature — and an account of the connections it discloses between the most different of their activities. (1932b, p. 156)

We are now beginning to realize that the "truths" contained in the account do not lend themselves to a list of propositions which can be tested against the evidence. The most ambitious attempt to codify the theory in this manner (Fisher and Greenburg, 1977) yielded very little in the way of useful information and goes largely uncited in the clinical literature. Calls by Grünbaum (1984) and Edelson (1984) to test the truths of psychoanalysis by the use of traditional experimental methods have failed to generate much in the way of research, largely because there is no agreement about how these "truths" should be formulated or in what manner they should be treated. And it is common knowledge that Freud himself had a somewhat scornful attitude toward experimental verification. In response to Saul Rosenzweig's first experiments on repression, Freud responded as follows:

> I have examined your experimental studies for the verification of the psychoanalytic assertions with interest. I cannot put much value on these confirmations because the wealth of reliable observations on which these assertions rest make them

independent of experimental verification. Still, it (experimental verification) can do no harm. (Freud, letter of February 28, 1934; reprinted in Postman, 1963, p. 703)

Rather than focus on what "truths" Freud had in mind, it might be wiser to develop an account of the "connections" which psychoanalysis reveals between "the different . . . activities." A knowledge of these connections is one way to represent psychoanalytic wisdom and to express the problem in these terms makes a virtue out of what is normally seen as a problem. What is the connection in the Brenner example between forgetting the name and everything else we know about the patient? The importance of context can be seen as a problem of connections, and the ways in which context is controlling probably follows the same rules as the way in which early childhood experience affects later behavior, the way in which outside reality affects our analytic attitude, and the way in which the moment of reporting a case and the texture of that moment affects the narrative voice of the author and his way of representing the clinical happenings. Facts do not stand alone; they are always and necessarily embedded in a web of circumstances, memories, and intentions; to pry them free of this web and to list them as a set of propositions is to violate the analytic attitude and show a significant disregard for its underlying assumptions.

In the Brenner example, we are given a putative explanation for a piece of forgetting which rests on the theory of the influence of childhood experience. The force of the explanation takes refuge, as it were, in the standing of this theory; if we are inclined to believe it, little more argument is needed; if we doubt the underlying proposition (that derivatives of early experiences can influence later behavior), then we find the explanation unconvincing. A fuller account of the connections embedded in the material would take greater advantage of the clinical material. It would attempt to draw maximal advantage from the separate details of the happening, to draw conclusions from these details, to provide alternative understandings and choices among these alternatives, and in the final accounting, to show how the final explanation is a necessary consequence of the antecedent findings. If forgetting the name of the handicapped acquaintance was indeed triggered by the patient's memory of his dying father, then we would like to have other examples of how this memory had surfaced in the analysis (and, if possible, in the transference) and how it had distorted his behavior. If forgetting is seen as a childhood derivative, then it would be useful to be referred to other instances in the clinical literature (in as much detail as possible) in which similar influences had been observed; the similarity among cases would help to add persuasiveness to the argument. If the explanation can be derived from the clinical material in convincing fashion, then this particular instance takes on archival significance and helps, in turn, to clarify our understanding of a particular kind of parapraxis. This type of explanation which is highly case specific must be distinguished from the more usual kind in which the explanation rests on theory.

The boundless domain of context described by Culler in Chapter IV (p. 90) can thus be seen, not as an interference, but on the contrary, as an opportunity to exercise the analytic instrument and increase the persuasive power of the material. As more connections become available and integrated into the account, the strength of any one reading should be correspondingly enhanced. Some contexts may clarify specific uncertainties. If we learn (for example) that the author of a clinical report was, at the time of writing, mourning the death of his father, we can more fully understand his reluctance to interpret certain details in the clinical material having to do with loss; we can make allowance for his punitive response to a series of unexplained cancellations; and we might even understand his fascination with memories of early childhood and the excitement of growing up (life instead of death). How present circumstances impinge on his perception and representation of the clinical material is not an interfering intrusion, to be set aside in the interests of clarifying the clinical problem; it *is* the problem, and because it sits more clearly in the author's here-and-now, it may be more accessible to clarification and elaboration.

If the focus is on connections rather than facts, then it stands to reason that repeated attempts to unpack the context (beginning with the analyst) will be more fruitful than one "final" account. Connections reveal themselves slowly. Some may appear only after the material is studied and restudied from a number of contexts and by a number of observers. In the process, the "facts" are not uncovered and set out to dry; on the contrary, the material is constantly being rearranged and repartitioned. In contrast to Freud's jigsaw puzzle, with a home for all the pieces, the more sophisticated synthesis may concentrate on only a portion of the material but inspect it from a variety of positions. The challenge faced by the clinical investigator is not that of assembling a jigsaw puzzle, decoding a rebus, or excavating a burial ground. Each of these metaphors confuses as much as it explains; each of them carries forward the myth of the world "out there" whose meaning can be revealed by means of a patient sifting of all the facts; each of them conceals the important way in which significance depends on who is looking, just as what qualifies as an answer depends on what question is being asked.

What is the proper metaphor for this search for connections? The law immediately (if somewhat surprisingly) comes to mind. In the first place, we are struck by the fact that it has the same orientation toward cases which we find in psychoanalysis.

The judicial analogy seems apt in that it suggests that different parties may have competing interests (whether legal, theoretical, or practical interests) which often seem to influence the course of debates surrounding particular cases, whether in courts of law, historical-political controversies, or scientific de-

> bates. For example, Freud's case of the Wolf Man was written partly in order to further his side of the argument with Adler and Jung about the primary importance of childhood sexual experience in adult neurosis. Similarly, Wolpe and Rachman's critique (1960) of Freud's study of Little Hans was written in order to criticize the evidential foundations of psychoanalytic interpretation, as well as to argue for the advantages of learning theory foundations. (Runyan, 1982, p. 444)

Secondly, the tradition of peer commentary, used so successfully in the law, would seem to lend itself to psychoanalytic case reports as well. By inviting commentary on specimen texts, we are choosing the metaphor of discovery through dialogue; we accept the fact that the first report is only a tentative approximation and that further understanding can only come from closely reasoned argument, projected into the future. This metaphor also helps to make clear why a case report cannot be reduced to a set of propositions, because its meaning always depends on the specifics of the situation. For the same reason, the law cannot be reduced to a list of rules. The history of the law shows that the truth of a rule grows with each new case.

Once we view case reports as tentative approximations of a very complex truth, we see more clearly the need for commentaries. To date, these efforts have been largely restricted to Freud's famous five cases — what Eissler calls the "five pillars on which psychoanalysis now rests" (1963) — together with the Irma, or "specimen," dream. Almost no criticism, elaboration, or clarification has been devoted to the contemporary clinical literature. Part of the reason for this oversight has been the belief, outlined in Chapter IV, that psychoanalysis is a science which rests on the evidence of the case reports, and evidence should be respected, not tampered with. As it becomes clear that outside observers can sometimes see more clearly than the treating analyst, that normative competence can sometimes contribute to privileged competence, then the way is open for a new genre of contemporary commentaries which seeks to increase our understanding by means of enlarging our context of discovery. Rather than feel his technique is being criticized, the analyst whose work is under discussion might even learn to appreciate the fact that he has been singled out as particularly worthy of notice, complimented by the attention because only his account is sufficiently rich to benefit from additional commentary. (In literature, after all, criticism is not wasted on minor authors.)

Commentary means dialogue and an exchange of views; as new voices join the conversation, new themes emerge from the clinical records and what was already richly overdetermined now becomes even more harmonically complex. As the new interpretations begin to accumulate, some are more telling than others; some are informed, even inspired, whereas others are merely conventional or stereotyped. But the commentary continues because the context, as we have seen, is boundless, and it is through the interplay of interpretation and formulation that the true wisdom begins to emerge — not as a final list of standard principles but as an open set of interpretative possibilities.

The accumulating commentaries on the Dora case which are now being published add perspectives to the material which were simply not available at the time it was written; for example, we now better understand the meaning of being a sick woman in a man's world as we move out from under the shadow of a traditional masculine authority. Feminist readings of the Dora case add to our understanding by enlarging the context of discussion as well as unearthing a specific piece of prejudice that Freud may have unknowingly practiced. In similar manner, future readings of the Dora case may well clarify technical mistakes that we are still in the process of discovering; they may even provide more illuminating metaphors for understanding the two dreams and perhaps give us a clearer conception of why the treatment was doomed to fail.

As the dialogue is broadened and participation becomes more open, we should see a gradual shift from argument by authority — the standard mode of reasoning in psychoanalytic discussions — to agreement through dialogue. Open discussion allows for the chance to reach what Habermas calls an "uncompelled consensus," and the overall aim is summarized by Geuss (1981):

> If an unrestricted community of rational agents investigate a state of affairs, under conditions of complete freedom and eventually reach a stable consensus, the judgment which expresses that consensus is the "objective truth" about that state of affairs. (p. 72)

While we may not agree that an objective truth has necessarily been reached, it seems clear that decisions under these conditions are clearly preferable to pronouncements by authority based on evidence which is not open to inspection — the usual state of affairs in clinical reports. The emphasis on open discussion has clear parallels with the democratic process, and Simon sees the way in which observation influences theory as similar to the way in which the will of the people influences the candidates elected to office.

> I am willing to see one theory or another win a democratic election, but refuse to have any as tyrant or absolute monarch. . . . The analogies in the psychoanalytic arena to democratic processes in the political arena are for me two-fold: first, the idea of free association — that fragile reed — that is the best guarantor we have to free the patient and the analyst from the tyranny of a theory. But, as we know, it is indeed subject to multiple pressures and multiple distortions. The second is free debate which, again, does not guarantee our liberties, but gives us a fighting chance to hear out all aspects of the *patient* in the face of the competing claims of our competing theories. (1983, pp. 9–10)

In the final reckoning, the interpretation or explanation which is arrived at through an extended dialogue is grounded in the plausibility it contributes to a certain sequence of events or a certain body of observation. Clinical accounts are concerned, above all, with what Berlin (in his essay on Vico) has described as the

> "intentional" awareness which humans have as actors, not mere observers from outside, of their own activities, of their own efforts, purposes, direction, outlook, values, attitudes, both present and past, familiar and exceedingly remote, and of the institutions which embody and, in their turn, determine them. This is certainly what [Vico] calls knowledge *per caussas — obtained by attending to the modificazioni* of our *mente*, and leads to knowledge of what men or societies are *at*, that is, not merely of what happens to them, or of how they react or behave as causal agents or "patients," but of those internal relationships and interconnections between thought and action, observation, theory, motivation, practice, which is precisely what observation of the external world, of mere compresences and successions, fails to give us. In the world of things, we see only similarities, conjunctions, regularities, successions or their absence; these can be summarized under laws and necessities in a Cartesian or Newtonian system; but this yields no knowledge of why things and events are as they are; for no one but the Creator of this world knows what is *at*, or for. This distinction between the "inside" and "outside" views, between mechanical cause and purpose; between understanding and knowledge, the human and the natural sciences, was made by later thinkers like Herder . . . Dilthey, Croce and to some degree Max Weber. . . . (Berlin, 1976, p. 106)

Where the "outside" view deals in regularity and predictability, the "inside" view is grounded in circumstance and the specific constraints of time and place. Almost any piece of clinical knowledge fails as a general law (despite Freud's ambition to write a general theory of the mind); conversely, the rules which work across situations are generally useless in persuasively accounting for a particular clinical happening. It follows that clinical accounts draw a special wisdom from detail. It is the accumulation of the here-and-now particulars that gives the full meaning to the episode, and it is the accumulation of commentaries on the incident that draws out the full range of implications. They allow us — the outside observer — to acquire an "inside" view and give the democratic process of theory formation its greatest chance for success. Public exposure of the full measure of clinical richness is the best antidote to dead metaphor, to argument by authority, and to incomplete explanation. Exhausting the contents of the specimen through extended dialogue would seem to be our shortest path to what Habermas calls an uncompelled consensus.

The usual tradition has been otherwise. Partly as a result of Freud's belief (1912, p. 114) that additional data would not change the reader's mind if he was not inclined to agree with the formulation, a custom has emerged which gives the author of a clinical paper the right to allude to the facts rather than state them in full. Because the evidential basis for the argument is only partly open to public inspection, the criteria for conviction are necessarily more relaxed than they would be in a field (such as law) where *all* the evidence must be presented. As a result, the skeptical reader cannot challenge any conclusion which he finds unpersuasive; on the other hand, even reasoned argument often falls short of total conviction because of the possibility that some of the evidence has been withheld.

As a result of this state of affairs, clinical accounts have almost no evidential standing, and as a result, matter very little in the profession or in the history of ideas. Clinical evidence, as a result, contributes almost nothing to the formation of theory; and theory, as we have seen, is more often than not rooted in dead metaphor which is uncoupled from the clinical findings.

The fact that *all* the evidence is never available for public scrutiny not only affects the grounds for conviction but must necessarily affect the standards of argument as well. Just as Freud regretted his decision to accept a patient who would not report everything (for the reason that he was bound, by his occupation, to keep certain professional secrets—see Freud, 1913, p. 136, footnote), so the field of psychoanalysis can hardly function in optimal fashion so long as its reasoning rests only on partial data—and for exactly the same reason. Just as Freud's patient would be quite free to reclassify all of his difficult moments into a category marked Top Secret and therefore exempt from discussion, so the reluctant author, faced with a piece of fuzzy reasoning or a doubtful interpretation, is able to simply omit the embarrassing detail from publication. Given the tradition just cited, he does not even need to supply an explanation.

Journal editors frequently collude in these omissions by agreeing to publish an incomplete account; in so doing, they merely reinforce the familiar tradition of argument by authority which we have found to be so detrimental to open discussion. By agreeing to a literature founded on omission and disguise, we have, in effect, opted for a double standard: Behavior we would not accept from a patient we readily tolerate in our colleagues.

Parallels Between Psychoanalysis and Law

In arguing for an accumulation of commentaries rather than the excavation of a session (or a person's mind), we are saying goodbye to the archeological metaphor and substituting something much closer to an open conversation. We are suggesting that wisdom does not emerge by searching for historical truth, continually frustrated, as we have seen, by a lack of clear specimens and context-free data; rather, wisdom emerges from the gradual accumulation of differing readings of the same situation and the accumulating overlay of new contexts. Notice how the metaphor has changed. No meaning attaches to any one piece which is buried in the past, in the unconscious, or in the clinician's incomplete records; no excavation is necessary. Instead, the meanings are constantly in flux, seen each time against a different context which provides a change of emphasis; figure and ground are constantly in motion.

This kind of clinical discovery has many parallels with legal discovery and the way in which a new ruling grows out of a series of cases.

> The basic pattern of legal reasoning is reasoning by example. It is reasoning from case to case. It is a three-step process described by the doctrine of precedent in which a proposition descriptive of the first case is made into a rule of law and then applied to a next similar situation. The steps are these: similarity is seen between cases; next the rule of law inherent in the first case is announced; then the rule of law is made applicable to the second case. . . . It cannot be said that the legal process is the application of known rules to diverse facts. Yet it is a system of rules; the rules are discovered in the process of determining similarity or difference. . . . It appears that the kind of reasoning involved in the legal process is one in which the classification changes as the classification is made. The rules change as the rules are applied. More important, the rules arise out of a process which, while comparing fact situations, creates the rules and then applies them. (Levi, 1949, pp. 2–4)

There are no clear procedures for this process. "Very often the decision to include a new case in the scope of a rule or to exclude it is judged by the sense that this is the 'natural' continuation of a line of decisions or carries out the 'spirit' of a rule" (Hart, 1967, p. 271). There are further parallels. Law rests on an accumulation of instances; "psychoanalytic knowledge," writes McIntosh, "rests on the practice of psychoanalysis . . . I have tried to show how the nature of factual and theoretical statements and their interrelations, as well as the nature of explanation—all derive from this practice" (1979, p. 428). Law depends on a combination of inductive and deductive reasoning, but it is the opinion of many commentators that these principles are applied with a liberal amount of flexibility and that strict rules of logic are almost never applied. Psychoanalysis could make the same claim. The following distinction between hard and soft reasoning in legal argument could be applied almost word for word to psychoanalysis:

> . . . the crucial difference remains between the search for general propositions of fact rendered probable by confirming instances but still falsifiable by future experience, and rules to be used in the decisions of cases. An empirical science of the judicial process is of course possible: it would consist of factual generalization about the decisions of courts and might be an important predictive tool. However, it is important to distinguish the general propositions of such an empirical science from the rules formulated and used by courts. (Hart, 1967, p. 269)

And further:

> For any rule, however precisely formulated, there will always be some factual situations in which the question whether the situation falls within the scope . . . of the rule cannot be settled. . . . Such cases can be resolved only by methods whose rationality cannot lie in the logical relations of conclusions to premises. Similarly, because precedents can logically be subsumed under an indefinite number of general rules, the identification of *the* rule for which a precedent is an authority cannot be settled by an appeal to logic. (p. 270)

Both psychoanalysis and the law depend on procedures which are rule-governed (but not rule-bound). Both are influenced as much by the circumstances of a particular happening as by an abstract set of laws. Of particular interest is the way in which respect for the law (or rule) is always tempered, in the best opinions and the best interpretations, by respect for the specifics. Also significant is the law's overarching respect for the public record: All arguments are publicly argued and no refuge is taken in private testimony, privileged evidence, or in argument by authority. Psychoanalysis suffers considerably by comparison.

To say that parallels exist between law and psychoanalysis is to make the claim that legal metaphors are more fitting than natural science metaphors: in other words, that cases are sacred and must be preserved; that argument must be shaped to suit the situation; and that the sheer accumulation of facts is less important than the context into which they are fitted. The legal metaphor also highlights the importance of an accumulated, public record of cases, highly codified and cross-indexed, resting on a rich bed of commentary, both present and past. It highlights the respect for circumstance over respect for rule; it tolerates a disregard of strict rule in situations where other circumstances are privileged (see Hart, 1967, p. 272); and it underlines a respect for public discussion and public argument, as distinguished from argument by authority. Perhaps most important of all, the legal metaphor gives psychoanalysis a way of rediscovering and refining its true nature, making the best use of its past history, and making the most considered use of its accumulated wisdom without falling prey to the idols of science.

We have said that psychoanalysis (like the law) is rule-governed but not rule-bound; we are now in a position to expand on this distinction. Both analysts and judges are very much guided by rules; to a considerable degree (analysts less than judges), they are guided by previous cases. Within these guidelines, both feel free to break the rule whenever it seems required by circumstance. This flexibility stands in clear contrast to the rule-boundedness of natural science. Rules in law are said to have an "open texture": They are subject to interpretation, they contain exceptions not predictable in advance, and deviation from the rule does not necessarily lead to bad law (whereas it often leads to doubtful science). Psychoanalysis follows the same set of distinctions.

Rules do not predict the behavior of either psychoanalysts or judges. In both fields, the rules operate suggestively, not automatically; they provide standards against which decisions or interpretations are shaped.

> . . . predictions of what a court will do . . . rest ultimately on an appreciation of the non-predictive aspect of rules. . . . Though the existence of rules in any social group renders prediction possible and often reliable, it cannot be identified with them. (Hart, 1961, pp. 143–144)

The word *often* in the last sentence is a telling clue that we are dealing with something quite different from a predictive science. The final authority rests with the individual implementing the rules — analyst or judge.

Rules — in either psychoanalysis or the law — are not frozen. "Out of psychoanalytic observation a stream of new propositions constantly emerges. . . . It cannot be a static process; it must be dynamic and continuous" (Kris, 1947, p. 23). The rules are interpreted anew each time they are applied, depending on the constraints of the situation. This is one way in which context is taken into account. Because context is all important, it becomes essential that careful records be kept — of all cases, in law; of the largest feasible number, in psychoanalysis — because the situation always has the last word.

> Even when verbally formulated general rules are used, uncertainties as to the form of behavior required by them may break out in particular concrete cases. Particular fact-situations do not await us already marked off from each other, and labelled as instances of the general rule, the application of which is in question; nor can the rule itself step forward to claim its own instance. . . . Canons of "interpretation" cannot eliminate, though they can diminish, these uncertainties; for these canons are themselves general rules for the use of language, and make use of general terms which themselves require interpretation. They cannot, any more than other rules, provide for their own interpretation. (Hart, 1961, p. 123)

Flexibility of application is both a requirement and a luxury; it allows a general rule to be modified according to circumstance, and it also gives the last word to analyst or judge.

Rules—in either psychoanalysis or the law—always remain partly unspecified. The law can be thought of as a general family of rules, but it is never exhausted by any list because the "law is what the courts decide." In similar fashion, psychoanalytic theory is only partly written down; it is not exhausted by any author (including Freud); it is also "what the courts decide"—represented by what analysts do as much as by what they say or write. For this reason, neither psychoanalytic theory nor the law can be used predictively; neither body of knowledge contains a set of axiomatic statements which can be manipulated and tested (as in science). The rules which make up these bodies of knowledge are always open to interpretation, and precedent is never final: "There is no authority or uniquely correct formulation of any rule to be extracted from cases" (Hart, 1961, p. 131).

Because rules are flexibly applied and may even come into existence as a function of circumstance, it is essential that cases be described in maximum detail. The history of law (and psychoanalysis) is nothing less than the archive of cases. Exhaustive reporting maximizes both understanding and persuasion; public accountability guarantees a high level of argument, as noted above, because bad logic cannot be hidden under the cloak of privacy. Psychoanalysis might do worse than to follow this example. We traditionally question the need for full disclosure (in the interests of protecting the patient's confidence), but a distinction can be made between material which is disguised to protect privacy and material which is disguised because of poor choice of language, lack of detail, and the temptation to shelter under the Sherlock Holmes tradition. To turn case reports into entertaining narratives is to turn psychoanalysis into a branch of literature (which it clearly is not, as we will soon discover), misrepresent the way it functions in reality, and enormously oversimplify both theory and practice.

The law changes over time; so does psychoanalysis—both in theory and in practice. But the law has codified these changes in an exhaustive compilation of all major decisions, cross-indexed for maximum accessibility, making it possible to trace the applicability of a particular rule over time and study how it is influenced by changes in context. Psychoanalysis is subject to the same kind of influence—consider how differently we see transference now compared to the way Freud saw it in 1905—but the crucial changes remain largely undocumented, putting us at a serious disadvantage with respect to our past, and greatly handicapping our attempts to learn from our history. In the belief that psychoanalysis is a science, we have tended to simplify rather than expand the account; we have tended to reduce particulars to the general, and in the process, the particulars are lost forever. We have a Concordance to the *Standard Edition*, but no concordance of creative specimen cases.

Interpretation is central to both law and psychoanalysis, and the core of interpretation is nicely illuminated by a metaphor from Dworkin (1986). He compares the long line of judges writing opinions to the authors of a chain novel, writing successive chapters. "In this enterprise a group of novelists writes a novel *seriatim*: each novelist in the chain interprets the chapters he has been given in order to write a new chapter, which is then added to what the next novelist receives, and so on" (p. 229). Both judges and authors aim

> to impose purpose over the text or data or tradition being interpreted. Since all creative interpretation shares this feature, and therefore has a normative aspect or component, we profit from comparing law with other forms or occasions of interpretation. We can usefully compare the judge deciding what the law is on some issue not only with . . . citizens . . . deciding what [the tradition of courtesy] requires, but with the literary critic teasing out the various dimensions of value in a complex play or poem. (p. 228)

How else are judges like authors of a serial novel—and like analysts writing up their cases? All three groups are constrained by what has gone before; they cannot introduce just any interpretation or twist of plot, but must pick an argument that "must have some general explanatory power." If the serial author chooses an account which "leaves unexplained some major structural aspect of the text, a subplot treated as having great dramatic importance or a dominant and repeated metaphor," then the account is flawed (p. 230).

It may also happen that more than one interpretation fits the bulk of the text. In that case, the author or judge or analyst must rely on which shows the text in the better light.

> He will form a sense of when an interpretation fits so poorly that it is unnecessary to consider its substantive appeal, because he knows that this cannot outweigh its embarrassments of fit in deciding whether it makes the novel [or judicial record or clinical case] better, everything taken into account, than its rivals. . . . We can appreciate the range of different kinds of judgments that are blended in this overall comparison. Judgments about textual coherence and integrity . . . are interwoven with more substantive aesthetic judgments. . . . Nor can we draw any flat distinction between the stage at which a chain novelist [or judge or analyst] interprets the text he has been given and the stage at which he adds his own [material], guided by the interpretation he has settled on. (Dworkin, 1986, pp. 231–232)

The metaphor of the chain novelists writing a continuous series of chapters can be applied to the long line of analysts, stretching back to Freud, who are engaged in making sense of their clinical material and publishing their conclusions. Multiple interpretations are always arising; they are justified by a sense of what seems fitting to the case and consistent with the theory. Specific readings may be justified by a reference to earlier cases (Freud's, in particular). The process looks both backward and forward. Transference is seen in the light of the Dora case, and yet in some (perhaps invisible) respects, it is radically different; current readings of transference will influence interpretations yet to come. Meanings are continually evolving because we have no handbook of standards; at the same time, continuity is preserved because we all adhere to a shared community of principles. Interpretation of the clinical moment is always a combination of principle and inspiration. History matters to a significant degree, but its application is flexible. To quote again from Dworkin

> [Reasoned interpretation] does not require consistency in principle over all historical stages . . . it does not require that judges [or analysts] try to understand the law [or practice] they enforce as continuous in principle with the abandoned law [or practice] of a previous century or even a previous generation. It commands a horizontal rather than a vertical consistency of principle across the range of legal [or psychoanalytic] standards the community now enforces. It insists that the law [or theory] . . . contains not only the narrow explicit content of [past] decisions but also, more broadly, the scheme of principles necessary to justify them. (p. 227)

Dworkin's metaphor can also be applied to the analytic process itself. Analyst and patient are also writing a continuous story in which each new chapter not only builds on the past (both the past of the patient, the earlier stages of the analysis, and the history of the psychoanalytic movement), but reaches forward into the future. Schafer (1983) has shown clearly how "psychoanalysts may be described as people who listen to the narrations of analysands and help them to transform these narrations into others that are more complete, coherent, convincing, and adaptively useful than those they have been accustomed to constructing" (p. 240). The metaphor of the chain novel helps to highlight the idea of multiple authors and the unending nature of the task. The identity of the authors is continually changing as a result of fluctuations in the transference: Now the patient/writer is living in the present; now he or she is creating something out of the past. Now the analyst/

author is the stern father; now he is an understanding colleague. But the story is always a joint product, and it is the story of this story that needs to be documented in greater detail.

Three Specimens and Their Commentaries

For an example of how external commentaries can expand our understanding of a clinical happening, consider the following dream and its presumed meaning. It was drawn from a recent case report by Reiser (1985). It was dreamt by a patient in the last months of a four-year analysis. At the start of the analysis, the patient told the following story:

> When she was thirteen years old, she and her brother, on a rainy afternoon, were in the kitchen making tapioca pudding. She put a large pot of boiling water on the refrigerator to cool. Her brother opened the refrigerator door, the pot fell over, and he was seriously scalded. A neighborhood physician was called who sent Carol to the drugstore to get an emergency medication to be applied before the ambulance arrived. She "awoke" three hours later, sitting on a bench in the park with total amnesia for the intervening time. She had had a major hysterical dissociative fugue. She could not even remember the name of the medication she was supposed to get — in fact, she had never been able to remember it though she had tried many times — a major disturbance of memory. (Reiser, p. 21)

Dream:

> In the first part of the dream, she was planning a trip to Europe and wanted to go to a certain city in or near Germany but could not remember the name no matter how hard she tried. Then the scene shifted; she was in the kitchen of her fiancé's home with the whole family sitting around the kitchen table. She was naked but felt no shame or embarrassment. Her brother-in-law said, "That's a wonderful tan you have." At this point, she felt intensely embarrassed, and felt both guilty and

ashamed for the first time in her dream. She asked for a robe and replied, "Well I am tan but not nearly as tan as Danny (her fiancé)." (Reiser, p. 21)

The analyst made the interpretation that the second part of the dream was concerned with remembering, to balance the first part (which was concerned with forgetting), and that, further, she was trying to remember the name of the forgotten medicine. He wondered if the name came to mind, and the patient replied, "tannic acid."

First commentary. I was struck by the "rightness" of the interpretation and by the fact that it was corroborated by the patient's response (tannic acid was a well-known remedy for burns during the time the patient was growing up). If the words "tannic acid" were actually encoded in the dream, it should be possible to carry out a small experiment by presenting dream and background information to knowledgeable clinicians and asking them to come up with the medicine. To that end, I presented this material to three different audiences all acquainted with psychiatry. A sizable number from each group thought of the words "tannic acid"! At least one of the respondents did not know (because of her age) that tannic acid was a remedy for burns!

Second commentary. The dream served to undo a longstanding repression and bring into awareness a long-forgotten name. Because the original forgetting was part of the hysterical fugue, it would naturally follow that details of this forgotten interval would also come into awareness after the dream had been interpreted. Could the treating analyst (Dr. Reiser) discover any material in his notes which might have a bearing on this issue? Was the question discussed in the analysis of the dream? Could the record be expanded to include this information?

Third commentary. In the original incident, the neighborhood physician sent the patient to the drugstore in search of tannic acid. In the analysis of the dream, the treating analyst "sent" the patient into her preconscious to recover the forgotten name. The successful retrieval has a bearing on the transference and on the fact that the treating analyst was a physician.

Fourth commentary. In the first part of the dream, the patient is trying to remember the name of a city in or near Germany. Did she try to associate to this piece of the dream? Did city-associations (e.g., Tannenberg, a city in East Germany) prepare the way for "tannic acid"? Could the record be expanded to include these details?*

It can be seen how the initial commentaries on a piece of clinical material would lead naturally to specific replies from the treating analyst, and how these replies provide glosses on the original dream and help to expand our understanding of it. The elaborated clinical incident might then bring about a second generation of responses; replies to these could be added to the original record. As a result of this kind of exchange, some of the original ambiguities would be clarified, some of the alternative explanations would be laid to rest, and the final account, enriched by later additions from the treating analyst and illuminated by peer commentary, would quite naturally acquire greater respect as an example of a clinical happening. If all ambiguities dropped out, the final account would become our equivalent of a benchmark case in the law, and could be cited as an example of the way in which correct interpretation can remove repression and the way in which the response to a correct interpretation can be used to corroborate its correctness.

Notice that the entire discussion is case-specific. No mention is made of which structural agencies participated in the remem-

---

*I am indebted to Dr. Julian Kassen for providing me with one of these commentaries, and to the third-year residents in psychiatry, Rutgers Medical School, for being subjects in an experiment which attempted to recover the name of the medicine.

bering or what defenses were abolished to permit the name to come into awareness. Abstract explanations of this kind are better left for the future and for a time when we have a collection of benchmark cases which can be used to generate a set of propositions. When enough cases have been collected and enough ambiguities resolved, it may then be possible to generalize to an analytic "rule" which would seem to account for the greater number of instances. Such a formulation would not only draw on a large number of examples — much larger than is presently the fashion — but it would also include the citation of specific cases; as a result, any uncertainty about the standing, interpretation, or scope of the "rule" could be settled by reference to the deciding cases.

Notice that the first commentary made use of what might be called the principle of replicated persuasion. By submitting part of the clinical material to a series of outside panels, I was able to corroborate the truth value of the analyst's interpretation that the name of the medicine was encoded in the dream. If outside judges were able to supply the name of the burn medicine, then we have further proof that the name was actually encoded in the dream; external validation minimizes the possibility that awareness of the name was triggered (in the patient) by some other set of circumstances. Replicated persuasion of this kind adds to the benchmark status of the clinical incident by significantly grounding the account in a framework of events that go beyond the original happening. In much the same way, a benchmark case in the law accumulates status when it is repeatedly cited in winning decisions, for this is a sign that other lawyers found the case convincing (a parallel mark of replicated persuasion).

As specific cases are accumulated which reveal similar phenomena, it then becomes possible to study them retrospectively and look for items in common. Suppose in a sample of dreams-leading-to-recovered-memories it was found that the theme of forgetting was explicit in some and implicit in others. It then becomes possible to look more closely at the first set and compare the nature of the remembering in those examples with the nature of remembering in the other cases. Experiments of this kind could be routinely carried out on the accumulated record and would carry significant weight because the cases are formulated independently of the hypothesis being tested (there is no danger of confounding one with another) and because it is possible to split the sample, use one part to develop the hypothesis and the second part to test it. It goes without saying that any inductive rule which was grounded on ten or more clinical examples would immediately acquire more authority than the majority of psychoanalytic propositions currently populating our theory.

If cases are collected with an eye toward the future and in full awareness that some ambiguities will be resolved as a result of peer commentary, then it is no longer so important for the author/analyst to explain everything. If the first report is recognized to be a first approximation of the final accounting, then the author/analyst no longer need pretend that he is another Sherlock Holmes. The open texture of the clinical material becomes more of an accepted reality and it becomes more natural to admit to ignorance or disbelief when subsequent responses may provide the answer. To speak too knowingly too soon may only choke off later clarification; still worse, it may expose the author's ignorance in the face of peer response.

For a second example, consider the following vignette by Paul Gray:

> A 40-year-old man, one year in analysis, began, midway in an hour, to relate a memory associated with events from the day before. He spoke of his wife's becoming explosively irritable over a trivial occurrence. He told of her yelling at him criticisms which hit on an especially painful set of memories. After describing this in detail, he recalled that some anger welled up in himself. He began to speak of how he had controlled his own outward response by reminding himself that she was premen-

strual at the time, and further, that on the previous night he had been sexually ungratifying to her in a way she must have found very frustrating.

This was a patient whose fear of his aggression in general was severe. His resistance to aggression against the analyst was only slightly worked through. Because of what had occurred earlier in the hour, I knew his associations *included* a displacement of potential criticism or anger having to do with me. The memory reported referred manifestly to a recent episode in which his narcissism had been cruelly hurt. However, the displacement from me to his wife failed to achieve any significant degree of conscious mobilization or expression of aggression even at the safer location. As one can see, additional defensive measures occurred as he began to describe the memory, which was the new location of the drive derivative. That is, his fear of revealing to the analyst his aggression against women . . . forced him to recapitulate, in memory, avenues of bringing his aggression under control — reason, thoughtfulness, self-examination. . . .

In brief, during an analytic hour in which this patient had to avoid anger with his analyst, his solution was a displacement to a memory of another figure who had aroused his aggression. In the presence of the analyst, even in the displacement, the experience of aggression again became unsafe, and the immediate solution was further control — almost to the point of assuming a masochistic orientation. Any reference on the part of the analyst to the memory material, as if he were speaking of the outside event itself, would not only neglect observations about the location of the drive conflicts of the moment and the details of the defensive measures being employed, it would also be taking as literally true something almost certainly distorted, condensed, and out of context. (Gray, 1973, pp. 481–484)

First commentary. The force of the argument depends on the possibility that anger toward his wife represents a displacement of anger toward the analyst; thus the force of argument requires evidence for the latter as much as for the former. But we are only indirectly told about the anger toward the analyst: Earlier in the hour, there had been "potential criticism or anger having to do with me." Was the anger clearly visible or only implied? A full description of the incident would make this distinction clear; if the anger were clearly directed at the analyst, then it seems quite straightforward to assume that it had been displaced from the wife and to concur in the thrust of Gray's argument. If the anger toward the analyst were, on the other hand, a matter of interpretation, then Gray's general line of reasoning seems more in doubt.

If the grounds for the formulation can be clarified, the incident would gain significantly in its power to persuade. The incident would then represent an example of how attention to a sequence of events *within the hour* takes fullest advantage of the analyst's position and draws the greatest significance from the clinical material, whereas a reference to events outside the hour tends to blur the focus, wrongly transform narrative truth into historical truth, and miss an important opportunity to widen the patient's awareness of the operations of his mind.

Gray's reactions to this commentary, along with the commentary itself, would be added to the original incident. Its future standing would depend on its power to persuade. Subsequent readers might find the enlarged presentation altogether satisfactory — in which case we would have another example of replicated persuasion and the case becomes a landmark specimen. On the other hand, skeptical readers might find that added information did not clarify the argument, perhaps feeling that evidence for anger toward the analyst was rather too indirect to qualify as fact. Greeted by a critical response, Gray might be motivated to come forward with a more persuasive specimen and the cycle of presentation and commentary would start all over. It stands to reason that Gray's second specimen would not only be more persuasive than the first, but it would also contain a more clearly defined clinical example, which would better serve to anchor the meaning of an "inside" interpretation and sharpen the distinction between *inside* and *outside* interpretations (see Gray, 1973). Future uses of these terms could, in turn, all make reference to the specimen case. Because they are anchored to a particular clinical happening, they are less likely to become free-floating metaphors: The meaning of *inside* and *outside* is referred to a specific clinical happening.

For our final example, we look at a fragment of Case C from Gill and Hoffman (1982). The patient, an actress, is talking about some problems with her director (J):

> *P*: Yes, sort of, except I — I know that. I think one thing that he resents about it is that he knows I'm — this may sound weird — but he knows I'm talking to somebody else instead of talking to him. And the reason I think that is because he likes to know what everybody's up to and he likes to, you know, know where they're at. And I think he considers it like a threat to him. Just the way he considers, you know, my talking to G about things a threat. Anytime anybody makes, you know, yells at the top of their lungs about my seeing a shrink, I don't like it. I was very embarrassed when T said it. I mean it's not something I'm particularly proud of, you know. [Pause] You know, with people, with people I know, it's cool but — or with people that I feel comfortable with I guess is a better thing. And I guess what it is, is people that I think are going to stick with me till I get fixed, you see. I remember the thing I didn't like about T saying it was that it's like I assumed that everybody else would say, "Oh we wouldn't, we're not going to have to pay attention to her, you know. Poor crazy girl."
>
> *A*: She doesn't have anything worth paying attention to.
>
> *P*: All right, if you want to put it that way. Or did I already put it that way? You know, I'm getting sick of this. Every time we come back to the same thing and then just stops there. Mental block. Done this routine many times before. I'm thinking of knocking all the books off the wall again. So what about it? (p. 56)

First commentary (Gill and Hoffman):

> The analyst now more clearly refers to the female genital. The patient's response provides us with data which make plausible the inference that the earlier material about the dictatorial man alludes to the analyst implicitly. Even her saying, "All right, if you want to put it that way," suggests that she feels he insists on directing every detail. She is sick of what she experiences as his reiterating this point which still leaves her "in the dark" — i.e., does not contribute to her progress in dealing with the issue. She responds with an angry wish to knock his books off the wall, perhaps because she feels he is mechanically following some formula taken right from a book. (p. 57)

Second commentary (the analyst, some minutes later): "I take the idea about knocking all the books off the wall as if you wanted to knock my penis off" (p. 57).

Third commentary (Gill and Hoffman):

> An almost unbelievably pat interpretation that exemplifies our point. Instead of finding out what she means by wanting to knock down his books, the analyst uses what she has said to reiterate his fixed conviction, which — however correct it may be — she has just characterized as unhelpful. It is far more likely that her conscious experience is that he is repeating a formula from his books and that that is why she wants to knock them down. (pp. 57–58)

Fourth commentary (Malcolm, 1984a):

> The analyst . . . may be the tyrannical prig the annotators say he is, but he could also be a perfectly workmanlike analyst who — following Freud's directive to listen with "closely hovering attention" in order to "put himself in a position to make use of everything he is told for the purposes of interpretation and of recognizing the concealed unconscious material" — had "heard" the patient's unconscious message and reported it accurately. While the literal meaning of the interpretation is outlandish,

> there is plenty of support, not only in psychoanalytic case material but in mythology, anthropology, art, and literature for the theory that a woman's unconscious life is beset by a profound sense of powerlessness, a gnawing dissatisfaction — a feeling for which the term "penis envy" is thoroughly inadequate, not to say extremely irritating to women. (p. 18)

Still missing are rebuttals by (a) the analyst and (b) the patient. The latter is particularly needed because of the ambiguities in the initial selection. The emphasis on being crazy and getting fixed make it sound as if the patient is more concerned with being thought mentally ill than being found defective (castrated), and the analyst, in his eagerness to give the material a standard interpretation, may have overlooked the former in preference for the latter. The second excerpt is equally ambiguous. Does the wish to knock his books off the wall refer to taking pat interpretations from books (as Gill and Hoffman suggest), or does it have a more private meaning? This is not the first time she had the thought; what was its first context and does that give us more insight into its meaning? Once again, the patient's commentary would be helpful.

The range of reactions represented in the commentaries shows once again the undecided nature of the "facts." What is happening depends on who is listening and what theory is being used to decode the material. Where Gill and Hoffman tend to dismiss the penis interpretation as "almost unbelievably pat," Malcolm wonders if perhaps it does indeed lie in the material. Was the analyst really listening carefully and empathically, or is he not listening at all, merely waiting for a chance to impose his interpretations on the patient? If the latter is more the case, the patient finds herself in the uncomfortable position of having just experienced in the transference the very thing she complained about at work — the feeling that she is not being listened to. Is there some lawful connection between her statement that "we're not going to have to pay attention to her" and the fact that the analyst, a few minutes later, did exactly that? Commentary by the analyst might shed light on this problem. Even without it, we have an interesting specimen of how an "outside" complaint turns into an "inside" experience.

The wide range of commentaries should make us particularly skeptical of the seamless narrative account. If there is no agreement on a small fragment of the hour, we have little reason to believe that cases written in the Sherlock Holmes tradition carry much in the way of either narrative or paradigmatic truth. But the commentaries do not merely disagree; what is more important from the standpoint of hermeneutics is the way in which different reactions enlarge our understanding of the text, providing us with a multiple set of meanings. Some of these the patient may have had in mind; some may be in her preconscious; and some may be only in the mind of the analyst or the commentator. A similar expansion takes place in the law.

> First and more obviously, a series of cases elaborating the tensions implicit in a central statement of value — say that of freedom of the press — gradually gives to its key terms a kind of richness and complexity and clarity, a location in our experience, that they could not otherwise have. The world often presents cases no mind could anticipate, in circumstances no one could wholly foresee, and in such instances the meaning the law gives to its governing words must be new (however the case is decided), for the meaning is in large part derived from a context that is new. (White, 1985, p. 117)

Many other commentaries could be added to this account; some have been published elsewhere without an explicit reference to the legal model. We have already noted the commentary on the Schwaber vignette (presented in Chapter IV; see Davison et al., 1986, pp. 286–288).

Psychoanalysis and Literature

If psychoanalysis bears some similarity to the law and if the application of legal metaphors helps to show more clearly the nature of psychoanalytic wisdom, the process of carrying out this comparison makes clear why psychoanalysis is not literature—even though it has some literary qualities and is often represented in a partly fictitious manner. Or to put it the other way around, literature, as represented by the Sherlock Holmes tradition, is a bad metaphor for either theory or practice. Literature is a bad model because it pretends to a kind of narrative smoothness which can never be achieved; furthermore, it pretends to a kind of detective-story mastery of all the details whereas in practice many details are never understood. Literature is a bad model because it rests on the assumption that there are any number of ways of representing the world and that any one of them will do, that we know nothing for certain, and that, in the last analysis, narrative truth carries the day.

Psychoanalysis, on the other hand, does not take the position that anything goes; it is clearly governed by certain restraints which are transmitted through theory and training and by certain procedures which are instantiated by cases. Certain interpretations are preferred over others; certain strategies of interpretation are wiser than others; some patients get better and some get worse. This is hardly the case with literature, which is always searching for new combinations of fact and fiction, for new forms of telling a story, and for new ways of fooling and entertaining the reader. Although literature is related to reality, the relationship is highly variable, depending on the genre and the intentions of the author. Its coverage of the world tends to be anecdotal rather than systematic, and although beauty is truth, it is never the whole truth.

Psychoanalytic theory is also related to reality, but in a much more dedicated fashion. Many analysts would agree with McIntosh when he writes that "it is the context of the practice of psychoanalysis which supplies the key rationale for the structural theory." A somewhat smaller number, however, would agree that "as long as this theory is useful to the analyst in the conduct of therapy, its epistemological basis is solid" (1979, p. 427). For reasons just discussed, theory can be loosely mapped onto clinical happenings with no likelihood that the latter will change the former. Bad theory, particularly when couched in evenly suspended metaphor, can easily coexist with any number of clinical happenings which have no bearing on the theory. It is more than a little wishful to define epistemology in terms of usefulness and to do so puts theory in the same class as myth and folklore.

If theory grows out of practice (and it is defined by practice as much as by defining proposition), then it would seem all the more important to make the clinical accounts as detailed as we can manage. Only then will discovery be possible; only then will the clinical findings lead to new theory. If building theory is similar to electing candidates, as Simon (1983) has suggested, then we need an informed electorate with access to the full range and richness of the clinical encounter. The democratic process of theory-making is not served by narratized accounts which rely mainly on metaphor. If theory is to grow beyond metaphor, it must be exposed to the specifics of the clinical encounter. The previous section provides one model; the Hampstead Index, organized by Anna Freud and her colleagues, provides another; Rapaport's commentaries on selected papers (1951) provides a third.

Because the specifics do not always lend themselves to tellable stories, literature is clearly not the metaphor of choice. Specifics are important because precedent and tradition are almost as important in psychoanalysis as in law; a rule or concept is often, as we have seen, formulated in terms of the clinical account. Literature is much less bound by history, and does not return to the same issue, over and over, in an attempt to clarify and understand. Repetition (after a certain point) gets in the way of a good story.

If psychoanalysis, in common with law, rests on both cases and rules, then it becomes urgently important that we expand our case reports and develop a new genre of informed peer commentary. The open texture of the clinical account thrives on this kind of dialogue, and its very lack of closure stands out in contrast to the false finality of the Sherlock Holmes adventure. It should be apparent by now that the two traditions cannot coexist: If we continue to read and write narratized case reports, we will never have the kind of multilayered archive necessary to bring about systematic change in theory and we will never have the data base needed to distinguish between live and dead metaphor. In the absence of a rich heritage of clinical records, our theory runs the risk of becoming more and more uncoupled from the data, and changing, inevitably, from live to dead metaphor and from dead metaphor to myth.

When Freud told us, fairly late in life (1933), that he was more interested in psychoanalysis as a body of truths than as a method of treatment, he was clearly hoping to develop a list of axioms which would provide the foundations for a theory of the mind. These truths, as we have seen, are hard to formulate apart from the specifics of the clinical encounter. When we move too quickly into abstractions, we end up with half-truths in the form of metaphors, and unless we are careful, these metaphors will gradually change, in the course of time, from live to dead. But psychoanalysis is not rule-bound; it is case specific. We come back to the law as the best guiding metaphor; it reminds us that rules can never stand alone and that it is the specifics of the here-and-now which make all the difference. Those who wanted science may be disappointed; on the other hand, if we adopt a metaphor which more truly fits the problem, we may be edging toward the algebra which forms the beginning of science.

CHAPTER VII

The Post-Freudian
Metaphor

Until we came to realize that the Freudian approach is only one of many possibilities, it would have been unthinkable to define it as a metaphor. Until that step was taken, it would have been unthinkable to seriously consider the subject of the present chapter. But if there is reason to stand back and see the current Zeitgeist as reflecting a specific climate of opinion, then it becomes possible to consider other metaphors as well. In this chapter, we will take a hard look at one of the more compelling alternatives.

We have seen throughout the book how easy it is to project meaning onto meaninglessness. We noted, in Chapter II, that one of the primary supports for the substantive unconscious was the need to find order beneath the surface of disorder. The need to find some kind of order, even if illusory, is one of the forces which tends to perpetuate the Freudian metaphor, often to its disadvantage. But there is growing evidence, from a number of directions, that there is more randomness in the world than we like to imagine, that the scrambled surface is not always deceptive, and that the complete account of a happening may sometimes never be discovered. We are used to hearing this argument applied to situations in the physical sciences in which many variables are operating simultaneously (e.g., meteorology), but it is now becoming clear that randomness can occur quite rapidly (and unpredictably) even in cases which use relatively few variables (see Crutchfield et al., 1986).

To say that not everything can be explained raises once again the possibility of not knowing, and this condition carries unpleasant connotations. It was rarely confronted during the Freudian Age because of the belief that *the answer* could always be found, buried beneath layers of surface distortion or behind years of past experience. It was this belief in an underlying order which increased our tolerance of the bizarre and the problematic, and which fueled ever-longer analyses and increased the number of re-analyses. These repeated attempts to find *the answer* frequently only postponed the inevitable and put off, as long as possible, the possibility that perhaps there is, in some situations, no good answer after all. The modern, post-Freudian theory of dreams makes this position quite clear (see McCarley and Hobson, 1977). This theory argues that the stream of images we experience during the night are the result of random firings of the pontine reticular neurons. These images are then subjected to the sense-making properties of the forebrain and we wake up with a semi-believable narrative which, in turn, is further streamlined by the familiar functions of secondary revision. It would be interesting to apply a similar theory to the contents of free associations because here, too, the appearing structure may often be the final common pathway of many contributing factors and not evidence for one underlying pattern. The fact that the patient or analyst can make sense of these productions says nothing about the presence of an overall structure.

To begin to admit that for some events there is no explanation and that the surface of the world is frequently devoid of meaning is to come face to face with a terrifying possibility.

This is the challenge posed by the post-Freudian metaphor, and the terror behind this challenge accounts for many of the more recent efforts to salvage the system at whatever cost (see Brenner and his firm belief that psychoanalysis is a "science like any other"; see Wasserman, 1984, and his determined critique of the post-Freudian theory of dreams). To be faced with an unknowable world brings us back, once again, to the spiritual crisis of the Middle Ages, when it was recognized that the Hand of God was not accountable for everything, and to the crisis of the Renaissance, when the power of the alchemists began to give way to the search for real causes by the new breed of experimentalists (see Vickers, 1984).

The fear of the unknowable has been described by Bernstein (1983) as the Cartesian anxiety—the fear that nothing is fixed and that, in the last analysis, nothing is known. The choice is familiar:

> Either there is some support for our being, a fixed foundation for our knowledge, or we cannot escape the forces of darkness that envelop us with madness, with intellectual and moral chaos. . . . At the heart of the objectivist's vision, and what makes sense of his or her passion, is the belief that there are or must be some fixed, permanent constraints to which we can appeal and which are secure and stable. (Bernstein, 1983, pp. 18–19)

But we are now coming to realize that the options are somewhat less polarized. New investigations of randomness and chaos in the physical sciences have introduced some important distinctions. It is now widely believed that what is random is not necessarily accidental. Current theory forces us to grapple with the paradox that "chaos is deterministic, generated by fixed rules that do not themselves involve any elements of chance . . . [In other words], there is order in chaos" (Crutchfield et al., 1986, p. 46). The more sophisticated approach teaches us that much of what is seemingly random can ultimately be explained in terms of quite simple laws, but that in many cases these laws remain to be discovered. Conversely, it makes us aware that a combination of even a small number of principles, given enough time, will produce an indeterminate pattern.

> Chaos brings a new challenge to the reductionist view that a system can be understood by breaking it down and studying each piece. This view has been prevalent in science in part because there were so many systems for which the behavior of the whole is indeed the sum of its parts. Chaos demonstrates, however, that a system can have complicated behavior that emerges as a consequence of simple, nonlinear interaction of only a few components. (Crutchfield et al., p. 56)

Given the importance of the total system in deriving its underlying principles (even if this derivation may be ultimately incomplete), it becomes all the more important to respect the details of the clinical encounter — to treat as almost sacred the particular features of any specific happening. Tracy reminds us of J. B. S. Haldane's famous admonition: "Nature is not only stranger than we imagine; it is stranger than we can possibly imagine" (Tracy, 1981, p. 359). In the search for understanding, there is developing, on many fronts, a widespread interest in the concrete and the everyday. Tracy makes us realize a growing awareness of what he calls the "extraordinariness of the ordinary" (p. 382). We are participating in a "journey of intensification into the concreteness of each particular reality," sharpening our "astonishment at the contingency, the need-not-have-been-ness of each particular reality" (p. 382). Edelson reminds us of the special significance of idiosyncratic detail in the search for evidential support of the theory (1984, p. 137).

Details are sacred because they contain the wisdom of the clinical happening; this wisdom may not be Freud's wisdom, and for that reason, we must be open to what the specimens have to tell us and find ways of making them available for study from a variety of different points of view. The new theory of chaos is paradoxically reassuring because it suggests that the patterns waiting to be discovered may be much simpler than what appears on the surface; at the same time, they may not belong to the received wisdom of psychoanalytic theory and they may not, when finally discovered, explain *all* features of the clinical event. The new theory teaches us that random is a more relative term than we had been taught; that it does not necessarily connote the forces of darkness; and that it is amenable to investigation — there are, in other words, several orders of randomness. But it also teaches us that knowledge is lost if we leap too quickly at explanation.

The post-Freudian metaphor would suggest that we must find ways of separating the domain of possible discoveries from the domain of apparently random happenings, and that the Freudian approach, invaluable and irreplaceable in some contexts, may be misguided and inappropriate in others. Orthodox psychoanalytic theory excludes the random; the seemingly meaningless, according to theory, also has a pattern which merely takes somewhat longer to be discovered. And the search can be endless as we have seen, because the lack of discovery is frequently used as justification for continuing to look. While certain kinds of interpretations are falsifiable, it is never possible to falsify the assumption that the true meaning lies somewhere beneath the surface — and so the search continues.

Under what conditions can we apply the Freudian metaphor and what signs do we have that this approach is useful? The preceding discussion of the tannic acid dream makes quite clear the importance of replication. If an underlying sequence or interpretation can be repeatedly documented, we have the same kind of redundant confirmation that underlies the experimental sciences. Replicated manifestations in our clinical work lead to replicated persuasion, and we need look no further to know that we have found a convincing way of accounting for surface discontinuity. We can, if we wish, expand this explanation into a full-fledged theory which moves us beyond metaphor and, with luck, into science. But there are many times when no redundancy appears and when each new event calls for a new interpretation. We hear samples of these one-time interpretations in public discourse all the time and they represent a gross misuse of the Freudian metaphor. "He broke his leg while skiing because he had an argument with his wife." "He forgot the appointment because he didn't want to come." "He mispronounced his boss's name because he didn't want the raise." *Post hoc, ergo propter hoc*; these are all misapplications of the Freudian metaphor because they play on the maxim that contiguity is causal. Sometimes this form of explanation is true — but not in every case. Because of their one-time nature, these examples lack the certainty that comes from repeated manifestations; what is more, they are all devoid of context and they never make any appeal to alternative forms of explanation.

If replication, convergence, or recursion are all positive indicators in support of the Freudian metaphor, what should be listed as inconclusive evidence? We have already mentioned the suspicion we should attach to the rule of one behavior — one hypothesis. Not only does it clearly fail the replication test, but we have seen in Chapter V how easily two disparate pieces of data can be linked together and how few of these soft pattern matches are truly the two sides of cause and effect. Because soft pattern matches are so easy to discover, their appearance cannot be used to support the Freudian metaphor.

Suspicion should also be attached to mere associations and the uncritical tendency to give them all equal weight as evidence. We discussed in Chapter V the difference between primary and secondary associations. This confusion overlaps with what Grünbaum (1984) has labeled the Thematic Affinity Fallacy. He makes it clear that associations to a dream or a slip of the tongue or some other piece of target behavior arising *after* the event are not necessarily from the same domain as associations which *caused* the event (see also Spence, 1981). To put the point another way, we can no longer assume that free association provides privileged access to the substantive unconscious and, as a consequence, no longer assume that whatever emerges in the way of clinical material has a necessary bearing on the target event. (Once we admit that the substantive unconscious is more metaphorical than real, we may be less tempted to commit this error because we no longer assume that associations after the fact are necessarily pointing to something inside the head.)

At the same time, the attempt to distinguish between primary and secondary associations does not lead to the conclusion that all associations are suspect. Here is where the archival record comes into its own. We have seen that the law is "what the courts decide"; by the same token, psychoanalysis is what psychoanalysts do. The richness of the clinical encounter has more to tell us about the nature of human beings than the bare bones of our theory, particularly when the theory rests on unfalsifiable metaphor which carries little more than narrative appeal. The richness of the clinical encounter can only be understood by studying what goes on within the session. The interchange must first be illuminated by the treating analyst and then opened up to a range of clinical commentaries which will identify ambiguity, clarify problems of reference, add further interpretations which lie beyond the horizon of the treating analyst, and in this and other ways, progressively clarify and unpack the underlying happening. Specimen happenings, when and if they occur, could have the standing of landmark cases in the law; they could serve as anchors for specific concepts and benchmarks for theoretical discussion. (Consider how the discussion of the concept, therapeutic alliance, might have prospered if a clear-cut instance had been available for discussion—see Spence, 1982a, pp. 201–211, for what happened when no specimen case was available.)

As specimen cases are identified, they provide the referents for specific theoretical concepts. As the concepts change (because of new observations or because of refinements of theory), the standing of the specimen case may change as well; in some cases, it might be superseded by a new specimen; in others, it would be clarified by a new series of commentaries. The study of the law makes clear that cases are always determining and that it is usually a mistake to generate a rule by drawing an inference from a set of examples; psychoanalysis would seem to follow the same approach.

To return to the unpacked data of the clinical session would help map out the domain of material that seems accessible to the Freudian metaphor. We need to establish the boundary between this domain and those of other regions which seem more governed by random events. This, too, is a relative judgment, depending on time and context; what is not understood today may well become quite simple tomorrow; what seems random today may be lawful tomorrow. But there is a difference between declaring lawfulness by default, relying on unpublished evidence and argument by authority—and convincing the reader that lawfulness really follows from the nature of the evidence—i.e., allowing the reader to participate in the "conversation." In similar fashion, there is a difference between admitting ignorance in a case where no clear pattern exists, and conjuring up an explanation because of an outmoded axiom that everything can be explained. That line of argument takes us back to the Middle Ages and marks a retreat from metaphor to mythology.

The full meaning of the clinical report will not, it is clear, be revealed by any simple combination of internal unpacking and external commentary. A new kind of hermeneutic discipline must also be developed which takes nothing for granted, which cares less about standard theory than new formulation, and which takes the task of interpretation more seriously than any other endeavor. This new brand of tough-minded hermeneutics assumes that not everything has a pattern, or more specifically, it assumes that no pattern exists until it is discovered. We will call this approach the null position (comparable to the null hypothesis in statistics); it asserts that no regularities can be assumed until they have been established beyond reasonable doubt (a more elaborated presentation can be found in Spence, 1987). The null position has much in common with the realist view of science set forth by Bhaskar (1975) and more recently by Manicas and Secord (1983). Their position assumes that there is "no pre-interpreted 'given' and that the test of truth cannot be 'correspondence.' Epistemologically, there can be nothing *known* to which our ideas can correspond" (p. 401). They go so far as to argue that only one science is grounded on specific causal regularities, and that science is celestial mechanics.

The null position demands relentless suspicion of all possible contaminating conditions, a skeptical attitude which doubts all findings until they are replicated and/or independently arrived at, and a steadfast openness to new discoveries and new findings. It sees true explanation as the exception rather than the rule, but jealousy guards any explanation which meets all necessary requirements because it has the status of a true discovery, a landmark specimen. It is important to realize the bearing of the null position on the context of discovery. If I make no assumptions about lawfulness or pre-existing pattern, then the pattern which *does* emerge — the pattern which I generate inductively from a series of non-chance differences — is more likely to be something truly new and different. Thus the strict adoption of the null position allows me to see the world in a radically new manner. It goes without saying that too-slavish adherence to the Freudian metaphor tends to perpetuate the same old patterns. So long as we assume that certain patterns are waiting to be discovered, we will always be able to find them; in so doing, we are engaged in pseudo-confirmation and, ultimately, in pseudo-science.

To accept the null position is to assume that there are few, if any, givens "out there" against which our stories can be checked; as a result, we must give up the correspondence theory of truth. How, then, do we arrive at firm conclusions? One of the most persuasive answers comes from Habermas (see Thompson and Held, 1982) in his belief that truth is arrived at through dialogue and argumentation leading to consensus. Theory statements, he would claim, are not true because they perfectly describe the world, but because they achieve better and better interpretations of it.

The dialogic nature of truth-seeking puts a special premium on public discussion; it replaces experiment by conversation.

> Real conversation [writes Tracy in his recent discussion of religious pluralism] occurs only when the participants allow the question, the subject matter, to assume primacy. It occurs only when our usual fears about our own self-image die: whether that fear is expressed in either arrogance or scrupulosity matters little. That fear dies only because we are carried along, and sometimes away, by the subject matter itself into the rare event or happening named "thinking" and "understanding." For understanding *happens*; it *occurs* not as the pure result of personal achievement but in the back-and-forth movement of conversation itself. (1981, p. 101)

In the tough-minded hermeneutics which is grounded in the null position — and which makes up the core of the post-Freudian metaphor — argument by authority must necessarily give way to open dialogue, sufficiently accessible to encourage wide public involvement. Second, there must be public criteria for success or failure of any particular line of reasoning; arguments cannot be settled, as is usually the case, by appeals to authority. Third, there must always be the possibility for free assent to the argument — the chance to reach what Habermas calls an "uncompelled consensus."

In the context of the post-Freudian position, we can look back on the changing face of psychoanalytic theory. We have seen how Freud began his work by invoking certain tentative metaphors which could be seen as temporary scaffolding for the larger structure, to be exchanged for others more appropriate because "they are not the bottom but the top of the whole structure, and they can be replaced and discarded without damaging it" (1914, p. 77). But they were not replaced, as we have seen; they soon became a part of the structure and their description changed from the language of observation to the language of mythology. When the id could be defined as a "cauldron of seething excitations" and when Sterba described how impressed and fascinated he was "by the id contents which psychoanalysis enables us to discover" (1953, pp. 17–18), we have moved to the domain of folklore and speculation. By the time the id is described in frankly metaphorical language, it has been effectively disconnected from the data of observation and from that point on, the theory is in the hands of the rhetoricians.

We can see the rush to reification as an all-too-human reaction against the endless nature of the search. It is many times more comforting to have a concrete image — the "seething cauldron" — in place of a bundle of uncertainties. It is much more reassuring to have a final set of structures or mechanisms than to admit that we are still in the early stages of theory formation and that our options must, at all costs, remain open. But short-term relief may be a long-term loss. To settle prematurely for *any* set of concepts is to blind ourselves to a multitude of observations which lie outside the metaphor. We are now beginning to realize that Freud was quite wrong when he said that "the foundation of science, upon which everything rests . . . is observation alone" (1914, p. 77). Observation is always guided by theory; where and how we look is always guided by metaphor.

The wisdom of the case method would seem to complement the wisdom of science. Working within a natural science model, we might accumulate a sample of observations in order to inductively generate a concept. This concept could then be tested — either inside or outside the session — and, depending on the outcome, further refined and then further tested. But the history of the law tells us that concepts of this kind make bad law because they do not fully represent what is common to all cases. The interplay of circumstance and intention has a subtlety which is always specific to the individual instance and to jump from the individual case to the general rule is to abandon the very subtlety we most highly cherish. For this reason, it would seem as if empirical research in psychoanalysis is somewhat premature because we are in no position to identify what propositions should be tested. There is certainly nothing to be achieved by attempts to validate metaphor.

The open texture of the law is an accepted part of the judicial tradition; we are only beginning to accept the open texture of psychoanalysis. This quality is troubling to many because it opens the way to ambiguity, multiple meanings, and a lack of certainty; by the same token, it opens the way to continuing conversation. Meanings are not fixed; at the same time, it is not true that anything goes. Psychoanalysis is caught up in the same need to get beyond the either/or, to get beyond objectivism and relativism, that is facing all aspects of contemporary thinking.

> Central to this new understanding [writes Bernstein] is a dialogical model of rationality that stresses the practical, *communal* character of this rationality in which there is choice, deliberation, interpretation, judicious weighing and application of "universal criteria," and even rational disagreement about which criteria are relevant and most important. It is an illusion to think that before the fact we always know (in principle) what will count as a decisive refutation of a proposed theory or that the epistemologist can discover fixed, permanent rules that are to be used to resolve differences. Various theories of "instant rationality" fail to capture what is distinctive about science as a rational activity. Yet alternative paradigms, theories, and research programs can be warranted by communal rational argumentation. (1983, p. 172)

To open up the conversation between clinical findings and received theory is to treat the observations of colleagues no differently from the observations of patients. In both cases, we must beware of premature closure and oversimplified narrative, be wary of facile formulation (which masquerades as explanation), and expect no easy answers. Where Holzman (1985) asks (quoting Freud) whether the therapy is destroying the science, we would turn the question around and suggest that without the therapy there can be no science. The therapy hides our wisdom, and the problem facing psychoanalysis is to find ways of extracting this wisdom — not to find ways of becoming more of a science. Because whether it is a true science, a half-science, or something that is still looking for a name,

> the task is always to find the resources within us to understand what confronts us as alien. And such understanding requires a dialectical play between our own pre-understandings and the forms of life that we are seeking to understand. It is in this way that we can risk and test our prejudices and we can not only come to understand what is "other" than us but also better understand ourselves. (Bernstein, 1983, p. 173)

Time, however, is running out. A misguided devotion to unsystematic story-telling, grounded in the Sherlock Holmes tradition, has left psychoanalysis with only a scanty set of archives and almost no reliable specimens. A profession noted for its fascination with the past is rapidly losing its own, and as the past disappears, anecdote, mythology and dead metaphor take its place. Can we reverse the process before it is too late?

References

Abend, S. M. (1986). Countertransference, empathy, and the analytic ideal: The impact of life stresses on analytic capability. *Psychoanalytic Quarterly* 55: 563–575.

Abrams, M. H. (1958). *The Mirror and the Lamp*. New York: Norton.

Barratt, B. (1977). Freud's psychology as interpretation. In T. Shapiro (Ed.), *Psychoanalysis and Contemporary Science, Volume 5*. New York: International Universities Press.

Berlin, I. (1976). *Vico and Herder: Two Studies in the History of Ideas*. New York: Viking.

———— (1981). The concept of scientific history. In H. Hardy (Ed.), *Concepts and Categories: Philosophical Essays by Isaiah Berlin*. New York: Penguin Books.

Bernstein, R. J. (1983). *Beyond Objectivism and Relativism*. Philadelphia: University of Pennsylvania Press.

———— (1987). Interpretation and its discontents: The choreography of criticism. In S. Messer, L. Sass, and R. Woolfolk (Eds.), *Hermeneutics and Psychological Theory: Perspectives on Personality, Psychotherapy and Psychopathology*. New Brunswick, N.J.: Rutgers University Press.

Bettelheim, B. (1983). *Freud and Man's Soul*. New York: Knopf.

Bhaskar, R. (1975). *A Realist Theory of Science*. Leeds, England: Leeds Books.

Black, M. (1962). *Models and Metaphors: Studies in Language and Philosophy*. Ithaca, N.Y.: Cornell University Press.

Blight, J. (1981). Must psychoanalysis retreat to hermeneutics? Psychoanalytic theory in the light of Popper's evolutionary epistemology. *Psychoanalysis and Contemporary Thought* 4: 147–205.

Bowers, K. (1984). On being unconsciously influenced and informed. In K. S. Bowers and D. Meichenbaum (Eds.), *The Unconscious Reconsidered*. New York: Wiley.

Breger, L. (1982). Insight and gurus (review of *Discovering the Mind, Volume 3*, by Walter Kaufman). *Contemporary Psychology* 27: 122–124.

Brenner, C. (1955). *An Elementary Textbook of Psychoanalysis*. New York: International Universities Press.

———— (1982). *The Mind in Conflict*. New York: International Universities Press.

Brooks, P. (1984). *Reading for the Plot*. New York: Knopf.

Bruner, J. (1984). Narrative and paradigmatic modes of thought. Invited address presented at the Annual Meeting of the American Psychological Association, Toronto, August 1984.

Carveth, D. (1984). The analyst's metaphors: A deconstructionist perspective. *Psychoanalysis and Contemporary Thought* 7: 491–560.

Cooper, A. (1986). Some limitations on therapeutic effectiveness: The "burnout syndrome" in psychoanalysis. *Psychoanalytic Quarterly* 55: 576–598.

Crutchfield, J. P., Farmer, J. D., Packard, N. H., and Shaw, R. S. (1986). Chaos. *Scientific American* 255: 46–57.

Cuddon, J. A. (1977). *A Dictionary of Literary Terms*. New York: Doubleday.

Culler, J. (1982). *On Deconstruction*. Ithaca: Cornell University Press.

Dahl, H. (1983). On the definition and measurement of wishes. In J. Masling (Ed.), *Empirical Studies of Psychoanalytic Theories*. Hillsdale, N.J.: Erlbaum.

Dahl, H., Teller, V., Moss, D., and Trujillo, M. (1978). Countertransference examples of the syntactic expression of warded-off contents. *Psychoanalytic Quarterly* 47: 339–363.

Davison, W. T., Bristol, C., and Prag, M. (1986). Turning aggression on the self: A study of psychoanalytic process. *Psychoanalytic Quarterly* 55: 273–295.

Dewald, P. A. (1972). *The Psychoanalytic Process*. New York: Basic Books.

Doyle, A. Conan (1938). *The Complete Sherlock Holmes*. New York: Garden City.

Dreyfus, H. and Wakefield, J. (1987). Alternative philosophical conceptualizations of psychopathology. In *Hermeneutics and Psychological Theory. See* Messer et al., 1987.

Dworkin, R. (1986). *Law's Empire*. Cambridge: Harvard University Press.

Eagle, M. (1980). A critical examination of motivational explanation in psychoanalysis. *Psychoanalysis and Contemporary Thought* 3: 329–380.

Edelson, J. (1983). Freud's use of metaphor. *The Psychoanalytic Study of the Child* 38: 17–59.

Edelson, M. (1983). Is testing psychoanalytic hypotheses in the psychoanalytic situation really impossible? *The Psychoanalytic Study of the Child* 38: 61–109.

——— (1984). *Hypothesis and Evidence in Psychoanalysis*. Chicago: University of Chicago Press.

Eissler, K. (1963). Freud and the psychoanalysis of history. *Journal of the American Psychoanalytic Association* 11: 675–703.

Felman, S. (1983). Beyond Oedipus: The specimen story of psychoanalysis. *MLN* 98(5): 1021–1053.

Fisher, S. and Greenberg, R. (1977). *The Scientific Credibility of Freud's Theories and Therapy*. New York: Basic Books, Inc.

Fodor, J. (1983). *The Modularity of Mind*. Cambridge: MIT Press.

Freud, A. (1937). *The Ego and the Mechanisms of Defence*. London: Hogarth Press.

Freud, S. (1900). The interpretation of dreams. *Standard Edition* 4, 5. New York: Norton, 1953.

——— (1905). Fragment of an analysis of a case of hysteria. *Standard Edition* 7: 7–122. New York: Norton, 1953.

——— (1909). Analysis of a phobia in a five-year-old boy. *Standard Edition* 10: 1–149. New York: Norton, 1955.

——— (1912). Recommendations to physicians practising psychoanalysis. *Standard Edition* 12: 111–120. New York: Norton, 1958.

——— (1913). On beginning the treatment (Further recommendations on the technique of psychoanalysis I). *Standard Edition* 12: 121–144. New York: Norton, 1958.

——— (1914). On narcissism. *Standard Edition* 14: 73–102. New York: Norton, 1957.

——— (1915a). Instincts and their vicissitudes. *Standard Edition* 14: 109–140. New York: Norton, 1957.

——— (1915b). Repression. *Standard Edition* 14: 141–158. New York: Norton, 1957.

——— (1915c). The unconscious. *Standard Edition* 14: 161–215. New York: Norton, 1957.

——— (1923a). The ego and the id. *Standard Edition* 19: 3–66. New York: Norton, 1957.

——— (1923b). Remarks on the theory and practice of dream-interpretation. *Standard Edition* 19: 107–121. New York: Norton, 1957.

——— (1925). An autobiographical study. *Standard Edition* 20: 7–74. New York: Norton, 1959.

——— (1932a). The dissection of the psychical personality (New introductory lectures on psycho-analysis). *Standard Edition* 22: 57–80. New York: Norton, 1964.

——— (1932b). Explanations, applications and orientations (New introductory lectures on psycho-analysis). *Standard Edition* 22: 136–157. New York: Norton, 1964.

——— (1933). The question of a Weltanschauung. (New introductory lectures on psycho-analysis). *Standard Edition* 22: 158–182. New York: Norton, 1964.

Gadamer, H-G. (1975). *Truth and Method.* London: Sheed and Ward.

Gardner, H. (1983). *Frames of Mind.* New York: Basic Books.

Gaylin, W. (1982). *The Killing of Bonnie Garland.* New York: Simon and Schuster.

Geuss, R. (1981). *The Idea of a Critical Theory.* Cambridge, England: Cambridge University Press.

Gill, M. M. and Hoffman, I. Z. (1982). *Analysis of Transference, Volume II.* New York: International Universities Press.

Glover, E. (1931). The therapeutic effect of inexact interpretation. *International Journal of Psycho-Analysis* 12: 397–411.

Gray, P. (1973). Psychoanalytic technique and the ego's capacity for viewing intrapsychic activity. *Journal of the American Psychoanalytic Association* 21: 474–494.

———— (1982). "Developmental lag" in the evolution of technique for psychoanalysis of neurotic conflict. *Journal of the American Psychoanalytic Association* 30: 621–655.

Greenacre, P. (1952). Re-evaluation of the process of working through. *International Journal of Psycho-Analysis* 33: 6–77.

Greenson, R. (1967). *The Technique and Practice of Psychoanalysis.* New York: International Universities Press.

Grice, H. P. (1967). Logic and Conversation. Unpublished manuscript, William James Lectures at Harvard.

Grünbaum, A. (1984). *The Foundations of Psychoanalysis.* Berkeley: University of California Press.

Habermas, J. (1983). Paper presented to the Conference on Hermeneutics and Critical Theory, Bryn Mawr College.

Hart, H. L. A. (1961). *The Concept of Law.* London: Oxford University Press.

———— (1967). Problems of philosophy of law. In P. Edwards (Ed.), *The Encyclopedia of Philosophy, Volume 6.* New York: Macmillan.

Harth, E. (1982). *Reflections on the Physical Basis of Consciousness.* New York: Morrow.

Hartmann, H. (1951). Technical implications of ego psychology. In *Essays on Ego Psychology.* New York: International Universities Press, 1964, 142–254.

Hertz, N. (1983). Dora's secrets, Freud's techniques. *Diacritics,* Spring, 65–83.

Hesse, M. (1980). *Revolutions and Reconstructions in the Philosophy of Science.* Bloomington, Ind.: Indiana University Press.

Hirsch, E. D., Jr. (1967). *Validity in Interpretation.* New Haven: Yale University Press.

Holt, R. R. (1962). Individuality and generalization in the psychology of personality. *Journal of Personality* 30: 377–404.

———— (1984). The current status of psychoanalytic theory. Invited address, American Psychological Association, Toronto.

Holzman, P. S. (1985). Psychoanalysis: Is the therapy destroying the science? *Journal of the American Psychoanalytic Association* 33: 725–770.

Jacobsen, P. B. and Steele, R. S. (1979). From present to past: Freudian archeology. *International Review of Psychoanalysis* 6: 349–362.

John, E. R., Tang, Y., Brill, A. B., Young, R., and Ono, K. (1986). Double-labeled metabolic maps of memory. *Science* 233: 1167–1175.

Kanzer, M. (1981). Freud's "Analytic Pact": The standard therapeutic alliance. *Journal of the American Psychoanalytic Association* 29: 69–87.

Kaplan, A. (1981). From discovery to validation. *Journal of the American Psychoanalytic Association* 29: 3–26.

Kosinski, J. (1970). *Being There*. New York: Harcourt Brace Jovanovich.

Kris, E. (1947). The nature of psychoanalytic propositions and their validity. In *Selected Papers of Ernst Kris*. New Haven: Yale University Press, 1975, pp. 3–23.

Lakoff, G. and Johnson, M. (1980). *Metaphors We Live By*. Chicago: University of Chicago Press.

Langs, R. (1981). Modes of "cure" in psychoanalysis and psychoanalytic psychotherapy. *International Journal of Psycho-Analysis* 62: 100–214.

Levi, E. H. (1949). *An Introduction to Legal Reasoning*. Chicago: University of Chicago Press.

Malcolm, J. (1984a). The patient is always right. Review of Gill and Hoffman's Analysis of Transference. *New York Review of Books* 31(20): 13–18.

———— (1984b). *In the Freud Archives*. New York: Knopf.

Manicas, P. T. and Secord, P. F. (1983). Implications for psychology of the new philosophy of science. *American Psychologist* 38: 399–413.

Marcus, S. (1977). Freud and Dora: Story, history, case history. In T. Shapiro (Ed.), *Psychoanalysis and Contemporary Science*,

McCarley, R. and Hobson, J. (1977). The neurobiological origins of psychoanalytic dream theory. *American Journal of Psychiatry* 134: 1211–1221.

McIntosh, D. (1979). The empirical bearing of psychoanalytic theory. *International Journal of Psycho-Analysis* 60: 405–432.

Messer, S. B., Sass, L. A., and Woolfolk, R. L. (1987). (Eds.), *Hermeneutics and Psychological Theory: Perspectives on Personality, Psychotherapy, and Psychopathology*. New Brunswick, N.J.: Rutgers University Press.

Messer, S. and Winokur, M. (1980). Some limits to the integration of psychoanalytic and behavior therapy. *American Psychologist* 35: 818–827.

Morison, S. E. (1942). *Admiral of the Ocean Sea*. Boston: Little Brown.

Neu, J. (1976). Thought, theory, and therapy. In D. P. Spence (Ed.), *Psychoanalysis and Contemporary Science, Volume 4*. New York: International Universities Press.

Ornston, D. (1985). Freud's conception is different from Strachey's. *Journal of the American Psychoanalytic Association* 33: 379–412.

Pepper, S. (1948). *World Hypotheses: A Study in Evidence*. Berkeley, California: University of California Press.

Popper, K. R. (1963). *Conjectures and Refutations: The Growth of Scientific Knowledge*. New York: Harper and Row.

Postman, L. (1963). (Ed.), *Psychology in the Making*. New York: Knopf.

Quine, W. V. and Ullian, J. S. (1978). *The Web of Belief*. Second Edition. New York: Random House.

Rapaport, D. (1951). *Organization and Pathology of Thought*. New York: Columbia University Press.

Reiser, M. (1985). Converging sectors of psychoanalysis and neurobiology: Mutual challenges and opportunity. *Journal of the American Psychoanalytic Association* 33: 11–34.

Ricoeur, P. (1970). *Freud and Philosophy: An Essay on Interpretation*. New Haven: Yale University Press.

———— (1983). Reply to Habermas. Conference on Hermeneutics and Critical Theory, Bryn Mawr College.

Rorty, R. (1979). *Philosophy and the Mirror of Nature*. Princeton, N.J.: Princeton University Press.

Rossner, J. (1983). *August*. Boston: Houghton Mifflin Co.

Runyan, W. M. (1981). Why did Van Gogh cut off his ear? The problem of alternative explanations in psychobiography. *Journal of Personality and Social Psychology* 40: 1070–1077.

———— (1982). In defense of the case study method. *American Journal of Orthopsychiatry* 52: 440–446.

Schachtel, E. (1947). On memory and childhood amnesia. *Psychiatry* 10: 1–26.

Schafer, R. (1976). *A New Language for Psychoanalysis*. New Haven: Yale University Press.

———— (1983). *The Analytic Attitude*. New York: Basic Books.

Schwaber, E. (1981). Empathy: A mode of analytic listening. *Psychoanalytic Inquiry* 1: 357–392.

Shepherd, M. (1985). *Sherlock Holmes and the Case of Doctor Freud*. New York: Methuen.

Shevrin, H. and Dickman, S. (1980). The psychological unconscious. *American Psychologist* 35: 421–434.

Simon, B. (1983). The Oedipus Complex is a hard act to follow. Paper presented at panel, The Oedipus Complex Revisited. Spring Meeting, American Psychoanalytic Association, Philadelphia, May 1983.

Spence, D. P. (1981). Toward a theory of dream interpretation. *Psychoanalysis and Contemporary Thought* 4: 383–405.

———— (1982a). *Narrative Truth and Historical Truth*. New York: W. W. Norton.

———— (1982b). Narrative truth and theoretical truth. *Psychoanalytic Quarterly* 51: 43–69.

———— (1987). Tough and tender minded hermeneutics. In *Hermeneutics and Psychological Theory*. *See* Messer et al., 1987.

Stein, M. (1985). Irony in psychoanalysis. *Journal of the American Psychoanalytic Association* 33: 35–57.

Sterba, R. (1953). Clinical and therapeutic aspects of character resistance. *Psychoanalytic Quarterly* 22: 1–20.

Thompson, J. B. and Held, D. (1982). (Eds.), *Habermas: Critical Debates.* London: Macmillan.

Tracy, D. (1981). *The Analogical Imagination.* New York: Crossroad.

Vickers, B. (1984). (Ed.), *Occult and Scientific Mentalities in the Renaissance.* New York: Cambridge University Press.

Wallerstein, R. S. (1986). *Forty-two Lives in Treatment.* New York: Guilford.

Wasserman, M. D. (1984). Psychoanalytic dream theory and recent neurobiological findings about REM sleep. *Journal of the American Psychoanalytic Association* 32: 831–846.

White, J. B. (1985). *Heracles' Bow: Essays on the Rhetoric and Poetics of the Law.* Madison: University of Wisconsin Press.

Whyte, L. (1960). *The Unconscious Before Freud.* New York: Basic Books.

Index

Abend, Sandor, 45
Abrams, M. H., 120
Adler, Alfred, 174
Alternative explanation, 124, 130, 134, 137, 149, 151, 156, 162, 165, 172, 174, 186, 190, 197, 208, 213
  see also peer commentary; uncompelled consensus
Analyst as sleuth, 192, 199
  see also Sherlock Holmes tradition
Archival account, 113-14, 117, 184
  see also clinical specimen; unpacking; detail, wisdom in
Argument by authority, 73, 86, 118, 120-21, 131-32, 136, 155, 162, 166, 175, 179, 182, 195-97, 210, 212
  see also singular solution

Barratt, Barnaby, 149, 150, 155
Benchmark case, 190-91, 209, 211
  see also clinical specimens; archival account

Berlin, Isaiah, 2-3, 177; on nature of history, 109-10
Bernstein, Richard, 23, 205, 214-15
Bettleheim, Bruno, 1, 3
Bhaskar, R., 211
Black, Max, 1, 4, 78
Blight, James, 77
Bohr, Niels, 11
Bowers, Kenneth, 18, 39
Brenner, Charles, 26, 71, 73-75, 77, 161-62, 164-66, 171, 205
Brentano, Franz, 13
Brooks, Peter, 78, 116, 119, 121, 149
Bruner, Jerome, 142-43

Carveth, D., 6
Case histories as fiction, 119-20, 125, 127, 141, 145, 169, 184
  see also analyst as sleuth; narrative truth; Sherlock Holmes tradition
Case History genre, 113-14, 119, 122, 136
  see also Sherlock Holmes tradition

Chaos, theory of, 205–07
Clinical specimen:
  Appearance of toilet seat, 81
  Cutting liverwurst, 60
  Displacement of anger toward analyst,
    192–95
  Forgetting a man's name, 161–69
  Forgetting name of medication,
    188–90, 207
  Girl in playpen, 55
  Labor Day cancellation, 83–84
  Last session before vacation, 91–109
  Shame of being analyzed, 195–98
Clinical specimens, absence of, 67,
    79–80, 138, 140, 152, 168, 179,
    181, 185, 215
  importance of, 79, 174, 184, 206, 209
Clinical wisdom, 177, 206
Context, boundless domain of, 172, 175
Context of discovery, 52, 149, 153
Context of understanding, see under-
    standing, how context controls
Convergent evidence, 126, 165, 167,
    172, 189, 191, 206, 208
  see also peer commentary
Conversational Implicatures, 87–89
Cooper, Arnold, 74
Correspondence theory of truth, 211–12
  see also positivistic world view
Croce, Benedetto, 177
Crutchfield, J. P., 204, 206
Culler, Jonathan, 90, 106, 172

Dahl, Hartvig, 82, 100, 139
Davison, W. T., 100, 198
Decoding meaning, 148, 151, 156, 191
  see also unpacking
Derrida, Jacques, 106
Descartes, René, 13
Detail, wisdom in, 177, 185, 200, 206
Dewald, Paul, 55, 64, 67
Dialogue, expansion of, 175–76, 182,
    210, 212
  see also argument by authority; singular
    solution
Dickman, Scott, 18, 27
Dilthey, Wilhelm, 76, 177
Disclaimed action, 94–95
Dora Case, 122–23, 130, 133, 144, 147,
    149–50, 154, 175, 186

Dreyfus, Herbert, 13
Dworkin, Ronald, 185–87

Edelson, Marshall, 7, 77, 148, 170, 206
Empathy, 197
  as immaculate perception, 45, 59
  as sympathetic projection, 63
  compared to pathetic fallacy, 63
  mischievous role of, 67
    see also projective fallacy
  nature of, 44, 62
  translation of Einfuhlung, 62
Evenly suspended attention, 157
  as complement to free association, 52
  as conventional belief, 69
  as impartial calculus, 43, 56, 58, 67–69
  as metaphor, 43–69
  standing of, 43

Fabula, 121
Felman, Shoshana, 158
Fisher, Seymour, 170
Foreunderstanding, 90, 146
Free association, as guide to explanation,
    162–65
Free association, as metaphor, 14
Free-floating metaphor, 159, 168
  see also uncoupled metaphor
Freud, Anna, 139, 200
Freud, Sigmund:
  compared to Heidegger, 13
  on Dora Case, 124–26, 128, 138; on
    Little Hans, 59
  on evenly suspended attention, 52; on
    free association, 43
  on grammar of transformations, 20
  on meaning of symptoms, 18
  on metaphor, 1, 3, 8, 57, 78, 117
  on explanation, 9; on observation, 10,
    58–59; on experimental
    verification, 170
  on psychoanalysis as general theory,
    170, 201; as science, 72
  on ego and id, 38; on the id, 11; on
    repressed contents, 38; on the
    unconscious, 12, 31–32
  Standard Edition of, 1, 185

Gadamer, Hans-Georg, 47, 66, 88, 90,
    146, 150, 152

Gardner, Howard, 40
Gaylin, Willard, 105
Geuss, Raymond, 176
Gill, Merton, 99, 135–36, 139–40,
    195–97
Glover, Edward, 108
Gray, Paul, 139, 140, 151–54, 192–95
Greenberg, Roger, 170
Greenson, Ralph, 20–25, 156
Grice, H. P., 87–89
Grübaum, Adolph, 7, 72, 76, 135–37,
    141, 165, 170, 208

Habermas, Jurgen, 47, 49–50, 64, 68,
    176, 178, 212
Haldane, J. B. S., 206
Hart, H. L. A., 180–84
Harth, Erich, 37
Hartmann, Heinz, 139
Heidegger, Martin, 13
Held, D., 212
Herder, Johann Gottfried, 177
Hermaneutic approach, 7, 77, 118, 134,
    141–42, 149, 150–51, 154, 198
  tough-minded, 210–12
Hertz, Neil, 133, 149
Hesse, Mary, 5–6
Hirsch, E. D., 34
Historical truth, 116, 123, 151, 156,
    179, 194
  absence of, 106
  search for, 77–91
  see also clinical specimens; archival
    account
History vs. science, 109–10
Hobson, J., 204
Hoffman, Irwin, 99, 135–36, 139, 140,
    195–97
Holt, Robert, 35, 72, 75–76
Holzman, Philip, 7, 158, 215
Horizontal vs. vertical, consistency of
    principle, 187
  listening, 147–48, 152
  reading, 121

Inside vs. outside interpretation, 194–95,
    198
Interpretation, evidence for, 82, 86, 149
  mistaken, 55, 64, 84–85, 89
  task of, 51

vs. explanation, 132–34, 136, 167, 176

Jacobsen, P. B., 18, 106
James, Henry, 116, 150
James, William, 27
John, E. Roy, 40
Johnson, Mark, 2–4
Jung, Carl Gustav, 174

Kanzer, Mark, 84
Kaplan, Alex, 16
Kassen, Julian, 190
Kosinski, Jerzy, 53–54
Kris, Ernst, 183

Lacan, Jacques, 158
Lakoff, George, 2–4
Langs, Robert, 20–22, 34
Levi, Edward, 180
Listening, between the lines, 45, 144,
    146–47
  for newness, 146, 153
  mishearing while, 45–46, 94, 96–97
  model of, 152
Little Hans Case, 174

Malcolm, Janet, 140, 196–97
Manicas, Peter, 211
Mann, James, 61
Marcus, Steven, 122–23, 127
McCarley, R., 204
McIntosh, D., 180, 199
Merleau-Ponty, Maurice, 13
Messer, Stanley, 27
Metaphor, alive vs. dead, 6, 8, 15, 201
  and algebra, 1, 201
  archeological, 23, 57, 78–79
  as defined by Royal Society, 2
  by Freud, 8
  by Hesse, 5
  by Vico, 2
  as free-floating concept, 10, 12, 15, 39
  see also uncoupled metaphor
  as obstacle to wisdom, 4, 9, 10, 42,
    167–68
  as used by Chance the Gardener, 54,
    62
  fear of, 3
  in physics, 11
  in psychoanalytic theory, 1–16, 76

Metaphor (*continued*)
  in the service of understanding,
    60–61, 68, 212
  literalization of 6–7, 169
  post Freudian, 203–15
    see also chaos, theory of
  transparent nature of, 5
  undeveloped nature of, 1
Metaphor of:
  Chain novel, 185–87
  Going beneath the surface, 30, 76
  Horse and rider, 41
  Innocent analyst, 43–69, 87
  Jigsaw puzzle, 57, 173
  Legal method, 173, 180, 182
  Passenger on the train, 14
    see also free association
  Science, 72, 75, 79
  Seething cauldron, 10, 38, 213
  Timeless unconscious, 12
Model of the mind, breadth vs. depth,
    13–14
Morison, Samuel, 50–51
Multiple interpretation, 57

Narrative explanation, 116, 153
Narrative home, 126, 173
Narrative mode, 143, 145, 162, 164,
    166–67
    see also paradigmatic mode
Narrative persuasion, 116, 120–24, 126,
    130, 138, 144, 161, 164–65, 209
    see also narrative home
Narrative smoothing, 65, 123, 133–42,
    137, 139–40, 143–45, 148, 151,
    153, 155, 158–59
  in service of justification, 133–35
  in service of discovery, 135
    see also singular solution
Narrative tradition, 119–21
Narrative truth, 106, 123, 127, 156, 167,
    194, 199–200, 204
Narrative vs. theory, 112
Neu, Jerome, 61
Nomothetic-idiographic debate, 36
Normative competence, 130, 174

Open texture, 192, 200, 214
Ornston, Darius, 1

Paradigmatic mode, 142, 146, 167
    see also narrative mode
Pathetic fallacy, 62–64, 68
    see also empathy
Pattern match:
  and unconscious fantasy, 19
  failure of, 46
  hard, 22, 27
  interpretation of, 22
  soft, 20, 208
  verification of, 22
Pattern-finding, 117, 207, 211
Peer commentary, 174–75, 179, 188–98,
    200, 209
    see also dialogue, expansion of
Pepper, Stephen, 131–32
Poe, Edgar Allen, 116
Popper, Karl, 31
Positivistic world view, 118, 154
    see also singular solution; transparency
      of meaning
Postman, Leo, 171
Privileged:
  competence, 130, 174
    see also normative competence
  narrative, 124
  withholding, 118, 178
Projection, in the service of understand-
    ing, 44, 46, 59, 61, 64, 86–88
  nature of, 44
  of assumptions, 64
  of feeling, 61
  role in clinical listening, 44, 46, 59
  unwitting (projective fallacy), 46, 50,
    53, 55–56, 58–60, 67, 96–97
Projective fallacy, *see also* unwitting
    projection
Psychoanalysis:
  and law, 179–88, 198, 200, 210, 214
  and literature, 198–201
  as science, 26, 71–112, 154–56, 174,
    185, 205
Psychoanalytic:
  explanation, independent evidence for,
    25
  inflexible nature of, 24
  imperialism, 66, 68
  theory, truth of, 4, 7, 26, 62, 73–74,
    76, 170

Public vs. private explanation, 125, 127, 129–30, 168, 176, 181, 184

Quine, W. V., 79

Randomness, 207, 210
    illusory vs. veridical, 203–05
Rapaport, David, 200
Reader's participation in narrative, 127, 129
    see also alternative explanation; dialogue; normative competence
Reconstruction vs. construction, 77, 92–93, 95, 100, 102–05, 108, 136
Reiser, Morton, 188–89
Replicated persuasion, 191, 194, 207
    see also convergent evidence
Ricoeur, Paul, 66, 149–50, 155, 170
Rorty, Richard, 145, 157
Rosenzweig, Saul, 170
Rule:
    of law, 180
    scope of, 182
Rule-bound, 181–82, 201
Rule-governed, 149, 181–82, 191, 199–200, 209
Runyan, Bruce, 131, 174
Ruskin, John, on pathetic fallacy, 62–63

Schachtel, Ernst, on infantile exprience, 15
Schafer, Roy, 27–28, 61, 78, 94, 106, 108, 169, 187
Schools of therapy, 61
Schwaber, Evelyn, 91–100, 107, 198
Science, as metaphor, 155
Scope of the rule, 180, 182, 191, 214
Secord, Paul, 211
Shepherd, Michael, 149
Sherlock Holmes, 114, 116, 118, 149–50
    as therapist, 115
Sherlock Holmes tradition, 113, 117–19, 122, 133, 137, 141, 145, 153–58, 161–62, 167, 169, 184, 198–99, 201, 215
    see also case study genre; narrative persuasion
Shevrin, Howard, 18, 27
Simon, Bennett, 76, 176, 200

Singular solution, 114, 117, 119, 120, 124, 131, 156
    absence of, 104–05, 107
    axiom of, 57–58, 81, 83–86, 100, 104
Snow, C. P., 71, 76–77
Spence, Donald, 52–53, 135, 165, 208–09, 211
Standard interpretation, 196–97, 211, 215
Steele, Robert, 18, 206
Stein, Martin, 27
Sterba, Richard, 139, 213
Suggestion, role of, 59
Sujet, 121
Surprise in clinical listening, 148
Suspension of disbelief, 120–21

Therapist as sleuth, 114, 116, 141
Thompson, J. B., 212
Titchener, Edward, 62
Tracy, David, 206, 212
Transference, as repetition, 197
    positive, 62
Transformation rules, 20, 33, 75, 79, 128–29, 148–49, 156, 189–90
    calculus of, 79
Transparency of meaning, 56, 81–83, 90–91, 101, 103, 107, 113, 115–16, 135, 141–44, 154, 166, 197, 214

Ullian, J. S., 79
Uncompelled consensus, 176, 178, 212
Unconscious,
    as defense against skepticism, 27–28
    against unknown, 29
    as defined by Freud, 10, 31
        as exempt from contradiction, 31
    as explaining behavior, 19, 29, 35
        role in pattern match, 19
    as having fixed content, 21, 26, 32
    as parallel processor, 40
    as postulate, 24–25, 34
    as potentially knowable, 18, 21, 26, 30, 32, 35
    descriptive nature of, 17, 34
    uncovering contents of, 33
    as metaphor, 17–42, 129, 132, 156, 164

Unconscious as metaphor. (*continued*)
    as autonomous and willful, 39
    as exempt from disconfirmation, 35,
        75
    as exerting continuous pressure, 38
    as ghost in machine, 41
    derivatives of, 32, 171–72, 189
Unconscious fantasy:
    and pattern match, 19
    form of, 20
    half-life, 27
Unconscious, substantive, 17–18, 22,
        36–37, 75, 203, 209
Uncoupled metaphor, 69–70, 169, 178,
        200–01, 213
Understanding, experience of, 44–48, 65
    failure of, 44–45, 48–49, 51, 55, 64,
        67, 83–84, 86, 89, 91, 94, 96,
        98–99, 101
    see also unwitting projection
    how context controls, 47, 52, 66–67,
        85, 87, 90–91, 102, 108, 111,

        140, 146, 153, 166, 171–72, 179,
            183, 185, 198
    literal, 46
    true vs. false, 49, 105
Unpacking, 80, 84, 91–109, 124, 134,
        152, 173, 189, 210
Unwitting interpretation, 53, 81, 83, 93
Unwitting projection, 82, 86, 101, 111

Vickers, Brian, 205
Vico, Giambattista, 2, 177

Wakefield, Jerome, 13
Wallerstein, Robert, 122
Wasserman, M. D., 205
Web of belief, 171
White, James Boyd, 198
Whyte, L., 39
Winokur, Meir, 27
Wolf Man Case, 1, 119, 174
Wolpe, Joseph, 174